THE
NEW
DEMOCRATS
AND THE
RETURN TO
POWER

THE
NEW
DEMOCRATS
AND THE
RETURN TO
POWER

AL FROM

WITH ALICE MCKEON

FOREWORD BY BILL CLINTON

palgrave
macmillan

First published in 2013 by PALGRAVE MACMILLAN® in the United
States—a division of St. Martin's Press LLC, 175 Fifth Avenue, New
York, NY 10010.

Where this book is distributed in the UK, Europe and the rest of the
world, this is by Palgrave Macmillan, a division of Macmillan Publishers
Limited, registered in England, company number 785998, of Houndmills,
Basingstoke, Hampshire RG21 6XS.

Palgrave Macmillan is the global academic imprint of the above
companies and has companies and representatives throughout the world.

Palgrave® and Macmillan® are registered trademarks in the United
States, the United Kingdom, Europe and other countries.

ISBN 978-1-137-27864-7

Library of Congress Cataloging-in-Publication Data

From, Al, 1943–
  The New Democrats and the return to power / Al From.
    pages   cm
  Includes bibliographical references.
  ISBN–13: 978-1-137-27864-7
  ISBN–10: 1-137-27864-1
  1. Democratic Party (U.S.)—History—20th century. 2. Democratic
Leadership Council (U.S.)—History—20th century. 3. United States—
Politics and government—20th century. I. Title.
JK2316.F76   2013
324.273609045—dc23

                                                    2013014702

A catalogue record of the book is available from the British Library.

Design by Letra Libre Inc.

First edition: December 2013

10 9 8 7 6 5 4 3 2 1

Printed in the United States of America.

To Ginger, Ginny, and Sarah

New conditions impose new requirements on government and those who conduct government.

—Franklin D. Roosevelt

What's so damn liberal about wasting money?

—Edmund S. Muskie

CONTENTS

FOREWORD

by Bill Clinton

My journey as a New Democrat began in 1972. In the midst of my studies at Yale Law School, I became a staffer on Senator George McGovern's presidential campaign, traveling the South to court delegates for the primary and eventually, with the help of two other faithful McGoverniks, leading the general election campaign in Texas. It was an exhausting, whirlwind adventure that I'll never forget, and by the time the dust had settled on election night, November 7, 1972, McGovern had won just Massachusetts and Washington, D.C. President Richard Nixon had run away with the other 49 states.

I loved McGovern, and Hillary and I kept in touch with him until his passing in October 2012, but it was clear that the campaign had failed on several fronts. I was only 26 by the time the general election ended, and I was full of frustration, angst, and excuses for why it hadn't gone our way. In a letter I sent to a trusted friend and mentor, I wrote that if we wanted to improve social and economic conditions for all Americans, we had to find a way to meet the valid needs of the middle class and enlist them in our cause, or we would "be out of the White House and many state houses for a good long time."

Twelve years later, it happened again. President Ronald Reagan, the incumbent, defeated Walter Mondale in the general election, and once again the Democrats suffered an embarrassing 49-to-1 defeat, this time winning only Mondale's home state of Minnesota. It wasn't Mondale's fault, just as it wasn't McGovern's in 1972. Our party was out of touch with the demands and desires of the American people. We were losing ground, and something had to be done. With the exception of Jimmy Carter's election in 1976, the White House had eluded the Democrats ever since Richard Nixon's first victory in 1968.

But 1985 marked a turning point in the Democratic Party. Many young Democrats, inspired by the Civil Rights Movement and the legacies of Presidents Roosevelt, Truman, and Kennedy, were determined to show America, once again, that ours was the party of the people. Out of our steadfast desire to turn the party around, the Democratic Leadership Council (DLC) was born. Led by Al From, the DLC set out to renew the party's appeal with new policies rooted in its original values. Al always had a sense about where we were and where we ought to go, and we felt good about following his lead.

The DLC wasn't a popular group at first, but we were a determined one. In 1990, the economy had gone from bad to worse—the deficit was high, the debt had exploded, income was flat, and poverty and crime were rising. Washington seemed to be stuck in ideological trench warfare: Republicans said the government was the problem, and Democrats said it was the solution. Every issue in Washington was obscured by ridiculous false choices: economy or environment; business or labor; impoverished or entitled.

In response, our small but growing group developed an outline of what needed to be done. Our approach, which came to be known as the Third Way, was rooted in common sense, a common devotion to our party's oldest values of opportunity and responsibility, and a common vision of the new era in which we were living. The New Orleans Declaration, as we called it, outlined the 15-point credo of the New Democrats.

The DLC believed that the Democratic Party's fundamental mission was—and still is—to expand opportunity, not government; to recognize that economic growth is a prerequisite for expanding opportunity; to invest in the skills and ingenuity of our people in order to build shared prosperity; to expand trade, not restrict it; and to reform welfare and reduce crime. And we called for an end to the era of false choices. We were pro-growth and pro-environment; pro-labor and pro-business; pro-work and pro-family; pro-middle class and pro-antipoverty efforts that work.

When I was elected president in 1992, I knew I owed a great deal to the DLC and to Al From. Together, we put stale partisan rhetoric aside and replaced it with the ideas and policies that actually mattered to our people. From the start of my first term until the day I left office, I promoted the policies of the New Democrats.

Just 26 days after my inauguration, I signed my first piece of legislation, the Family and Medical Leave Act, which was prominently supported by the DLC. The New Democrats believed in the importance of the family and the dignity of work, and the bill highlighted exactly that. FMLA allowed employees to take up to twelve weeks of unpaid leave to care for a newborn or a sick family member without the risk of losing their jobs. American workers no longer had to choose between the employment they needed and the family they loved. By the time I left office, 35 million Americans had claimed the benefits of FMLA. It sent a clear signal that we were trying to give the government back to the American people.

In 1993, we passed an economic plan that raised the income tax of the top 1.2 percent of wage earners, created a higher tax rate for corporations, cut spending, and eliminated unnecessary programs to reduce the deficit and lower interest rates. That bill, along with the 1997 Balanced Budget Act, the Telecommunications Act, our education legislation, nearly 300 trade agreements, and other economic initiatives, helped create 22.7 million jobs, the lowest unemployment rate in 30 years, and the highest home ownership rate and longest economic expansion in history. Most importantly to me, it helped move 7.7 million Americans out of poverty and into the middle class; one hundred times as many people as had moved up from poverty in the Reagan years.

We also believed in preventing crime and punishing criminals. That idea was turned into action through the Violent Crime Control and Law Enforcement Act, which provided 100,000 new police officers and an assault weapons ban, and the Brady Handgun Violence Prevention Act, which kept more than 500,000 felons and fugitives from getting handguns. By the end of 2000, our nation had the lowest crime rate in 25 years, the lowest homicide rate in 30 years, and a 35 percent reduction in gun crime since 1993.

Through all the ups and downs, I knew that the New Orleans Declaration had played a tremendous role in my administration's success. It gave us a platform on which to stand and a framework from which to work. It let the American people know that we were working for them, not trying to stir conflict or score ideological points.

In 2000, when I spoke at President Franklin D. Roosevelt's estate at Hyde Park, I said that "it would be hard to think of a single American citizen who, as a private citizen, has had a more positive impact on the progress of American life in the last 25 years than Al From." It was true then, and it's still true now.

When I addressed the delegation at Hyde Park, I knew that someday someone would write an entire book on how the New Orleans Declaration laid the foundation for the resurgence of the Democratic Party and for the successes of the American people in last decade of the twentieth century. It seems only fitting that Al From would write that book—this book. After all, he was the defining architect of the Third Way and the resolute leader of the New Democrats.

—April 2013

ACKNOWLEDGMENTS

Writing this book was both an enjoyable and an arduous undertaking. It tells the history of the Democratic Leadership Council (DLC) and the New Democrat political movement as seen through my eyes.

While it tells my story—and I am solely responsible for the contents and views expressed in it—I could not have written it without the help of many others.

Most important was Alice McKeon who worked with me on this book from the very beginning until the very end. Alice, who was my press secretary at the DLC, encouraged me to write my story and helped me frame the book, develop my proposal, and organize my research. She spent long hours editing my verbose prose into a coherent story line. In a real sense, she managed my book project.

Writing this book was all encompassing: seven days a week for 12 or more hours a day for nearly four months. Thanks to my wife, Ginger, for putting up with me not just during the writing of this book, but during the three decades during which this story took place. When I reviewed my schedules for those 30 years as I was writing this book, I came to appreciate anew the burden I placed on her to raise our two daughters while I was too often at work or traveling around the country.

Thanks to President Bill Clinton for his wonderful foreword, to Doug Band and Bruce Lindsey of the Clinton Foundation, and to members of the president's staff including Steven Rinehart, Hannah Richert, Amy Kuhn, Laura Graham, and Tina Flournoy.

I am indebted to Jason Allen Ashlock, my agent at Movable Type Management, who made this book possible, to my editors at Palgrave Macmillan, Laura Lancaster and Emily Carleton, and to others at Palgrave including Christine Catarino, Katherine Haigler, and Allison Frascatore, who worked so hard on this book. Laura, in particular, did an excellent job of editing my manuscript.

I appreciate the help of my assistant, Jenifer Callahan, and of my long-time colleagues at the DLC, Holly Page and Debbie Boylan, who helped pull together materials for this book. Also thanks to Stephanie Benedict, who helped with research for this book.

Thanks to my many colleagues at the DLC and Progressive Policy Institute who played such a big role in this story and in helping with the book, including Will Marshall, Bruce Reed, Elaine Kamarck, Bill Galston, Rob Shapiro, Don Baer, Tom Freedman, Linda Moore, Kiki McLean, Deb Smulyan, David Rothkopf, and Mark Dunkelman.

Thanks to Hillary Clinton and Tony Blair who played such a major role in taking the New Democrat movement international, and to the chairmen and political leaders of the DLC during the period of this book, including Chuck Robb, Dick Gephardt, Sam Nunn, John Breaux, Dave McCurdy, Joe Lieberman, Evan Bayh, Mike Espy, the late Lindy Boggs, Harold Ford, Jr., and Tom Vilsack. And a special thanks to Bob Strauss and to the late Gillis Long, who inspired me to start the DLC.

Thanks, as well, to Michael Steinhardt, Bernard Schwartz, Bob Kogod, Lew Manilow, Bill Budinger, Jim Kiss, Barrie Wigmore, Sandy Robertson, Rich Richman, John Dyson, Peter Joseph, Steve Rattner, David Roth, Chris Gabrieli, Bill Podlich, Jon Corzine, Jonathan Tisch, Peter Mathias, the late Howard Gilman, and the late Adam Solomon. Their support and generosity, and that of so many others, made the DLC story possible.

Though the DLC closed its doors in 2011, I'm appreciative of those who are continuing to promote New Democrat politics, including Will Marshall, who, with great steadfastness, has continued the intellectual work of the Progressive Policy Institute and Jon Cowan, whose organization, Third Way, carries on our political mission.

INTRODUCTION

With unemployment hovering at nearly 8 percent and most Americans believing the country was on the wrong track, the Republicans expected to win the 2012 presidential election. Instead, President Obama's reelection marked the fifth time in the last six national elections that the Republicans lost the popular vote for president. Voters have come to see the Republicans as out of ideas and out of touch with a changing America. Much of the political discussion during the next three years will focus on what the Republicans need to do to reverse their fortunes in 2016.

Political memories tend to be short, but just 25 years ago the fortunes of the two parties were reversed. In 1988, the Democrats lost an election they expected to win, their fifth defeat in six presidential elections. Twice, in 1972 and in 1984, the Democratic candidate lost 49 states.

In 1985, out of the political rubble arose the Democratic Leadership Council (DLC), the birthplace of the New Democrat political movement. Less than eight years later Bill Clinton won the presidency, having prepared for his White House run by chairing the DLC.

Today's Republicans will have to find their own formula. But they would be wise to start by rebuilding their party intellectually. Until they begin standing for ideas the American people want to support, voters are unlikely to return them to national power.

That is a lesson they can learn from us. The New Democrat movement was an idea movement that reconnected the Democratic Party with its first principles and grandest traditions:

- Jackson's credo of equal opportunity for all, special privileges for none;
- Jefferson's belief in individual liberty and the capacity for self-government;

- Kennedy's ethic of civic responsibility;
- Truman's tough-minded internationalism; and
- Roosevelt's thirst for innovation.

Based on those core Democratic beliefs, the New Democrat approach was fundamentally different from what had become Democratic orthodoxy over the previous quarter century.

At its best, the Democratic Party was the party of upward mobility. Democrats believed that social and economic progress in America is built on the talents and efforts of all Americans, not just the wealthy elites.

But as New Democrats, the centerpiece of our message was economic growth. The party's first imperative was to revive the American dream of expanding opportunity by fostering broad-based economic growth led by a robust private sector generating high-skill, high-wage jobs. We understood that the private sector, not government, is the primary engine for economic growth. Government's proper role is to foster private sector growth and to equip every American with the opportunities and skills that he or she needs to succeed in the private economy, not to pick "winners" and "losers," and not just to redistribute wealth.

As Democrats, we believed in tolerance and inclusion. We were proud of our heritage as the party that helped tens of millions of immigrants, including my father, to work their way into the economic and social mainstream. We were the party of civil rights and equal rights and human rights.

As New Democrats, we understood that tolerance and inclusion in an era of rapid change can best be preserved by a common civic culture grounded in the values most Americans believe in: work, family, responsibility, individual liberty, and faith. We anchored our policies in these mainstream American values.

As Democrats, we believed in community—that we are all in this together, and that we can only achieve our individual destinies if we share a common commitment to our national destiny.

As New Democrats, we understood that living in a community is a two-way street. We rejected the Right's ethic of every man for himself and "if you don't make it, so be it." But we also rejected the Left's ethic of something for nothing. We believed in an ethic of mutual responsibility—that government has a responsibility to its citizens to create opportunities, and that citizens have an obligation to their country to give something back to the commonwealth.

As Democrats, we believed that America has a special responsibility to lead the world, by example and diplomacy, toward political and economic freedom.

As New Democrats, we understood that the most important challenge to our role in the world today is to continue and strengthen America's leadership in the global economy, showing the world that freedom can work to our mutual benefit, and that peaceful competition can lift the standard of living in every part of the globe. We rejected calls for a new isolationism from both political extremes and committed Democrats to an internationalist foreign policy that defended American interests and promoted democratic values in the world.

As Democrats, we believed in activist government, that government can and should play a positive role in our national life. Unlike the Republicans, we don't believe government is an alien institution: It is the agent of our collective will and our instrument for helping Americans help themselves and each other.

As New Democrats, we understood that government must be modernized constantly to deal with the fast changing circumstances of the information age. We believed, as Franklin Roosevelt did, that "new conditions impose new requirements on government and those who conduct government." That's why we must consistently modernize government to make sure it equips people with the tools they need to get ahead.

As New Democrats, we called for a revolution in government to take power away from entrenched bureaucracies and narrow interests in Washington and put it back in the hands of ordinary people by making government less centralized, more flexible, and more accountable, and by offering more choices in public services.

This book tells the inside story of the historic resurrection of the Democratic Party from the brink of political extinction. The period of the book's main focus is recent, but it is important for today's reader to understand that while a central premise of this book—that message and ideas matter in presidential politics—has not changed, much about the political world is very different. In 1992, there was no internet, no email, no blogs, no iPads, and there were very few cell phones. I often received Clinton's campaign speeches for review over an old Telecopier machine, a predecessor of the fax machine, at the rate of a page every four minutes. When we traveled, we scheduled time to return calls from airport pay phones. Newspapers were still important, and a small number of key political reporters from major papers could set the tone and context of the campaign.

Finally, the electorate was much different than it is today. White voters were nearly 90 percent of the electorate, blacks about 10 percent, and Hispanics barely voted at all. For Democrats, the key to their political comeback was to win over the working and middle-class white voters—Clinton called them the forgotten middle class—who had deserted the Democratic Party in droves in the three previous presidential elections.

America has seen dramatic changes demographically, socially, and technologically in the last two decades. The challenges today are different than those in the 1990s, and so the policies must be different to meet them. But the core principles of the New Democrat movement—opportunity for all, an ethic of mutual responsibility, the core value of community, a global outlook, an emphasis on economic growth and empowering government—and its embodiment of values such as work, family, faith, individual liberty, and inclusion are as viable and useful for meeting today's challenges as they were for meeting the challenges of the 1990s.

In those principles and in the history of the New Democrat movement, there are lessons for both political parties today. I believe that if either party—and I certainly hope it will be the Democrats—would put together an agenda for the future that furthered those principles, it would both break today's polarized political gridlock and build an enduring political and governing majority. And America would be the better for it.

ONE

THE WILDERNESS

1968–1992

On the night of the 1980 election, I had a party and nobody came. By the time the party was to start, it was clear that the Democrats had lost the White House and were well on their way to losing control of the Senate and dozens of seats in the House. I had lost my job in the White House, and most of those invited to the party had lost their jobs, too.

There was no reason to celebrate. And so it was throughout the 1980s. The Democrats spent the 1980s wandering in the political wilderness. In 1980, 1984, and 1988, the Republican candidate won landslide victories, gaining on average 54.1 percent of the popular vote and nearly 90 percent of Electoral College votes. The Democratic Party's performance in national elections during the decade was the worst in the party's history. According to political writer and analyst Ron Brownstein, the Democratic candidates won a smaller percentage of the Electoral College vote in those elections than any party's candidates had won in three consecutive elections since the advent of modern parties in 1828.[1]

In 1980 incumbent President Jimmy Carter lost 44 states to Ronald Reagan. But it was in 1984 that the party truly reached its nadir. On November 6, 1984, former Vice President Walter F. Mondale lost 49 states, the second 49-state shellacking in four elections. Only by winning the overwhelmingly Democratic District of Columbia and his home state of Minnesota by a mere 3,761 votes did Mondale avoid losing every state. Four years later, when Massachusetts Governor Michael Dukakis was routed by Vice President George H. W. Bush, it marked the fifth

Democratic defeat in six presidential cycles, a losing streak interrupted only by Jimmy Carter's narrow victory in 1976 in the wake of the Watergate scandal.

The party of Roosevelt, Truman, and Kennedy had reached bedrock.

Members of my generation, born around the Second World War and the end of Franklin Roosevelt's presidency, grew up believing that Democrats were the majority party, the dominant party of American politics. We were the children of the New Deal era of American politics, an era dominated by Democrats and driven by Democratic policies. Our party had won seven of nine presidential elections between 1932 and 1964. During those nine elections, we won a majority of the popular vote for the White House, and we dominated Congress, too.

How had the Democratic Party, that had been the engine of economic and social progress for so much of the twentieth century and had been so politically successful during the New Deal era failed so badly in the 1980s?

Until we answered that question, it was unlikely that we could turn the party around. Before we could shape new ideas and launch a comeback, we had to understand why Democrats were getting blown away in presidential elections. Otherwise, as smart as we thought we were, we were bound to fall into the same traps and repeat the same mistakes as the candidates before us. As Bill Clinton would often remind me: Doing the same thing over and over again and expecting a different outcome is the definition of insanity.

In 1985, along with about three dozen governors, senators, and congressmen, I formed the Democratic Leadership Council (DLC) to analyze the party's precipitous decline and make it competitive again in presidential elections.

Our diagnosis was not earthshaking: When voters again trusted the Democrats to grow the economy and expand opportunity, to defend the country, and to support values most Americans believed in, they would turn to us for national leadership. During the New Deal era, Democrats were identified as the party that helped America recover from the Depression, saved the country and the world from fascism, and represented the interests and values of ordinary Americans.

That identification was strong enough to hold together a party that was, in reality, a broad and disparate coalition that often disagreed on specific issues. The harsh reality of the New Deal era—the nine elections between Roosevelt's in 1932 and Johnson's in 1964—was that it was the anomaly, not the norm. By the 1980s the Democrats had fallen back into their pre-New Deal ways.

From 1860 to 1932, Democrats were largely the remainder party of American politics—a confederation of disgruntled constituencies with little sense of national purpose. During that period, Republicans won 14 of 18 presidential elections. The only Democrat to win a majority of the popular vote was New York Governor Samuel B. Tilden, who lost the controversial 1876 election when an electoral commission appointed by Congress voted along party lines and awarded the election to Rutherford B. Hayes. The only Democrats to win the White House were Grover Cleveland and Woodrow Wilson, who both won twice but never won a majority of the popular vote. Over those eighteen elections, Democrats averaged around 43 percent of the popular vote.

In late 1987 in a speech in Houston, Charles S. Robb, then chairman of the DLC, articulated the historic plight of the party:

> Except for the New Deal era, Democrats have won the White House only when the Republicans have split, gotten themselves embroiled in scandal, or presided over a national calamity. In fact, between the Civil War and the Great Depression, Democrats were less a national party than a rather feckless confederation of disparate and often aggrieved constituencies: white southerners, Midwestern farmers, and ethnic workers in the East. What held this improbable collection together was a common fear of being ground down by America's transition from an agrarian to an industrial society.
>
> As Republicans became identified as the party of national dynamism, expansion, and progress, Democrats became identified as the party of those who were left behind, who often found their interests at odds with unfettered capitalism, technological progress, and the relentless forward movement of the nation. We became a party of protest, of habitual and seemingly permanent opposition.

Franklin Roosevelt changed that. Under FDR, Democrats offered a broad agenda for economic and social progress. Policies begun under the New Deal and boosted by the war effort rebuilt the American economy, created the great American middle class, conquered fascism, and saved the free world. The New Deal message was crystal clear: economic progress and upward mobility for the greatest number of Americans and antitotalitarianism on the global scene. Democrats reaped the political benefits. Between Roosevelt's victory in 1932 and Lyndon Johnson's in 1964, Democrats averaged about 52.5 percent of the popular vote.

Throughout this period the liberal agenda drove the Democratic Party, fueled economic and social progress, tempered the harshness of untrammeled capitalism, tipped the balance of economic power from the privileged few to the striving many, and benefited our core constituencies. It forged a collection of distinct interests—working men and women, retirees, farmers, and, later, minorities—into a purposeful national party dedicated to expanding opportunity and stimulating upward mobility for the greatest possible number.

But as the 1960s passed into the 1970s, the liberal agenda ran out of steam, largely because of its own success, and the intellectual coherence of the New Deal began to dissipate. The Democratic coalition split apart over civil rights, Vietnam, economic change, culture and values, and the great cause of liberal government that had united the Democratic Party for three decades degenerated back into a collection of special pleaders. The party was no longer seen as the party of prosperity, opportunity, and national strength. Not surprisingly, Democrats began losing presidential elections again—five out of six after Johnson's victory in 1964 until Clinton's in 1992.

The beginnings of the two schisms over civil rights and antitotalitarianism that shattered the New Deal coalition became apparent in the years immediately after World War II.

The party first included a civil rights plank in its 1940 platform, but Franklin Roosevelt never put civil rights high on his agenda, focusing instead on economic recovery and building what his 1944 platform boasted was the strongest military in the history of the world. That kept white southerners firmly in his camp. President Truman took a much more aggressive stance. In 1948 he established a highly publicized Commission on Civil Rights and ordered the integration of the armed forces. At the 1948 Democratic Convention, a group of liberals, led by Minneapolis Mayor Hubert Humphrey pushed for and won a strong civil rights plank in the party's platform. During Humphrey's speech supporting the plank, southern delegates walked out. They formed the States' Rights Democratic Party, known as the Dixiecrats. The Dixiecrats purported to support what they called "the southern way of life" but were primarily for segregation and against federal intervention to enforce integration. They nominated South Carolina Governor Strom Thurmond to run against Truman. The Dixiecrats won just four states—Louisiana,

Alabama, Mississippi, and South Carolina—but the fissure in the solidly Democratic South never healed.

In 1947 the founders of the Americans for Democratic Action (ADA)—a liberal organization founded shortly after FDR died by Eleanor Roosevelt, John Kenneth Galbraith, Walter Reuther, Arthur Schlesinger, and Reinhold Niebuhr to keep the New Deal vision and values alive—decided to take a firm stand against communism and Soviet expansionism. Concerned that liberals were sowing the seeds of their own destruction by avoiding the Soviet challenge to the West, the ADA decided to back President Harry Truman for the Democratic nomination in 1948 against Henry Wallace, FDR's vice president before Truman, who was a hero to many liberals and saw communists as allies in the fight for domestic and international progress.

Because it reconnected Democrats with the antitotalitarianism of FDR, that decision had a profound impact on the party's course over the next two decades and likely delayed the demise of the New Deal coalition until Vietnam shattered the consensus on anticommunism. The tough stance against communism kept many southern conservative Democrats in a strained alliance with the party as it became a louder champion of civil rights. It also defined the Cold War and played a major role in Democratic presidents involving the country in the wars in Korea and Vietnam.

In 1960 the first 12 sections of John F. Kennedy's party platform were devoted to defense and international policy. It wasn't until the section on economic growth that the platform even addressed a domestic issue. And, in his famous inaugural address, Kennedy made clear his commitment to the prevailing Democratic strand of tough-minded internationalism:

> Let the word go forth from this time and place, to friend and foe alike, that the torch has been passed to a new generation of Americans—born in this century, tempered by war, disciplined by a hard and bitter peace, proud of our ancient heritage—and unwilling to witness or permit the slow undoing of those human rights to which this nation has always been committed, and to which we are committed today at home and around the world. Let every nation know, whether it wishes us well or ill, that we shall pay any price, bear any burden, meet any hardship, support any friend, oppose any foe, in order to assure the survival and the success of liberty.

Then came Vietnam. President Eisenhower had first authorized military and economic aid to South Vietnam and sent a few hundred military advisors there. President Kennedy, in line with the promise of his inaugural address and his belief in the "domino theory" (if one state in a region fell to communism, surrounding countries would follow) expanded that aid and by 1963 had increased the number of military advisors to 16,000. When President Johnson escalated the effort to a full-fledged war, large-scale opposition arose in the country, on college campuses, and, most significantly, within the Democratic Party. In 1967 Senator Robert Kennedy came out against the war, and in January 1968 he announced his intention to challenge Johnson for the White House. The party consensus on muscular anticommunism no longer existed.

Running as an anti–Vietnam War candidate, Minnesota Senator Eugene McCarthy challenged the incumbent Johnson in the 1968 New Hampshire primary and won an astonishing 42 percent of the vote. Though Johnson actually won the vote with 49 percent, the close contest convinced him not to seek reelection. Vice President Hubert Humphrey, essentially Johnson's stand-in, won the nomination at a raucous party convention split asunder over Vietnam. Antiwar demonstrators who had no votes at that Chicago convention spilled out onto the streets where they had violent conflicts with the city's police. Humphrey never recovered and lost a close election to Richard Nixon.

Four years later, when South Dakota Senator George McGovern rode anti–Vietnam War sentiment to the nomination in 1972, ultimately losing 49 states to Nixon, the Democratic faithful could argue that, as an insurgent candidate, he represented the party's left fringe. With McGovern's nomination the party became identified with antiwar activists and the peace movement, hardly favorites among its working-class base. As a result, Democrats lost their advantage on national security issues built by Roosevelt, Truman, and Kennedy, a problem that would plague the party for two decades.

The image of Democratic weakness was reinforced during the Carter administration, particularly by the Iranian hostage crisis. On November 4, 1979, Iranian militants loyal to the Ayatollah Khomeini stormed the U.S. embassy in Teheran and for more than 400 days held 52 Americans hostage inside the building. The United States appeared to be a helpless giant taunted by a pip-squeak dictator. The low point came on April 24, 1980, when eight American servicemen were killed and two American aircraft were lost in the Iranian desert during a failed rescue mission. Not one of the hostages was rescued. At a time before cable news, the respected news anchor Walter Cronkite began every broadcast of the CBS Evening News by intoning the number of days our hostages were in captivity, cementing an image of American weakness that voters transferred to President Carter and the Democrats. On January 20, 1981, shortly after President Reagan's inauguration, the hostages were freed. Polling showed that at the time Johnson escalated the Vietnam War, voters had trusted Democrats and Republicans equally on national security. By 1980 twice as many trusted the Republicans as trusted the Democrats to keep our country safe.

As the image of Democrats as the party of strength dissolved, so did the glue that held together an unholy alliance between a party committed to civil rights and white southern segregationists who had made up a core constituency since the Civil War. Ironically, the crackup began around 1964, the year Johnson won 61.1 percent of the popular vote, the highest percentage in 144 years, when white southerners began to defect to the Republicans in droves over civil rights. Johnson lost only six states to Senator Barry Goldwater, the GOP candidate. One was Goldwater's home state of Arizona. The others—Louisiana, Mississippi, Alabama, Georgia, and South Carolina—were the core of a segregated South that had voted solidly Democratic since the Civil War. With the exception of Carter's post-Watergate victory in 1976, most Southern states have voted overwhelmingly Republican in presidential elections ever since.

In the 1970s the Democrats also lost credibility on the economy, another important strand of the New Deal promise. The failed Carter administration was a major culprit. In 1979 and 1980, the inflation rate increased by a total of 25 percent and interest rates rose to 20 percent. Ordinary people found their incomes and savings devalued and their ability to afford a mortgage dramatically reduced. This undermined the party's economic consensus, as policies demanded by leaders of constituency groups, including unions, began to conflict with those needed to fix the economy and promote widespread prosperity. The result was devastating for Democrats in industrial states. In the 1980s Democrats lost Illinois, Michigan, Indiana, Ohio, Pennsylvania, and New Jersey in all three elections.

I saw this crisis firsthand as the deputy advisor to the president for inflation in the Carter White House. What struck me was that I was different than Carter's talented aides. Many were young, single, living in small apartments, and spending almost every waking hour working in the White House. They seemed virtually oblivious to the devastating impact inflation had on middle-class families. Being a little older, married, trying to raise a family and pay a mortgage, I felt the punishing sting of high inflation in a way they did not. My wife and I struggled and cut back our budget to pay our bills. To me, our inflation policy wasn't about memos or meetings or events to show we were working on the problem; it was about bringing down inflation. Nothing else mattered.

But the Carter administration never understood that. Once in early 1980, when Mobil Oil was raising gasoline prices far in excess of the voluntary wage-price guidelines Carter had established, I went to Alfonso McDonald, the White House staff director, to urge him to have the president publicly call out Mobil Oil as John Kennedy had blasted the leaders of the steel industry for raising their prices against the public interest in 1962. McDonald told me that I was plain wrong. Instead, he said, we should bend the guidelines to find Mobil Oil in compliance. "That way," he said, "people will know the president's program is working."

"You're out of your mind," I responded, "all people have to do is to fill up their tank and they'll know the president's program is not working."

Carter's failed economic record took a terrible toll on the Democratic Party. According to the Gallup poll in 1976, the year Carter was elected, voters trusted Democrats more than Republicans to keep the country prosperous by a 47 to 23 margin. In early 1981, after Carter's single term in office, that number was nearly reversed—41 to 28 the American people now trusted the Republicans more. Clearly, Democrats were no longer viewed as the party of prosperity.

The final blow came when the party split on cultural issues just as it had on civil rights. In the late 1960s and 1970s, many life-long Democrats believed their party that had once symbolized prosperity, expanding opportunity, and unambiguous opposition to communist totalitarianism had become identified with Hippies and the drug culture, a breakdown of discipline and passivity toward crime, alternative lifestyles, and fervent denunciations of the use of U.S. power abroad—ideas, causes, and values alien at that time to most Americans and to important New Deal constituencies such as urban ethnics and Catholics.

It was clear that the nominating process which had been controlled by party bosses was out of date and in need of serious reform. In 1964, for example, Mississippi sent an all-white delegation to the convention in Atlantic City. The Freedom Democratic Party, led by legendary civil rights activists Fannie Lou Hamer and Aaron Henry, challenged the seating of the segregated delegation. The convention turned down the challenge but offered the Freedom Democrats two seats, which they refused. Their demonstrations focused attention on the issue and after the enactment of the Voting Rights Act of 1965 Mississippi never sent another segregated delegation to a convention.

In 1968 the party bosses delivered the nomination to Humphrey who had not competed in a single primary. After the violence at the Chicago convention, the party formed a commission chaired by McGovern and Minnesota Congressman Don Fraser to democratize the presidential nominating process by reducing the power of elected leaders and by bringing in new participants. The purpose was noble, and the overall impact of the commission's report was to increase the power of voters in picking the party's nominees through primaries and caucuses. But an unintended consequence of the reforms was to supplant elected and party officials with a new elite—interest group leaders and party activists who could organize voters behind their particular causes and dominate the primary process. Elected leaders had in the past served to moderate interest group demands. But under the new system the interest group leaders were the new convention brokers—and their demands began to define the party's agenda and undermine its sense of national purpose.

By the beginning of the 1980s, it was clear that the Democrats had run out of ideas—and liberalism was in great need of resuscitation. Liberals confused expanding government with expanding opportunity. They forgot what John Kennedy had taught—that opportunity and responsibility must go hand in hand. They worried more about police power than public safety at home and more about American power than America's enemies in the world.

The American people said, "No, thanks." Politically, and intellectually, the Democratic Party was in a state of near collapse.

In 1984 special interest politics defined the Democratic Party. Walter Mondale was a good and decent man, and having served as Humphrey's successor in the Senate and as Carter's vice president, he embodied what the party had become. As the establishment candidate, he fended off the insurgent candidacy of Senator Gary Hart en route to the nomination. But, in the general election, despite the support of the party's interest group leaders, he lost the constituencies those leaders purported to represent. Although he won the endorsement of every major women's organization, including the National Organization for Women, he lost the women's vote. Organized labor worked tirelessly on his behalf, and 51 percent of blue-collar workers and 62 percent of white-collar workers voted for Reagan. According to the ABC News exit poll, fully 45 percent of labor union households and half of white labor union members supported Reagan.

In 1988 Democrats lost a presidential election that they thought they would win. Dukakis had left his party's convention in Atlanta with a 17-point lead in the public opinion polls only to see his advantage evaporate during the fall campaign as Bush romped to a 40-state victory.

So it was little wonder why, throughout the second half of the 1980s, respected political analysts were writing about a permanent Republican lock on the Electoral College. The Democratic Party had ceased to be a competitive national party in presidential elections and was in grave danger of going the way of the Whigs. We were out of power, out of ideas, and out of hope.

The 1988 defeat showed that the party's losing streak would not end when Ronald Reagan left the White House. Democrats could no longer blame their electoral problems on a charismatic president. Democrats had to face reality. Too many Americans had lost faith in the party's ability to manage the economy, project mainstream values, and defend our country.

After 1988, some Democrats urged the party to reaffirm its commitment to New Deal liberalism while others argued that it should turn to the right. But neither course made sense. Moving left would only make the party's problems worse—voters already thought it was too liberal. But moving right was really not an option since it was doubtful the party would nominate a candidate unacceptable to liberals. Democrats needed a tough liberal in the tradition of Roosevelt, Truman, and Kennedy. The party needed a New Democrat.

TWO

FORMATIVE EXPERIENCES

The New Democrat philosophy is built on a basic understanding that John Kennedy had taught: opportunity and responsibility must go together. Government's responsibility is to provide opportunity for everyone to rise as far as his or her talent would allow. The people's responsibility is to take advantage of that opportunity. I had learned that philosophy firsthand during my very first job out of college, working in the Deep South for the War on Poverty.

"You can write about poverty or you can do something about it," Edgar May said to me as I prepared to leave Washington and return to Chicago in the spring of 1966. May was a Pulitzer Prize–winning journalist who had written on welfare and poverty. I was completing my graduate degree in journalism from Northwestern University's Medill School of Journalism and about to follow my chosen career path as a reporter. I had already signed on to join the *Chicago Daily News*, Chicago's most highly regarded newspaper, after I returned from a final semester in the nation's capital.

I reconnected with May, a fellow Medill graduate whom I had previously met when he spoke at our Washington program. When President Johnson asked Sargent Shriver to run the War on Poverty, Shriver enlisted Ed May in the battle. And Ed May enlisted me.

I took up Ed's challenge and went to work in the War on Poverty. The prospect of working for R. Sargent Shriver, President Kennedy's brother-in-law, was too enticing. Sarge Shriver was a lawyer and a businessman who ran the Merchandise Mart in Chicago for the Kennedy family, but he was best known for starting the Peace Corps. At the War on Poverty he didn't trust bureaucrats to assess the success or failure of his programs. Instead, he hired a bunch of young lawyers and journalists to report back to him from the front lines.

I was lucky enough to be one of them and even luckier to be assigned to the Southeast region, which included Alabama, Mississippi, and Georgia, hotbeds of civil rights activity in the 1960s. My job in the War on Poverty was to find out what was really going on in its Office of Economic Opportunity (OEO) programs in the Deep South and send missives back to May and Shriver that read more like in-depth articles in the *New York Times Magazine* or *New Yorker* than stodgy government reports.

Contrary to the conventional wisdom today, the War on Poverty was not a big welfare program. Just the opposite: it was an empowerment program. We hated welfare. In the Deep South, welfare was the tool of a controlling and detested white power structure. The OEO, the agency that ran this war, worked to empower poor people, to give them a say in their own futures—and that was a "no-no" in the Deep South in the mid-1960s. The white power structure might agree to give them welfare, as long as it was controlled by the powers-that-be. But give power to poor people? Never.

At OEO I learned an important lesson: Everyone, no matter how poor or disenfranchised, wanted a piece of the American dream. Everyone wanted his or her children to have a better life than he or she did. And I learned that if you wanted to help the poor, the most effective strategy with the broadest reach was to empower them, to give them a chance to get ahead by helping themselves.

I also learned that government must play an important role. Government can be an agent of powerful and positive change when it offers citizens opportunity, but citizens need to do their part and take full advantage of that opportunity. Simply put, if people can help themselves, government should empower them to do so, not keep them on the dole forever.

With the Voting Rights Act, the right to vote came to millions of blacks previously disenfranchised in the segregated South. With the War on Poverty, economic power came to previously dirt-poor communities. In some of the poorest counties in America in the 1960s I witnessed the enormity of the changes brought about when people were empowered— both economically and politically—*and* they took advantage of the opportunities they were given.

I saw it in Sunflower County, Mississippi, where empowered poor blacks fought their way into the local antipoverty program. When I first visited the county in 1967, it was two-thirds black but totally controlled by a white power structure, largely segregated, a focal point for civil rights activity, and one of the poorest counties in America. The birthplace of the supremacist White Citizens' Council, it was also the home of both segregationist Senator James O. Eastland, the wily chairman of the Senate Judiciary Committee where civil rights legislation had died for decades, and Fannie Lou Hamer, the golden-tongued civil rights icon best known for her speech on behalf of the Mississippi Freedom Democratic Party at the 1964 Democratic Convention in Atlantic City.

Shriver sent me to Sunflower County to investigate a dispute between two Head Start programs, one run with federal funding by the white powers of the county—the Eastland forces—the other run on a volunteer basis by civil rights activists and local black citizens, followers of Hamer. Ostensibly fighting over control of the funded Head Start program, in reality the two groups were fighting for an important prize in the political balance of power in the county. As long as Eastland forces administered antipoverty program funds, the civil rights activists, a major threat to the established political leadership of the county, remained in check.

I recommended to Shriver that OEO try to bring Hamer's group into the county program with the responsibility of running a number of Head Start centers. Eventually, the two sides reached an uneasy agreement. As a result, all poor children in the county were able to benefit from the higher quality, federally funded Head Start. But even more importantly the agreement changed the power arrangements in the county. Now previously disenfranchised blacks were empowered with a piece of the antipoverty program pie, and that became a platform to drive further social and economic change.

I visited Lowndes County, Alabama, a dirt-poor region with a history of violence during the Civil Rights Movement. In the summer of 1967 Shriver sent me to investigate a charge by Governor Lurleen Wallace (segregationist Governor George Wallace's first wife, who was elected as his surrogate when he could not succeed himself) that John Hulett, leader of the Student Non-Violent Coordinating Committee, was taking money from the antipoverty program. That charge was false, but Hulett, as the leader of the black community, did work closely with the antipoverty program. He also led efforts to win the vote for the county's black majority, which was Wallace's real concern. I watched as Hulett's efforts and the War on Poverty empowered the local black residents. They took advantage of their newfound opportunity and power. Three years later, Hulett was elected sheriff of Lowndes County. Once in office, even his old adversary George Wallace courted him, and years after that, he delivered the county's black votes to a reformed George Wallace in his last run for governor.

I went to Wilcox County, Alabama, where 80 percent of the residents were black, but not one black was registered to vote in 1965 when Martin Luther King's Southern Christian Leadership Conference (SCLC) came into the county. There, in the summer of 1967, I was introduced to my wife, Ginger, by the Reverend Tom Threadgill, one of Dr. King's lieutenants. Between her sophomore and junior years in college, she was running a youth center in Wilcox County run by SCLC and funded by the War on Poverty. The FBI kept a watchful eye over this young white woman living with a black family. One of the local residents who watched out for her was an old black sharecropper named Jesse Brooks. Ginger and I were married in 1968, and a few months later, Brooks visited us at our home in suburban Washington. Blacks had taken advantage of their newly won right to vote and had just elected Jesse Brooks to be tax collector of Wilcox County. How things can change.

And, in Holmes County, Mississippi, where Shriver sent me in 1968 to look at a work-study program, I found poor black kids gaining "valuable work experience" by building segregation academies for the white power structure. A quarter century later, when Mike Espy, Mississippi's first black congressman since Reconstruction, and I were launching the Mississippi DLC chapter in Jackson, I told that story to illustrate how much the state had changed. After I finished speaking, an older black woman introduced herself. "I'm Jessie Banks, the mayor of Tschula, Mississippi, in Holmes County, and that white family that ran the Chevy dealership and built those segregation academies has been run out of the county."

In those four counties and so many other places I visited during my nearly three years in the War on Poverty, I learned how economic and political empowerment could change lives when people took advantage of their new opportunities. I never forgot those lessons. The belief in opportunity and responsibility became the cornerstone of my political philosophy—and the cornerstone of the New Democrat philosophy.

When we founded the DLC in 1985, we built a governing philosophy on a foundation of opportunity and responsibility.

Our enduring purpose was equal opportunity for all, special privilege for none. Our public ethic was mutual responsibility. Our core value was community. And, our modern means was an empowering government that equips people with the tools they need to get ahead. Our mantra, as President Clinton best articulated, was opportunity, responsibility, community, and empowering government. We stood for traditional Democratic values and modern means.

Over the next 15 years, adherence to those principles and advocating for the ideas to further them would resuscitate progressive politics in the United States and around the world.

THREE

INTELLECTUAL AND POLITICAL ROOTS OF THE DLC

The intellectual and political roots of the DLC stretched back to the aftermath of George McGovern's 49-state shellacking in 1972.

While the Vietnam War and McGovern's antiwar stance were prominent in that campaign, inflation and the federal deficit also emerged as important issues. In 1970 inflation briefly jumped to a then-unthinkable 6 percent, and it stayed persistently above 4 percent throughout 1971.

As federal deficits grew in the early 1970s, voters became concerned that deficit spending was a cause of inflation. Democrats and liberals worried that cutting spending would undermine social gains and often seemed indifferent to the growing deficits. They were slow to grasp the potency of the inflation issue with middle-class voters who saw their purchasing power diminished. As a result, they increasingly became associated with profligate spending.

McGovern's campaign reinforced that image. He proposed a negative income tax that would have given every American, regardless of income, a $1,000 refundable credit. The idea didn't go anywhere. But, in combination with his calls for immediate withdrawal from the war, amnesty for draft resisters, an end to the draft, and a guaranteed job for every American, his proposals painted a picture in the minds of many voters that equated liberals and the Democrats with weakness abroad, and a lack fiscal responsibility and the welfare state at home.

In this context Maine Senator Edmund S. Muskie, whom McGovern had defeated for the Democratic presidential nomination in 1972, sowed the first intellectual seeds of the New Democrat movement. Muskie delivered a blunt message during a 1975 Liberal Party dinner speech: To preserve progressive governance, we had to reform liberalism.

"Why can't liberals start raising hell about a government so big, so complex, so expansive, and so unresponsive that it's dragging down every good program we've worked for?" Muskie asked. "Our challenge this decade is to restore the faith of Americans in the basic competence and purposes of government. . . . Well-managed, cost-effective, equitable, and responsible government is in itself a social good. . . . Efficient government is not a retreat from social goals. . . simply a realization that without it, those goals are meaningless."

Muskie's arguments for fiscal discipline and government reform would become important underpinnings for the New Democrat movement more than a decade later.

I joined the staff of Muskie's U.S. Senate Subcommittee on Intergovernmental Relations in April 1971 and served as its staff director from December 1971 until the end of 1978 when I left to work in the Carter White House. When I signed up with Muskie, I was sure he would be elected president of the United States in 1972.

A tall, Lincolnesque figure with an exceptional mind, Muskie was fiercely independent. His outward calm and reassuring demeanor hid a mercurial personality and an easily triggered temper. On one occasion, walking in the hall of the Russell Senate Office Building on the way to a markup on the Congressional Budget Act, Muskie launched into me for agreeing on his behalf to accept an amendment by Senator Chuck Percy. Screaming at me while we walked down the hallway, he recognized some constituents from Maine walking toward us. Muskie immediately ceased yelling and introduced me to his fellow Mainers as if I were the most important person in the world. The minute they had walked past us and were out of hearing range, Muskie picked up his rant in midsentence. When we finally made it to the committee meeting, Muskie went inside and accepted the Percy amendment exactly as I had proposed. As we were leaving the meeting, I asked Muskie why, if this amendment was the stupidest amendment he could think of, did he accept it? "Because," he said, "if I'd have rejected it, you would never be able to deal on my behalf again."

In 1954 Muskie was the first Democrat elected governor of Maine in twenty years. Four years later, in the 1958 Democratic landslide, he was elected to the Senate. He quickly got in trouble with Majority Leader Lyndon Johnson. When Johnson asked the new senator if he could count on his vote for reforming the filibuster rule, Muskie responded that Johnson would know when they got to the "M's." Muskie paid for that remark when Johnson banished him to the committees on Public Works and Government Operations, considered two of the Senate's least desirable committees.

From those relatively obscure committees, Muskie built a reputation over the next two decades as one of the Senate's finest legislators. As a member of the Public Works Committee, he authored landmark environmental legislation to protect the air and water. As a member of the Government Operations Committee, he authored legislation that would profoundly impact both America's fiscal policies and politics for decades to come.

In 1968, a tumultuous year for the country and Democratic politics, Vice President Hubert Humphrey picked Muskie to be his running mate. The ticket lost, but Muskie emerged a star, largely because voters reacted positively to his steadfast New England demeanor.

Senator Ted Kennedy seemed poised to be the Democratic candidate in 1972. But after a female member of his staff died when Kennedy drove a car off a bridge on Chappaquiddick Island in July 1969, Muskie was catapulted to front-runner status.

On the eve of midterm elections in 1970, fearing they would lose the Senate, Democrats bought fifteen minutes of television time on the three networks simultaneously and asked Muskie to speak for them.

Seated in a wingback chair in his home in Kennebunkport, Maine, Muskie delivered a fireside chat that reassured nervous Democrats. Looking directly into the camera, Muskie accused President Nixon of falsely attacking incumbent Democratic senators. In his most remembered line, Muskie said that Nixon's charges were not only false but that the president knew it when he made them: "That is a lie, and he knows it is a lie."

Muskie's speech was credited with saving Democratic control of the Senate, and it firmly established him as the 1972 front-runner. When Muskie announced his candidacy in January 1972, the campaign distributed buttons reading "President Muskie—don't you feel better already?"

Had the 1968 nominating rules still been in effect, the old party bosses would have almost certainly delivered the nomination to Muskie.

But the McGovern-Fraser Commission had rewritten the rules to take the power away from the party bosses and put it in the hands of caucusgoers and primary voters. McGovern ran an insurgency candidacy grounded in his opposition to the Vietnam War. Knowing the rules he had written better than any other candidate, he aimed his campaign at younger voters and antiwar activists who would swell the party's left fringe and stream into the primaries and caucuses.

Just as Eugene McCarthy had stunned Lyndon Johnson in the New Hampshire primary in 1968, George McGovern surprised Ed Muskie in New Hampshire in 1972. The Muskie campaign told reporters before the primary that it would not consider New Hampshire a victory unless he won 50 percent of the vote. He did not live up to the expectations his campaign had set for him. He beat McGovern 46–37, but the political world considered McGovern the winner and that victory catapulted his campaign.

After New Hampshire, the Muskie campaign quickly unraveled, and McGovern went on to win the nomination at the party's convention in Miami. But the antiwar campaign that won him the nomination repelled many working-class and moderate Democrats. Nixon swamped him in the general election. Not only was his loss historic, but the Democratic Party was in shambles and in great need of someone to turn it around.

Much to Muskie's credit, despite his anger and disappointment about his aborted presidential campaign, he returned to the Senate with increased zeal. Over the next three years, I was at Muskie's side as he sowed the seeds for what would grow into the important underpinnings of the New Democrat movement through three paradigm-breaking pieces of legislation: the Congressional Budget Act, the Sunset bill, and Countercyclical Revenue Sharing.

Muskie wasted little time becoming immersed in the Congressional Budget Reform Act, which established the congressional budget and created the House and Senate Budget Committees and the Congressional Budget Office.

Up until that time, the country had no coherent budgeting process for managing its finances. The president submitted a budget to Congress in January or February, but it was just his recommendations and a political statement. Once the president's budget was sent to Congress, all hell broke loose. Spending decisions were made independently in 13 separate appropriations bills covering separate parts of the government, with no relationship to each other or to their overall impact on the country's

fiscal health. Congress had neither a process nor the institutional capacity to set priorities or make coherent taxing and spending decisions.

Without an overall budget, each spending program was decided on
its own merits with no consideration given to its priority. Most Democrats preferred that system. They could spend money for their favorite
constituencies and favorite programs without having to argue that those
expenditures were more important than other spending.

To make matters even more chaotic, if Congress appropriated
money for a program the president didn't like, he simply didn't spend the
money—a presidential power called impoundment that Richard Nixon
used with abandon. That action set off senators like Muskie and North
Carolina's Sam Ervin, the self-proclaimed country lawyer who led the
Senate's investigation of President Nixon's Watergate scandal. As consti-
tutionalists, Ervin and Muskie believed impoundment undermined the
congressional power of the purse.

The Congressional Budget and Impoundment Control Act attempted
to end that chaos. It created a timetable for considering a congressional budget, passing individual spending and tax bills, and fitting them
into the congressional budget. Budget committees in both houses would
shape the congressional budget and guide the spending and taxing decisions that would follow. Most importantly, it created the Congressional
Budget Office to give Congress the analytical and institutional capacity to make rational budget decisions and rival the president's Office of
Management and Budget. And, to protect the constitutional spending
powers of Congress, it created a process for dealing with presidential
impoundments.

Throughout 1973 and the first half of 1974, Muskie was the driving
force behind the budget reform act. In keeping with Muskie's belief that
major reform legislation should have bipartisan sponsorship, freshman
Senator Bill Brock of Tennessee, a conservative Republican, was our
principal ally. Day after day, Muskie, Brock, a Brock staffer, and I would
meet with Charlie Schultze of the Brookings Institution (he had been
President Johnson's budget chief) to draft the bill in Muskie's hideaway
office in the basement of the Capitol.

Nixon signed the Congressional Budget Act in late July 1974. Because I was one of a handful of Senate staffers who drafted the bill,
Nixon sent me a presidential pen (symbolizing the pen with which he
signed the bill) and a note thanking me for my work on the bill. That
note, sent from his San Clemente, California, White House was dated

July 22, less than a month before he was forced from office by the Water-gate scandal. I still have that letter and pen framed in my office together with a letter from Ervin, another sponsor of the bill whose investigation led to Nixon's resignation.

In August 1974, Senate Majority Leader Mike Mansfield rewarded Muskie for his work on the legislation by naming him chairman of the new Senate Budget Committee. His role as a budget reformer and the often-lone advocate for fiscal discipline among liberals in his own party represented the early intellectual seeds of what would become the New Democrat movement. "Why," Muskie asked in his 1975 Liberal Party speech, "can't liberals talk about fiscal responsibility and productivity without feeling uncomfortable?"

Nearly two decades later, the progressive fiscal discipline that Muskie preached would serve as a cornerstone of President Bill Clinton's New Democrat economic growth policy.

Muskie's other two pieces of reform legislation would also serve as foundations for the New Democrats. The concept behind the Sunset bill was simple and straightforward: Every federal program had to be re-enacted by Congress every four years or it would "sunset," that is, go out of business. The Budget Act helped Congress control spending on the macro level. Sunset would create a system for reconsidering indi-vidual programs. The idea was not new. A similar bill that Muskie had introduced in the mid-1960s went nowhere.

When Muskie introduced the Sunset bill in December 1975, he de-cided to go to the floor and read the introductory speech—an unusual practice for senators who usually just signed legislation they were bring-ing forward and filed them with the clerk. When he delivered the speech, Senators Hubert Humphrey of Minnesota, one the leading liberals, and Barry Goldwater of Arizona, the leading conservative, were on the floor. Both stopped what they were doing and made short remarks, then signed on as cosponsors of the bill. That colloquy was unusual enough that the *Washington Star*, then Washington's afternoon newspaper, did a short piece on it. The story caught the attention of freshman Congressman Jim Blanchard of Michigan, later the state's governor, who telephoned me that night. "You owe me one," Blanchard told me, "I was Muskie's in-state coordinator in [the] 1972 [presidential primary campaign] and he never made it to Michigan. I want to be the House sponsor of this bill." For the next three years, until he sponsored the Chrysler bailout bill, Sunset was Blanchard's major legislative initiative.

Despite the fact that 62 senators signed on as cosponsors, the Sunset bill had rough sledding in the Senate. When the General Accounting Office and the Congressional Budget Office combined to give us an inventory of federal programs, we found, not unexpectedly, that Congress had a lot easier time enacting federal programs than terminating them. Spending continued for programs begun during the Civil War that no longer served any purpose. The government was so complex and programs so overlapping, it would have been impossible for the committees to consider every program every four years, so we put all programs on a 10-year review schedule: 20 percent of government expenditures would be reconsidered in every two-year Congress.

As the bill moved through the Senate, entitlements—like Social Security and Medicare—were exempted from sunset procedures. So were tax expenditures—credits and deductions that constituted spending through the tax code.

Weakened sunset legislation passed the Senate in the fall of 1978 but got nowhere in the House. Nonetheless, the three-year fight over Sunset turned out to be well worth it. It brought tremendous attention to the need to constantly modernize government, and for Democrats, at least, that helped reconnect them with Roosevelt's legacy of innovation.

As Muskie eloquently said in testimony before the 1976 Democratic Party Platform Committee: "Some Democrats seem to accept waste and inefficiency as a cost of helping people—a commission we pay for a Faustian bargain to protect what little we have gained—and that attacking waste somehow amounts to a repudiation of the New Deal. Well, all I can say is, what's so damn liberal about wasting money? I never heard Franklin Roosevelt say we had to reject reform ideas because we had more to lose than to gain. Instead, I heard him call for 'bold, persistent experimentation,' and say in 1936 that 'government without good management is a house built on sand.'"

Countercyclical revenue sharing was legislation with a wonky name that introduced an important innovation to the New Democrat movement.

During periods of high unemployment like the 1974–75 recession, state and local governments often face both an increased demand for services and a decline in tax revenue that forced them to lay off policemen, firemen, teachers, and other government workers. Countercyclical revenue sharing provided federal aid to replace some of that lost revenue.

It was a quintessentially New Democrat idea. It was progressive—the formula provided the most assistance to those states and communities with the highest unemployment rates. And, it was innovative—the program was designed to terminate once the recession had ended. When the national unemployment rate fell below six percent, the program ended. If the national unemployment rate remained higher than six percent, but a locality's rate fell below it, the assistance to that community ended. The legislation was intended to provide aid during the recession, not permanent aid to states and localities.

Countercyclical revenue sharing was the brainchild of Bob Reischauer, then an economist at the Brookings Institution and later director of the Congressional Budget Office, and later still, president of the Urban Institute. With its provision to terminate when the recession ended, it represented a clear break in Democratic Party thinking about antirecession programs. Typically, when unemployment rose, Democrats proposed big public works programs, and the 1974 recession was no exception; Speaker Carl Albert introduced a public works bill that passed the House in 1975.

Some economists believed as Reischauer did that countercyclical revenue sharing was a better antirecession idea than public works because it spent out quickly while the recession was still going on, and thus was truly countercyclical. Public works programs, they argued, spent out slowly because there were long lead-times in getting projects off the ground and often the money wasn't spent until long after the recession ended. Besides, public works projects, often viewed as political "pork barrel," were more likely to be authorized in response to political power than actual needs.

We had plenty of allies, including big city mayors like Coleman Young of Detroit, Moon Landrieu of New Orleans, Ken Gibson of Newark, Kevin White of Boston, Tom Maloney of Wilmington, and Joseph Alioto of San Francisco—all powers inside the Democratic Party—and the American Federation of State County and Municipal Workers and its founder Jerry Wurf, among the most prominent union leaders both in New York and nationally. The American Federation of Labor and Congress of Industrial Organizations became an enthusiastic supporter once we attached it to the Speaker's public works bill.

Even with that powerful outside support, the route to enactment for countercyclical revenue sharing was difficult, complicated, and required some real legislative hocus-pocus. The problem was the House, where the Government Operations Committee that had jurisdiction refused to even consider it. To get around that roadblock, we decided to attach it as an amendment to the Speaker's public works bill which had already passed the House. So we needed to a get the House to agree to accept our amendment in the conference committee where differences in the House and Senate passed versions were reconciled. To do that, we enlisted the critical support of the powerful House majority leader and future Speaker, Thomas P. "Tip" O'Neill of Massachusetts.

When Speaker Albert's public works bill came up on the Senate floor, Muskie and Brock amended it to add countercyclical revenue sharing. When it went to the conference committee, Tip O'Neill persuaded the House conferees to accept it, and with his support the bill, including countercyclical revenue sharing, passed the House. But we were still not home free. President Ford vetoed the bill and we failed to override the veto in the Senate by a handful of votes. After making minor modifications to assure the votes to override in the Senate, Congress passed the public works-countercyclical bill again. Ford vetoed it again, but this time we overrode his veto and the bill became law.

Countercyclical revenue sharing had a short and tumultuous life.

When it came up for reauthorization in the Senate Finance Committee in 1977, Senator Lloyd Bentsen of Texas, the subcommittee chairman, pushed through a subtle but essentially killer amendment. Bentsen, like his full committee chairman, Louisiana's Russell Long, represented an oil-patch state that did relatively well during the 1974–75 recession and thus got minimal benefit from a needs-targeted countercyclical bill. So, in committee he amended the formula to base the allocations on the number of unemployed instead of the unemployment rate. That seemed benign, but the number of unemployed is essentially a measure of size while the unemployment rate is a measure of hardship. A big city at or near full employment, like Houston or Dallas, could have a large number of actual unemployed people simply because of its size, without experiencing any negative impact from a recession.

So to save the essence of countercyclical, we had to figure out a way to amend the bill on the Senate floor to reinsert the original formula, no small feat since either Long or Bentsen, the second ranking member of the committee, would manage the legislation on the floor. I arranged with Dan Leach, Majority Leader Mike Mansfield's staffer, to schedule the bill during a rare Saturday session when both Long and Bentsen would be out of Washington. That meant that New York Senator Daniel Patrick Moynihan, the third-ranking member of the Finance Committee, who had favored the original needs-based formula, would manage the bill. I then arranged for Senator John Danforth of Missouri, a moderate Republican freshman, to offer a floor amendment reinserting the original formula. Moynihan accepted the amendment and moved to pass the bill. Countercyclical was safe for one more year.

That turned out to be its last. With the impact of the recession waning, the mayors pushed to remove the needs-based formula so it would become just another aid program for the cities, rather than a targeted antirecession bill. Congress wisely refused to reauthorize it. But we had set an important precedent by showing that government programs could be designed to terminate when the need for them had passed.

A decade later, fiscal discipline and reforming government would become core elements of the New Democrat message. The work that Ed Muskie did in the 1970s served as the intellectual foundation for those principles. He taught us that efficient and effective government needed to be part of a reinvigorated liberal agenda.

FOUR

THE HOUSE
DEMOCRATIC CAUCUS

1981–1985

The first organized effort of the New Democrat movement began in the House Democratic Caucus shortly after the 1980 Republican landslide. In January 1981, I became staff director of the caucus, the organization of all House Democrats, working for Louisiana Representative Gillis Long, its newly elected chairman.

Gillis Long was, in many ways, the godfather of the New Democrat movement. He was one of my mentors and a real hero of progressive politics. Elected to the House in 1962 from rural central Louisiana, his first vote was to expand the Rules Committee, enabling civil rights legislation to get to the House floor where it eventually passed. Like the rest of his delegation, Long voted against final passage of the civil rights bill, but his vote to expand the Rules Committee was enough to sink him, and he lost his reelection bid in 1964 to his cousin, Speedy Long, who called Gillis "the man who voted against the South."

With the solid support of black voters newly enfranchised by the Voting Rights Act, who made up one-third of the electorate in his district, Gillis Long won back his seat in 1972. His support among African Americans never wavered. In January 1985, black constituents in his hometown of Alexandria, Louisiana, lined the curb three and four deep with their hands over their hearts as his funeral procession rolled through their neighborhood on the way to the cemetery.

When Long and I had dinner in the House Members Dining Room two days after the 1980 election, he confidently offered me the job of running the caucus even though the chairmanship election was a month away. When I went back to the White House the next day, my friends in the Congressional Liaison Office told me that Long didn't really have much of a chance of winning that post because Tip O'Neill was backing another candidate. But when the votes were counted, Long had won 146 votes, exactly the number he told me he would garner at our dinner.

When Long's victory was announced, I excitedly made my way for the first time onto the House floor, a place that I would spend thousands of hours over the next several years. As caucus director and his main political advisor, my job was to drive caucus strategy.

Our goals were to begin to redefine the party so that it could reverse its 1980 losses and to engage a new generation of younger, more reform-minded House Democrats in national party affairs. The House Democratic Caucus is the oldest political institution in the House of Representatives other than the speakership. Until 1824, it nominated the Democratic candidates for president. Throughout its history, the caucus had periods when it played a prominent role in national politics and periods when it was virtually dormant. I came in during one of its dormant periods. In the early 1970s, House liberals had used caucus meetings to oppose the Vietnam War and promote other causes. In 1976, a newly elected House leadership was not eager to have the party's deep divisions debated in public and essentially shut the caucus down. During the chairmanship of Washington Congressman Tom Foley, who preceded Long, the caucus seldom met other than to organize the House at the beginning of each Congress. Foley ran most caucus operations out of his congressional office and hardly ever used the caucus office.

When I became its director, I went to see the caucus office and found a windowless room on the seventh floor of the Longworth Building with nothing but a pile of rubble—telephones, telephone wires, and other junk—in the middle of the floor. So I cleaned out the rubble. A Republican congressman whose office was next door had placed a large conference table out in the hall while his office was being painted. Before he could reclaim it, I moved it into the caucus office. Around that table, we began the New Democrat movement.

December 1980, when Long became caucus chairman, was a somber and soul-searching time for the Democrats. Not only had we lost the White House a month earlier, but we had lost control of the Senate for the first time since 1952. We also lost 33 seats in the House, including the majority whip and a number of committee chairs. Though we retained a nominal margin in the House of 242–193, our majority included 30 to 40 "boll weevils," conservative southern Democrats who would vote with President Reagan on key budget and tax votes in 1981, giving the Republicans de facto control of the House on important votes.

Keeping those boll weevils in the Democratic Party was an important objective of our caucus strategy. If they switched parties, the Republicans would have outright control of the White House and both Houses of Congress. Gillis Long, a southerner well respected by both liberals and conservatives, was the perfect person for that job.

In 1980 only 37 out of 277 members of the Democratic Caucus were delegates to the party's convention in New York. Conservative southern House members in particular saw being associated with the national Democratic Party as a threat to their own political survival. It was in that context that a number of young members, led by Tim Wirth and Dick Gephardt, and including Al Gore, Geraldine Ferraro, Martin Frost, Les Aspin, Tony Coelho, and many others, organized a retreat in January 1981 to discuss how they could begin to resurrect their party. Long had unofficially become the guru to these emerging House leaders who would become major players over the next four years as we constructed the foundation for the DLC and the New Democrat movement.

The January retreat, at the Capital Hilton Hotel in downtown Washington, proved a pivotal event in what would become the New Democrat movement, not so much for the specific issues discussed there, but because members emerged from it with a renewed determination to keep the reform effort going.

Wirth and Gephardt wanted leadership support for their issues retreat. Majority Leader Jim Wright helped finance it, a not-insignificant contribution. And, Tony Coelho, the young, newly elected chair of the House Campaign Committee, led a session devoted to politics. But, for the most part, the top House leaders, Speaker Tip O'Neill, Leader Wright, and Majority Whip Tom Foley kept the conference at arm's length, worried that the young members' ferment would cause political difficulty with the older, staid, less reform-minded committee chairmen. The late Kirk O'Donnell, Tip O'Neill's counsel, attended the conference on the Speaker's behalf.

Long, on the other hand, saw the young turks as his political allies, and he was eager to be the convener of the conference. Throughout the three-day conference, he was the senior leadership person there and gave it his imprimatur.

On the last morning of the conference, Sunday, January 11, 1981, I said to Long, "This is too good. We've got the best young members in the House eager to undertake an effort to rebuild the party. We can't let it end with one weekend. We've got to keep this going." He responded, "Why don't you talk to Kirk and see if the Speaker would react terribly negatively if we put together a little group?" O'Donnell agreed, and the "little group" became the Committee on Party Effectiveness (Caucus Committee) which was the focal point of the reform effort in the House and, in many ways, a predecessor of the DLC.

During his campaign for chairman, Long had promised to restore the caucus to its past glory. But I suspect that the top leadership and the "old bulls"—the chairmen who had historically run the House committees as their own fiefdoms—had no idea what was in store. We knew that we would never achieve our goals if we worked through regular House channels; the old bulls had no interest in our new ideas or party reforms. Our audience was really the political world outside the House: the press, political strategists, intellectuals, and policy wonks who set the context of the national political debate. Since most members of our Caucus Committee had little seniority or official power in the House, our strategic challenge was to figure out a way to go around the powers-that-be in the House to reach that larger political world.

Tim Wirth told me a great story that explains the atmosphere in the House at the time. He was part of the large group of Democratic House members elected in 1974, in the wake of the Watergate scandal. The so-called Watergate babies class was full of young reformers and Wirth, who understands how to drive change as well as anyone I have worked with, was one of its ringleaders. At their first organizing caucus in 1975, the reformers challenged the seniority system and ousted three committee chairmen whom the reformers argued were old, ineffective, and out of touch.

As Tim Wirth tells it, on the final day of the three-day caucus meeting, a senior member of the House approached him, looked at him, and said, "Young man, I've seen you on national TV the last two nights. I've been in this House for 26 years, and I ain't never been on national TV." The senior member was sending him a message—in the old House, power was derived from seniority and working on the inside, not from appearances on television. But Wirth knew we were moving into a new era, and that was about to change. Two years later the House began experimenting with televised floor proceedings, and two years after that C-SPAN began gavel-to-gavel coverage. In the new era, the ability to make a persuasive argument before the television cameras or in the press would be as sure a route to power as making secret backroom deals. For reformers on the Caucus Committee, it was the best route since we had little ability to prevail in smoke-filled rooms.

The key to any successful reform effort is to avoid being crushed before you even get to the starting gate. That means picking early battles and battlegrounds carefully. That doesn't mean avoiding tough fights—if you do that you'll never bring about change—but it does mean not taking on battles before you're strong enough to win them. It also means fighting battles on the most favorable turf possible, essentially creating your own playing field on which the chances of winning are greatly enhanced. I never liked fighting on our opponents' home turf where our adversaries set the rules. Both at the caucus and later at the DLC, I followed two simple rules that proved critical to our success: Because first impressions matter, I picked a first battle I could win, and I created my own playing fields so that I would always have a home field advantage.

The caucus got off to a fast start. President Reagan had seized the political initiative early in his term. In 1981 he put Tip O'Neill and the Democrats on their heels when he came out with a proposal for a 30 percent across the board tax cut and biting budget cuts in domestic spending. Sympathy and support for the president grew in March 1981 when he was shot after delivering a speech at the Washington Hilton Hotel. Democrats needed a politically astute and substantive response. And with the White House and the Senate both under Republican control, that response had to come from the House.

The Democratic budget, drafted by the House Budget Committee, would be the official substantive response, but House committees were notoriously bad at delivering political messages, and I believed this case would be no different.

So the Caucus Committee came to the rescue. With Gephardt leading the effort while Gillis Long recuperated from open-heart surgery, we drafted a statement of principles on the budget that would become the Democrats' political response to Reagan. During March, a few nights a week, I would meet in the windowless caucus office with Gephardt, Wirth, Leon Panetta, and other House members. The Speaker's two young staff members, Ari Weiss, the staff head of the Steering and Policy

Committee, and Ari's top assistant Jack Lew (currently President Barack Obama's Secretary of the Treasury) sometimes joined us to shape a political policy statement that defined the Democratic response to the Reagan budget and economic policy.

While Reagan eventually won the fights over the budget and taxes in 1981, our statement made its mark. On April 9, 1981, the *New York Times* printed the full text of our statement.

The themes and rhetoric in that first budget statement later became cornerstones of the DLC-New Democrat message, demonstrating the remarkable consistency of the New Democrat movement. It began with a preface that tied our policies to the historic principles and accomplishments of the Democratic Party.

"For half a century, the Democratic Party has been an engine of equity and progress," we wrote. "It has stimulated upward mobility and achieved a better life for millions of Americans. It has been the voice of working men and women, winning for them the right to decent wages and working conditions. It has protected racial and religious minorities from injustice and discrimination. It has promoted quality education for all of America's young and has secured, for older citizens, a living income and adequate medical care. Democratic programs have been the catalyst for vibrant economic growth in the private sector of the economy."

The statement defined our goal as achieving sustained economic growth and called for an all-out effort to control inflation, two important breakthroughs for Democrats in 1981. It outlined a budget strategy that included controlling federal spending, reforming and cutting taxes, and reducing the federal deficit—all while promoting investments to encourage work rather than welfare, strengthen national defense, generate technological innovation, prepare workers for a new economy, and protect the social safety net. It specifically attacked Reagan's assertion that government was "the problem" and rejected the administration's tax plan.

The budget statement was the right first battle for us to take on. It left a good impression and gave us running room for later reform efforts. Because it was to a large degree a political exercise that the Democrats desperately needed, it allowed us to begin to develop and establish our new themes without fear of being crushed by the old bulls. Moreover, because we ran it through the steering committee, it gave our effort the credibility of Tip O'Neill and the leadership, who did not see it as a threat. That the *New York Times* chose to print it in full was icing on the cake.

We would need that credibility as the year wore on. After Reagan's victories on the budget and especially on his tax cut bill, we began to hear grumblings about Tip O'Neill's leadership in the Caucus Committee and the caucus generally. The Speaker started to get nervous that we were really a renegade group within the caucus. He responded by asking his close ally, Dick Bolling, chairman of the Rules Committee, to keep an eye on us. That turned out to be more form than substance. Bolling was a close friend of both Gillis Long and Dick Gephardt, whom he viewed as a protégé, and I can't remember one instance when he did anything to inhibit our work.

We diffused any potential conflict with O'Neill and the leadership by making the strategic decision not to challenge the legislative hegemony of the old bulls, implementing my second rule of creating our own playing field. It was clear from the outset, and became even clearer as time went on, that the committee chairmen couldn't care less about any new ideas we might come up with in the Caucus Committee, and if we tried to push those ideas in the legislative process, they would never see the light of day.

So we devised a different strategy. In 1974, 1978, and again in 1982, the Democratic National Committee held midterm party conferences. Instead of developing our policy ideas for the legislative process, I suggested to Gillis Long in an August 31, 1981, memorandum that we develop policy statements on a limited number of issues and package them in a "mini-platform" for presentation to the midterm conference the next summer in Philadelphia.

The strategy outlined in my memo created a political playing field for our work. It made clear that our purpose was to become a force for change in the national Democratic Party, and, importantly, it removed us from the day-to-day legislative workings of the House, eliminating any incentive for the House powers to hinder our efforts. Long readily agreed to the plan to present our ideas to the midterm conference, and in September we got Tip O'Neill's agreement as well. We even passed a resolution in the caucus authorizing it.

Over the next couple of months, Long appointed task forces on the economy, national security, the environment, small business, and women's issues to draft the ideas. The most important task force was on long-term economic policy, and we kept that one close in the family: Long, me working on his behalf, Wirth, and Gephardt. With input from Weiss and Lew, we set out to redefine Democratic economic policy.

That task force produced a groundbreaking report for Democrats called "Rebuilding the Road to Opportunity: A Democratic Direction for the 1980s." We called it the Yellow Book or the "yellow brick road" because the Government Printing Office printed it with a bright yellow cover.

Its centerpiece was private sector economic growth. That seems pretty basic, but in the 1970s, Democrats had shied away from talking about growth, focusing entirely on fairness. For example, in the 1980 Democratic platform written by the Carter White House, every economic plank was a public jobs program. While not ignoring fairness, the Yellow Book refocused on growth, and that would become a pillar of the New Democrat movement a decade later.

Many of the policies we recommended, including one for an economic coordinating council in the White House, would become staples of the New Democrat economic policies put in place in the Clinton administration. We called for creating an investment environment with fiscal and tax policies that reduced debt and encouraged growth, for investment in people, technology, and infrastructure, and for expanding trade. We also called for reducing our dependence on foreign oil, for more cooperative, less confrontational relations between business and labor, and for policies to help Americans manage the transition from the manufacturing economy to a new technology-driven economy.

For more than a year we worked through dozens of drafts in the Caucus Committee to come up with the Yellow Book. We discussed some of the ideas at the midterm conference in Philadelphia, but we formally released it at lunch with Dan Rather, Bill Curtiss, and Diane Sawyer, the three top talents at CBS News in New York in September 1982. Tim Wirth, who was chairman of the Telecommunications Subcommittee in the House, arranged the lunch.

In addition to that lunch, our team did a small media tour to introduce the report to the editorial boards of the *New York Times, Wall Street Journal,* and other national outlets. We got significant press for our new approaches. "This is a significant departure, I think, for the Democratic Party," Wirth said during our meeting with the *Times.* "We want to move away from a temporary economic policy of redistribution to a long-term policy of growth and opportunity."[1]

The *New York Times* editorialized: "Growth and fairness may be familiar Democratic Party goals—but purposeful investment in growth is not. The Democratic proposals could put new life in the old liberal agenda."[2]

With that media tour, we had effectively changed the playing field. Though we formally sent the report through channels to Speaker O'Neill, our audience was not a dozen or so disinterested committee chairmen but the political stage at large.

A few days after our New York trip, I had lunch with one of the top people I had worked with in the Carter White House. "How did you get labor to sign off on the report?" he asked. "It was easy," I responded. "We didn't ask them." The former Carter official assumed that the labor movement would object to our emphasis on growth rather than fairness. And, because of the labor movement's power in the Democratic Party, we seldom did anything in the Carter administration without running it by them. But we needed to change our policy, and I wasn't about to give the unions or any other constituency group a sign-off on what we recommended.

The Yellow Book with its focus on growing the economy was the key breakthrough. No matter how much establishment Democrats focused on fairness, private sector growth was and is the prerequisite to expanding opportunity, particularly for the middle class. When Democrats talked fairness, voters heard "they're going to take money from people who work and give it to people who don't." Years earlier, when I was in the Carter White House, Senator Paul Tsongas had said to me: "The problem with the Democratic Party is that we spend so much time worrying about passing out the golden eggs that we forget to worry about the health of the goose." In our Yellow Book, we were finally worrying about the health of the goose.

With Wisconsin Congressman Les Aspin (who would become Clinton's first Secretary of Defense) doing the heavy lifting, in the fall of 1982 we also produced a report on national security and defense issues. That report and another Aspin wrote for the caucus in 1984 were the forerunners to a major DLC paper two years later called "Defending America," written by the party's three most respected leaders on national security, Senator Sam Nunn of Georgia, Aspin, and Senator Al Gore of Tennessee. "Defending America" played a major role in redefining the Democratic Party's posture on national security and separated the party from its perceived antimilitary posture in the post-Vietnam era.

Taking our policy ideas outside the House proved to be the right strategy for us. That became crystal clear during organizing caucuses in January 1983. By that time, Speaker O'Neill had become an advocate of our efforts to reform the party. Under House rules near the beginning of each session, committee chairs were required to submit to the Budget Committee all legislative recommendations that they intended to pass that year that could impact the federal budget.

As we were organizing for the new Congress after the 1982 election, the Speaker said, "Why don't we take the recommendations of the Yellow Book and ask the committee chairs to move them?" So he went to the floor and offered a resolution in the caucus to have the committee chairs include the progress they'd made on the recommendations in the Yellow Book in their submissions to the budget committee that spring. The resolution passed. But not one of the committee chairmen followed through on even one of our ideas. They all had their own priorities for their committees and we weren't on their radar screens.

At the time of the 1982 election, unemployment was running at nearly 11 percent. Democrats were running on social security and a jobs bill that had passed the House in September, but died in the Republican-controlled Senate. After the election, in which we won 26 seats, Tip O'Neill went down to the White House and made a deal with Reagan: If we passed the same jobs bill, Reagan would support it.

The Speaker called a meeting of committee chairmen to inform them of the deal. For me, it was an eye-opening experience. "Fellas," Tip said, "I got the president to agree to our bill. So we need to pass it again, and then we'll send it down and he'll sign it."

Augustus "Gus" Hawkins, a liberal from Los Angeles and chair of the subcommittee that came up with the bill, responded: "Mr. Speaker, that's not even a start. We're not going to pass that bill again." If Reagan was going to give us that much, Hawkins wanted more. Tip and Hawkins went back and forth. Finally, in frustration, Tip said "Fellas, I need you on this. This is what you said you wanted. I went down and made this deal. I need your help on this." The Speaker had barely finished his plea when old Carl Perkins of rural Kentucky, the chair of the full Labor and Education committee, got up, walked out. As Perkins headed for the door, O'Neill said, "Carl, old buddy, where you going? I need your help on this." Without breaking stride, Perkins said, "Mr. Speaker, I'm hungry. I think I'll go get me a sandwich." That was the end of that meeting.

That was the House in 1983. Even a bill that the House had passed and was agreed to by the Speaker and the president was no sure thing. We needed a new strategy.

For me, the 1982 midterm election underscored the limitations of "the old-time religion" as a political message. The week before the vote, I had invited Ed Tufte, a professor at Yale who did political modeling, to come before the Caucus Committee. Based on economic conditions, his model showed the Democrats should win more than 50 seats. So when we won only 26, I believed we had badly underperformed. In the face of high unemployment, Reagan argued his policies were working and his campaign message of "Stay the Course" proved effective enough to cut projected Democratic gains in half.

In spring 1983, a group of Caucus Committee members met occasionally in our windowless room to talk about how we could pass a budget that year. In both 1981 and 1982, Democrats in the House had been unable to pass our budget and, despite winning back 26 seats, passage of the Democratic budget in 1983 was no sure thing.

During one late-night session we decided that our strategy should be what Long called "participatory democracy." We needed to get everybody in the caucus, or at least as many as would participate, engaged in shaping the Democratic alternative. Jim Jones, chair of the House Budget Committee, had created a nine-page memorandum listing all the big policy choices his committee would have to make to produce a budget. With his support, our plan was to have all House Democrats, not just budget committee members, fill out a choices memo. Then we would compile the results and use that information to guide Jim and his committee in shaping the Democrats' budget. We believed that if members were confronted with the actual choices the committee had to make, not the exaggerated rhetorical choices that dominated the debate, the choices would be so obvious that members of all philosophies in our party would likely agree.

We got more than 175 Democratic members of the House to respond to our choices memo. And the answers were exactly what we expected.

When the committee produced its budget, we launched an all-out campaign to sell it that culminated in a caucus meeting a few days before the floor vote. When a number of boll weevils, including their leader, Charlie Stenholm of Texas, spoke in favor of our budget, I knew we were home free. Our participatory democracy strategy had worked. For the first time since Ronald Reagan took office, we passed a Democratic budget in the House.

For much of the last half of 1983, the Caucus Committee pored over drafts of policy papers that refined, updated, and expanded our work on the Yellow Book and our policy task forces in 1981 and 1982. Every Tuesday and sometimes twice a week, Congressman Marty Sabo of Minnesota led what seemed like endless sessions as we drafted a policy booklet called "Renewing America's Promise: A Democratic Blueprint for Our Nation's Future," released in January 1984. This blueprint planted seeds of the New Democrat movement that would fully blossom a decade later. As Gillis Long wrote in his introduction, it

> demonstrates again the vitality of the Democratic Party. It is a prod-
> uct of what I believe is an emerging new force within our Democratic
> Party—made up of members of Congress, young in mindset if not in
> age, who will become the next generation of leaders in our country and
> in our party. These men and women are ready to risk new departures,
> to define new standards of excellence, to explore new ways to advance
> enduring Democratic commitments. . . . Their agenda is a strategy for
> American renewal throughout the 1980's and 1990's. . . . Grounded in
> the fundamental principles of the Democratic Party, our program seeks
> not to dwell in the past, but to seize and secure the future.

Long made it clear that the document was not intended to represent the "official position" of the Democratic Party. It was the voice of emerging leaders bent on changing the party message that kept losing national elections. He continued:

> Our program amounts to a clean break with the recent rhetoric—but
> not the traditional values of the Democratic Party. It aims at cement-
> ing a new national coalition around broad-based strategies to rekindle
> private enterprise, to restore the competitiveness of American industry,
> to regenerate our sense of community and mutual commitment and to
> rededicate America's strength to the cause of peace.
>   We mean to redirect the nation's energies toward investment and
> growth to redeem America's promise of equal and expanding oppor-
> tunity. . . . This volume helps Democrats to reestablish our identity as
> the party of growth, for growth is the prerequisite of opportunity, of
> widening horizons [for] our people. It reaffirms our commitment to a
> stronger America, for the Democratic Party always has been foremost
> in defense of liberty. It renews our standing as the party of peace, for
> Democrats historically have led the quest for arms control and stability.
> It serves notice that the Democratic Party has the compassion to care
> and the toughness to govern.

Near the end of 1983, Pat Caddell, who gained fame as pollster for both George McGovern and Jimmy Carter, conducted a series of innovative polls in Iowa, the state of the first Presidential Caucus. Caddell put a mythical candidate, a Mr. Smith who was armed with the message we were developing in the caucus, up against the front-runners, former Vice President Walter Mondale and Senator John Glenn of Ohio. Not surprisingly, Mr. Smith overwhelmed the leading candidates.

Convinced that we had the right message, all we needed was a candidate. The candidate in the field who came closest to Mr. Smith was Colorado Senator Gary Hart, who was running as the candidate of new ideas. But the ever-scheming Caddell had a better idea: Lure Delaware's Senator Joe Biden into the race. Caddell had done Biden's polling when he was first elected as a 29-year-old in 1972, and he was clearly Caddell's favorite potential candidate. More importantly, Biden had, in fact, advocated much of Mr. Smith's message.

Caddell's strategy, with which I was happy to go along, was to use his polling to convince a critical mass of House Democrats, many of whom had already committed to Mondale, to support Biden. Then in January 1984, on the night of the filing deadline for the New Hampshire primary, Biden would announce with the phalanx of supportive House Democrats standing behind him. In the end, Biden had the good sense to put a stop to our nonsense. We did not have our candidate, but we had a pretty good idea that our message grounded in the policy work of the Caucus Committee could prevail.

Developing a winning message became our primary goal. But we were also determined to make our group of emerging leaders an important force in the presidential nominating process. At a breakfast in the fall of 1981 in the House Dining Room in the Capitol, Gillis Long and I had hatched the idea of the super delegates with North Carolina Governor Jim Hunt and David Price. Hunt had been tapped by the Democratic National Committee to chair a commission to reform the presidential nominating rules for 1984. Price, now a member of Congress, served as Hunt's executive director.

The Hunt commission created the super delegates, elected officials and party leaders who would automatically become uncommitted delegates for the 1984 Convention. There would be no return to the pre-1968 conditions in which the party bosses dominated, but we wanted to temper the influence of interest group leaders and party activists in the nominating process. We believed Democratic fortunes in presidential races would increase if the elected officials whose outlooks were moderated by actually having to be elected took a bigger role in the conventions. Making them super delegates would give them that role.

Working with two House members on the Hunt Commission, Mo Udall of Arizona, and Geraldine Ferraro of New York (who would become the first woman on a national ticket in 1984), the Caucus Committee proposed that two-thirds of the Democratic House members and all Democratic senators and governors be automatic or super delegates. Our breakfast with Hunt and Price in the fall of 1981 was to close the deal.

But in Democratic Party politics, nothing is that easy. Worried that the addition of the super delegates would diminish their influence at the convention, leaders of women's groups and organized labor objected. A debate raged over the winter. I spent many Sunday nights on the telephone with Ferraro as she felt heat from opponents of super delegates when she went back to her district for weekends. Finally, a compromise was reached at a meeting in the spring of 1982: 60 percent of the House Democrats would be super delegates. That meant four times as many House members would be delegates in 1984 as in 1980.

The House super delegates were to be elected by the Democratic Caucus. At Tim Wirth's urging, we scheduled the election for January 1984 even before the Iowa caucus and the New Hampshire primary. Wirth was supporting Senator Gary Hart, whose campaign against Vice President Mondale and the Democratic Party establishment paralleled much of the work of the Caucus Committee. I'm sure Tim thought, as did I, the affinity many younger House members had with Hart would give the Colorado senator an early boost.

It didn't turn out that way. As good as Hart was at framing the debate—at challenging old orthodoxies and old arrangements with new ideas—he was bad at some of the fundamentals of politics. Hart never called House members to ask for their support. Mondale, on the other hand, was relentless in pursuing them. Mondale racked up endorsement after endorsement of House members, including many, like Dick Gephardt, whom I believed should logically have been a Hart supporter. As a result, the House delegates gave Mondale an overwhelming early delegate count lead. The *New York Times* reported that Mondale had gained the endorsement of 100 House delegates out of 164, while only four House delegates were committed to Hart. That number was large enough to keep the vice president in the delegate count lead even after Hart won upset victories in New Hampshire and other early primaries.

While Mondale benefited from our decision to elect the House delegates before the end of January, he was less pleased with another caucus decision.

In August 1983 Congressman Charles Schumer of Brooklyn asked me if I thought I could get Long to agree to have the caucus sponsor a televised debate among the Democratic presidential candidates. Schumer wanted to come up with a debate format that would be both informative and entertaining for the television audience. The brash Schumer, later elected to the Senate, was just 32 years old at the time and in his second term in the House after serving three terms in the New York State Assembly. He got 100 of his House colleagues to sign a letter urging the eight major Democratic candidates to participate in the debate and, with the help of Washington super-lawyer Berl Bernhard, arranged for Dartmouth College to host it and for the Boston public television station WGBH to produce and televise it.

With the site and television secured, we were ready to break the pattern of candidate debates. Up to that time, almost all presidential debates followed the same dull format. A panel of journalists or experts questioned the candidates, who had 90 seconds or two minutes to answer each question before moving on to the next. There was no opportunity for the candidates to debate each other or for the debate moderator to pursue a line of questioning.

Our new format called for a three-hour debate, twice the customary length. Instead of a panel of reporters or experts, we had two moderators, each in charge of half the debate: Ted Koppel of ABC News "Nightline" and Phil Donahue, popular talk show host whose specialty was roaming his audience and coaxing tough answers from his guests. The idea of Koppel, among America's most respected television newsmen, as the first moderator was an easy sell. But O'Neill and Long had to be convinced about Donahue, who had pioneered the daytime talk show concept. We arranged a luncheon in the Capitol for them and a handful of other caucus members to meet Donahue and reassure them that he was up to the task. Donahue had prepared exhaustively for the meeting, reading up on all of the current issues. During the lunch, Donahue rose from the table and began to pace up and down, emulating his style from his daytime talk show and leading a discussion of the serious issues that would arise during the debate. O'Neill and Long were convinced.

By Thanksgiving, we were ready to issue invitations to the candidates when we got word that Mondale no longer wanted to participate. In September and October, he had picked up the endorsements of just about every interest and constituency group in our party, and he was not eager to risk his front-runner status by appearing on equal footing with his seven opponents, especially for a three-hour debate.

The Mondale campaign put pressure on Schumer to cancel the debate or, at least, to change the format. They leaked a story to syndicated columnists Jack Germond and Jules Witcover accusing Schumer of trying to undermine the front-runner's campaign. And they had New York Assembly Speaker Stanley Fink, Schumer's mentor, tell him that if he went through with the debate, he would not be invited to the White House. When Schumer told me of Fink's threat, I responded: "You won't be alone. Mondale won't be invited either."

On December 1, 1983, Schumer called me to say he was feeling the pressure and he thought he and Long should meet with Mondale. Long wasn't particularly eager for the meeting, but told me if Schumer insisted to go ahead and schedule it.

We scheduled the meeting about a week later. Long wanted the meeting held not in his Capitol office but in the Board of Education Room, a couple of doors down the hall. I wasn't sure what he was up to, but since he was adamant about not meeting in his office, I moved the meeting site.

In December 1983, Gillis Long looked like death warmed over. Once stocky, by that winter he probably weighed less than 130 pounds. His heart was so weak that he could only walk about 50 feet before having to stop and rest. Many nights, he had to be taken from his Watergate apartment to Bethesda Naval Hospital to have fluid pumped from his lungs, a symptom of congestive heart failure.

Mondale didn't come to the meeting, but sent his campaign chairman, Jim Johnson, and his campaign manager, Bob Beckel. Long started the meeting by saying that we hoped Mondale would participate in the debate. Johnson objected to the debate format, saying it would undermine Mondale. "Are we treating Fritz any different than any other candidate?" Long asked. "No," Johnson responded, "but he deserves better for all he's done for members of the House."

Long cut him off: "You go back and tell Fritz we'll do what we damn well please." With that, he walked out of the room. I now knew why Long didn't want to have the meeting in his office. About half an hour later, Mondale called him to apologize for what Johnson had said. A few minutes later Bob Strauss, the influential former Democratic Party chairman, called to send the same message. After hanging up the phone, Long turned to me and said: "If someone in my condition can intimidate Fritz Mondale, imagine what [then-Soviet leader] Andropov could do." I'm sure that experience is why Long did not endorse Mondale until he had clinched the nomination.

Mondale agreed to participate, and on the night of January 15, 1984, we had all eight candidates in the debate hall on the campus of Dartmouth College: Mondale, Hart, Senator John Glenn, Senator Alan Cranston of California, Senator Ernest Fritz Hollings of South Carolina, George McGovern, the Reverend Jesse Jackson, and former Governor Reubin Askew of Florida.

The debate did not disappoint. In the final 30 minutes, the two leading candidates engaged in a shouting match. The "eight major Democratic presidential candidates engaged in the sharpest exchanges of the new campaign year today in a nationally televised debate that produced a shouted confrontation between Walter F. Mondale and Senator John Glenn," wrote Howell Raines in the *New York Times*.[3]

"The exchange between Mr. Glenn, an Ohio Democrat, and Mr. Mondale, the former vice president, centered on the cost of programs favored by Mr. Mondale and his call for legislation to protect the American automobile industry from foreign competition," Raines's story continued. "At one point, Mr. Mondale leaped to his feet, shouting 'Who has the floor here?' and condemned Mr. Glenn's figures as 'baloney.'"[4]

The real beneficiary of the debate was Gary Hart, who responded to the Mondale-Glenn spat: "Quarreling between the two of you as to whose mistakes were worst is not going to win the election or govern the country." Hart went on to finish a surprising second to Mondale in the Iowa caucus and used the momentum from that race to swamp the former vice president in the New Hampshire primary. While Mondale eventually won the nomination, Hart was his principal competition all the way to the convention.

The debate was a momentous event. Nearly 10 million people watched the caucus-sponsored debate, an enormous number for a political event at the time and especially for one not broadcast on any of the commercial networks. When it was over, we had changed the way that presidential debates were conducted forever.

FIVE

EARLY DLC

1985

The Mondale election debacle made it clear to me that we needed the Democratic Leadership Council (DLC). And I wasn't alone. On November 29, 1984, three weeks after the election, Gillis Long was asked to attend a dinner "to discuss the future of the Democratic Party" by Virginia Governor Chuck Robb, the head of the Democratic Governors' Association (DGA).

The guest list at the Robb dinner included fellow Governors Bruce Babbitt of Arizona, Mark White of Texas, and John Carlin of Kansas, Senators Wendell Ford of Kentucky and Lawton Chiles of Florida, Congressmen Jim Jones of Oklahoma, Steny Hoyer of Maryland, Tony Coelho of California, and Tim Wirth of Colorado, and former party chairs Bob Strauss and John White, both of Texas.

At the dinner, Robb wanted to discuss "lessons learned" from this election, and he let me know ahead of time that he intended to call on Gillis Long first. To prepare Long, I gave him a memo outlining six lessons he might want to discuss. (*It is important to note that the electorate in 1984 was very different than the electorate in 2012—so lessons that applied then would not necessarily apply today.*) These six lessons would be at the core of why we went on to create the DLC:

1. This election had confirmed what most of us suspected for some time: As a national party Democrats are in deep trouble. This was our fourth loss in the last five presidential elections. In those five elections, we have averaged 42 percent of the vote and only once in 1976 did we

exceed that percentage. For the first time since it began polling in 1975, the *New York Times* found in its postelection poll that more Americans identified themselves with the Republicans than with the Democrats, 47–44.

2. Putting together a coalition of liberals and minorities is not the way to win national elections and achieve majority party status. To win national elections, we have to do well among men, whites, independents, and young voters—exactly where the Republicans are making their biggest gains. This year, the Democratic ticket got just 37 percent of the male vote, 33 percent of the whites, barely one in four southern whites and 40 percent of the votes under 30. In short, the data suggest that in this election the Democrats hit bedrock: hard-core partisans, liberals, and minorities. And together they do not constitute a majority.

3. A winning coalition must be built around ideas, not constituency groups. If the Mondale campaign showed us anything, it was that we cannot put together a majority by appealing to specific constituencies. The only way for Democrats to reverse the Republican trend is to develop a message that has broad appeal to the American people, a set of ideas around which a coalition can form that will draw voters to it. The fact of politics in 1984 is that the party that seizes the idea initiative dominates the political process. We lost the idea initiative in 1978—and ever since the Republicans have set the political agenda.

4. We must develop a message with national appeal; we cannot write off large areas of the country—such as the South and the West—and continue as a viable national party. With the exception of President Carter, during the past five elections, our national ticket and our national message have been aimed at the Northeast and Midwest. As a result, we have not won an electoral vote in the West since 1964 and, except for 1976, we have been routed in the South.

5. We cannot afford to become a liberal party; our message must attract moderates and conservatives, as well. In an electorate where 17 percent of the voters identify themselves as liberals, 28 percent as conservatives, and 46 percent as moderates, Democrats are increasingly viewed as the "liberal" party. Our party has virtually severed its conservative wing, once a significant segment of the Democratic Party. That has hurt us particularly in the South. As we have become more liberal, we have diminished our appeal to moderates—we have lost them by an average of 15 points in the last five elections.

6. As elected officials and party leaders, we need to do a better job of steering our party away from trouble. This year the party establishment deserves a large share of the blame for our defeat. Elected officials and party leaders sought and won status as unpledged delegates at our convention. We argued that we deserved that status so that we could hold back and keep the party from nominating a candidate with little chance to win. But most elected officials and party leaders didn't hold back, they endorsed early and were in no position to exercise good judgment when our likely nominee sank like a rock during the month before the convention.

Those six lessons of this election all point to one thing: the need for our party to change, and change drastically. We need a new image; we need a new structure; and we need new spokesmen.

If we don't act now to develop and promote a new message, to rid the party of the cancer of single interest and single constituency caucuses, to showcase new leaders, to establish a nominating procedure that produces a candidate who can win a general election, then we are destined to become a minority party for the foreseeable future. If we try to stand pat waiting for the Republicans to save us, we will not be saved and what happened in the Senate elections in 1980 will happen in the House sooner than we think.

At the end of that memo, I suggested that the action agenda of the dinner should be an effort, led by the Democratic governors, to back a candidate for chairman of the Democratic National Committee (DNC), the official party organization responsible for the nominating process, the national convention, and servicing state parties. The job was open because the chairman, Californian Charles T. Manatt, stepped down after the Mondale loss. They took my advice. The next morning, Governor Robb asked me to be on an afternoon flight to Hilton Head, South Carolina, where the newly elected Democratic governors were meeting. A main topic would be the selection of the party chairman.

Only a handful of the newly elected governors came to Hilton Head and little was accomplished there. Over the next two weeks, a small group—Chuck Robb, Bruce Babbitt, who would succeed Robb as chair of DGA, Gillis Long, and Dick Gephardt—began a search for a candidate we could support. The two most promising possibilities were House Budget Committee chairman Jim Jones of Oklahoma and former Portland mayor and Transportation Secretary Neil Goldschmidt. Neither ran.

It quickly became apparent that we would not find an acceptable candidate—and that, even if we could, we had little chance of influencing the election for party chairman. Though we had the backing of the DGA and the House Democratic Caucus, we had few votes among the DNC membership which elected its own chairman.

So, as fast as we got into the DNC chairman's race, we got out. On Sunday, December 16, 1984, Robb and Babbitt called a meeting with the state party chairs at a hotel in Kansas City, Kansas, to pull the plug on the effort.

The night before, five Democratic operatives met for dinner in the back room of a Kansas City steakhouse—Fred Duval, top aide to Babbitt; Chuck Dolan, executive director of the DGA representing Robb; John Rendon, a veteran Democratic operative; Bill Romjue, who organized Gary Hart's 1984 campaign in Iowa and worked for me at the caucus; and, me. We agreed that we needed to start our own group—independent of the DNC—if we were to change the direction of the party.

The next day at a private premeeting of governors, Mike Dukakis pushed hard to get our support for Paul Kirk from his home state. Kirk, a Ted Kennedy confidant, was the clear front-runner among DNC members. Babbitt and Robb resisted supporting Kirk. Later, at the main session the seven governors and about 40 state party leaders who attended could not agree on a candidate. The only consensus was that we needed to redo the party's message and should set up a new policy council for that purpose.

Two weeks later, on January 2, 1985, I delivered a memorandum called "Saving the Democratic Party" to Robb, Babbitt, Long, Gephardt, and Senators Sam Nunn of Georgia and Chiles of Florida calling for "the establishment by elected officials, on their own authority, of a governing council for the Democratic Party, independent of the DNC." All except Long, who died of heart failure 18 days later, would be founders of the DLC.

The council's purpose, I wrote, "should be simple and direct: to develop an agenda strengthening the Democratic Party and making it competitive again in national elections. In a sense, the council would simply assume the role and the authority of the policy making, governing body of the party."

I emphasized that the council should be independent of the DNC—that it have its own staff, raise its own money, and operate under its own rules. I was acutely aware that an attempt in 1981 to create a Strategy Council inside the DNC to give elected officials a greater say in the direction of the party had failed after getting mired in party rules and red tape.

The proposal I outlined called for the council to be sanctioned by the DGA and the House and Senate Democratic Caucuses. Thankfully, we rejected that route. Instead, we decided to move forward on our own and create an organization composed of Democratic leaders, but not officially connected to any party, gubernatorial, or Capitol Hill entity. That meant we could operate without any party constraints at all.

Robb, Nunn, Chiles, Gephardt, and I met in Nunn's Senate office in mid-January to discuss how to turn my idea into action. The good news was that I had convinced them to follow my advice and start an independent organization. The bad news was that Nunn wanted me to do an in-depth outline that fleshed out how we'd organize our council. "No good deed goes unpunished," he said.

To help prepare the materials needed to launch the council, I enlisted Will Marshall, who had worked briefly for Gillis Long as a speechwriter before serving as press secretary for North Carolina Governor Jim Hunt in the 1984 Senate race he lost to Jessie Helms.

Throughout January 1985, I met regularly with Nunn, Chiles, Gephardt, and Robb to flesh out our plans. No one played a more important role than Chuck Robb. He regularly helicoptered in from Richmond, where he was beginning his last year as governor, to Washington to drive the effort to form the DLC. It was in his Washington office in the Hall of the States that we decided to name our group the Democratic Leadership Council.

I was still working for Long at the time. His term as caucus chair had ended—Dick Gephardt was the new chair—and I was working out of the offices of the Joint Economic Committee (JEC). Tip O'Neill had appointed Long to chair that committee for the next two years, and Long, whose health was failing fast, had asked me to run the committee for him as staff director.

Gillis Long died of a heart attack at halftime on Super Bowl Sunday 1985, six weeks before we founded the DLC and two days before his formal election as JEC chairman, so my position as staff director was no longer guaranteed. The week after Gillis died, Nunn, Chiles, Robb, and Gephardt asked me to found and run the DLC. I told them I'd have to think about it. It was big leap that I was not sure I was ready to take—running an organization where I'd have to raise the money to pay my own salary. For 18 years, I'd been on one federal payroll or another—either on Capitol Hill or in the executive branch—and the security of a federal paycheck was important to me with a wife, two young kids, and a mortgage.

Had Gillis Long lived, it would have been no decision at all. Out of friendship and loyalty to him, I would have stayed as the JEC staff director. But with his death, O'Neill had to appoint a new committee chair. It came down to a choice between Lee Hamilton of Indiana and Dave Obey of Wisconsin. Hamilton had asked me to stay on if he became chairman, but O'Neill chose Obey. And, while Obey asked me to stay on the JEC staff, he had his own staff director.

Still, I probably would have stayed with the security of the JEC had it not been for Chuck Robb—he promised to pay my salary for a year, even if the DLC didn't last that long. With that guarantee, I took the leap and agreed to start and run the DLC.

We quickly learned that our effort was not welcome on all fronts. Paul Kirk, who was elected DNC chairman in early February, made it clear that he opposed the new outside group and moved quickly to organize his own policy council. When we were not deterred, leaks accusing us of splitting the party and portraying us, and Chuck Robb in particular, as pouting over our failure to elect a national chairman started to appear in print.

"Less than two weeks after Paul Kirk's selection as Democratic National Committee chairman, big names and big money confront him with an independent party apparatus representing a direct challenge," wrote syndicated columnists Rowland Evans and Robert Novak in a mid-February 1985 column in the *Washington Post*.[1]

Behind the proposed DLC, they wrote, were Robb and leaders of the "unsuccessful fight to elect a moderate southerner or westerner as national chairman," citing our effort to find an alternative to Kirk. "Kirk faced a dilemma. If he ignored the new group, he risked isolation. If he joined it, he risked downgrading himself. The only option, said his supporters, was to abort it." And, according to Evans and Novak, Kirk's backers viewed the formation of DLC "as a Chuck Robb ego-trip."[2]

Not surprisingly, Robb was not deterred. Son-in-law of President Lyndon Johnson, the retired Marine captain who had led night movements of troops in Vietnam was not easily intimidated. On February 19, we scheduled a late afternoon meeting with organizers of the DLC and potential financial contributors. Both former DNC Chair Bob Strauss, a big supporter of the DLC and a mentor of mine, and Kirk were invited.

Robb asked Kirk to come an hour early and meet with him, Nunn, and me in Nunn's hideaway office on the Terrace Level of the Capitol.

At that meeting, after making the case for the DLC, Robb confronted Kirk about the leaks. The governor took Kirk into the hallway where, in no uncertain terms, he told the new chairman that he would not put up with such behavior.

When we went upstairs to our meeting in a small room underneath the House floor, with a curious press corps gathering outside the closed door, Strauss told Kirk that if he had a modicum of sense, he'd get out his checkbook right there and write "these fellas" a $25,000 check. He didn't. Instead, Kirk continued his efforts to prevent us from starting up at all.

Afterward, Robb and I, with a couple members of his staff, walked over to the Phoenix Park Hotel on the Senate side of Capitol Hill, to have dinner with Harriet Zimmerman, a major Democratic fundraiser from Atlanta, whom Sam Nunn had invited to join our meeting. When we sat down, Zimmerman pulled out her checkbook, wrote a $10,000 check to the DLC, and handed it to me. That was the biggest check I'd ever seen. Without a pause, Robb wrote a $1,000 check. I now had seed money to get started. Once I got a bank account and filed the incorporation papers, the DLC would open for business.

On Tuesday, February 26, Kirk announced his own policy council within the DNC. Two days later, Gephardt, Robb, Nunn, Babbitt, and about 20 others in the Dirksen Senate building announced the formation of the DLC.

The new fledgling organization had formidable assets. We had an idea and a clear sense of purpose. We had the benefit of the policy work in the House Democratic Caucus over the past four years. And, most important, we had a willing gaggle of elected leaders committed to turning our ideas into action.

But we had no operational capacity. We had no staff, no office, and just $11,000 in a newly opened bank account.

And, of course, we were facing opposition from leaders and activists in our own party, many of whom would have been happiest if we had just done nothing and gone away.

A front-page headline in the *New York Times* the day of our formation read: "Dissidents Defy Top Democrats; Council Formed."[3]

"In defiance of the national party leadership, a group of Democratic officeholders from the South and West today announced the formation of an independent council to help shape party policy and rules," wrote veteran *Times* political reporter Phil Gailey, "At a news conference on Capitol Hill, organizers of the group, the Democratic Leadership

Council, said many elected officials who viewed the national party as a political liability in their regions had expressed support for the initiative. . . . 'We view the council not as a rival to any other party entity but as a way station or bridge back to the party for elected Democrats,' said Representative Richard A. Gephardt of Missouri, who will serve as chairman."[4]

In the last paragraph of Gailey's story, a Kirk confidante explained the DNC chairman's real reason for trying to block the DLC. "I don't know how much of it is presidential politics and how much is parochial politics," said one Democratic strategist close to Kirk. "The fear of a lot of people is that this group wants to take the cream of the party's leadership and leave Kirk with Jesse Jackson and the single-issue groups. Kirk needs these moderate elected officials for leverage in dealing with the interest groups and building the broad-based consensus he wants."[5]

Despite the opposition we were underway. I filed the incorporation papers with Bob Bauer, my friend and lawyer who later became White House Counsel for President Obama, and Stewart Gamage, Governor Robb's Washington representative. Because we didn't yet have an office, our address on the incorporation papers was the Capitol Hill townhouse of Chuck Dolan, the executive director of the DGA who served under both Robb and Babbitt. I made Will Marshall, who had been so helpful in preparing the materials leading up to the announcement, the DLC's policy director. With the help of Stewart Gamage, I found Jody Brockelman, a remarkably talented young woman who had worked for Senator Paul Tsongas, to run the day-to-day operations.

Within a week, Brockelman and I located a three-room office on the fourth floor of the Fairchild Building at 499 South Capitol Street, just four blocks from the Capitol. The office was no palace. Its most notable feature was an ink stained carpet from a previous tenant, a printing company. Our first order of business was to print stationary with the DLC letterhead. We didn't even have a logo, but with a plain letterhead we were really up and running.

About a month later, I brought in the final member of the original DLC team—Melissa Moss, a fundraiser from San Francisco who had worked for Governor Jerry Brown during his first stint as governor, and for his chief of staff Gray Davis, later elected governor in his own right. Moss had an aura of elegance about her and the events she organized during her four years with the DLC helped build our reputation as a first-class operation. Though I was very impressed by her in an interview, she carried what seemed like a gigantic price tag, and I was nervous about taking on the obligation. Duane Garrett, a top Democratic fundraiser from San Francisco, quickly brought me to my senses. "She'll raise her annual salary in a month," he said, "and everything else she raises in a year will be gravy."

For me, running the DLC was a radically new adventure in uncharted territory. It was my first experience in the private, albeit nonprofit, sector. Up to that point, every job I had was in the public sector, either in the executive branch or on Capitol Hill. Running the caucus or the Intergovernmental Relations Subcommittee was in some ways good experience, but unlike on the Hill, if I wanted furniture or office supplies for the DLC, I actually had to pay for them. I couldn't just find furniture in the hall and move it into our office. And there was no federal deficit to cover the payroll. If we didn't raise the money, we couldn't pay salaries.

The Democratic Leadership Council was not an ordinary political operation. It was an entrepreneurial enterprise. Unlike the DNC or the Senatorial and Congressional Campaign Committees, the DLC had no official responsibilities that it had to carry out. The DNC had to run the presidential nominating process, run the convention and service state parties. The DLC had no official duties. Our critics argued we had no real purpose. Columnist Jack Germond, a DNC loyalist who was openly hostile to the DLC, and his partner Jules Witcover, made that point succinctly in a column entitled "Kirk shows up the soreheads" in the *Baltimore Sun* in the fall of 1985: "No one has ever claimed that the fate of the republic—or even that of the Democratic Party—was likely to rise or fall on the success of the DLC."[6]

To me, that fact that there was nothing that we *had* to do was a great advantage. We were unencumbered of any kind of institutional responsibility. We could create and drive our own agenda and succeed on our wits and imagination.

In a number of ways, the DLC was different from other political or advocacy groups. First, it was built around ideas. We believed that the way to resuscitate the Democratic Party was not to promote a particular candidate, constituency, or narrow interest, but rather to build a coalition around workable ideas—a political philosophy and governing agenda with broad national appeal.

Second, it was an organization made up of elected officials who could actually put the philosophy and ideas into action. That was critical because the DLC members, as elected officials, could serve as high profile spokespersons, putting the DLC point of view in the center of the political marketplace. And, by their collective actions promoting and enacting DLC ideas, they could bring new definition to the Democratic Party.

Third, when I organized the DLC, I made sure that only our true believers set the agenda, not financial contributors or even the politicians who joined for political cover. We were on a mission to save a political party, and I wanted to make sure that only those most committed to that mission could pilot the ship. The DLC was organized like a congressional committee. Like the chair of a congressional committee, the DLC chair set the tone and the agenda for the DLC. While the DLC staff served all the DLC members and we had regular meetings, like most congressional committee staffs, it worked primarily with the chair and helped him set the agenda. Unlike most nonprofits in which the donors constitute the governing board, I kept the donors out of policy-making positions. That structure was probably not ideal for fundraising, but it served us well, particularly during the years of Clinton's chairmanship because it gave us the freedom to shape the agenda on which he ran for president.

From day one, the clear mission of the DLC was to forge a forward-looking national agenda that would make Democrats competitive again in national elections. That agenda would be grounded in the first principles of the Democratic Party—growing the economy, expanding opportunity, defending freedom, and asking citizens to give something back to their country—the principles that were the core of our national majority during the New Deal era and of our work in the House Democratic Caucus.

But while that purpose would drive us, we were a long way from achieving it when we opened our doors in the spring of 1985. I had two much more practical goals in mind for our first year. The first, and most important, was simply to stay alive. And, second, in line with my rule that first impressions matter, I wanted to get off to a fast start and make a mark on the national political scene.

Staying alive was a major challenge. To our allies, we were a lifesaver. To our detractors we were a threat. Since we were so clearly viewed as an insurgent or "splinter" group—and many of our early supporters were disenchanted with the DNC—party officials and DNC loyalists including union and interest group leaders were eager to drive us out of business.

From the outset resistance was strong. Kirk's policy council within the DNC was chaired by former Utah Governor Scott Matheson, a politician with similar ideas to ours. That raised the question of why the party needed two policy councils. Our critics charged that we were simply being divisive.

Moreover, our adversaries seized on what they believed were our vulnerabilities—the lack of diversity in our initial membership and our focus on appealing to the white middle-class voters who had deserted the Democratic Party in droves, which our critics saw as abandoning traditional Democratic constituencies. We were called the "southern white boys' caucus." The Reverend Jesse Jackson famously labeled the DLC "Democrats for the Leisure Class."

Finally, while the press was intrigued with our founding, the conventional wisdom among the Washington political reporters was that we'd have little impact on the party and that the most important action would be inside the DNC. So over the next couple of months, we were virtually ignored in the national press, a big problem for an insurgency that needed attention to survive.

As it turned out, Kirk's policy council proved to be blessing in disguise for two reasons. First, it quickly got ensnarled in DNC rules that required nearly every party constituency to be part of the council. It took months for Matheson to figure out representation that kept all the constituency groups happy and navigate the party's rules, giving us a head start. Second, the DNC's policy council staff was headed by a DLC friend, so when it finally produced its first report 18 months later, it reflected a point of view already identified with the DLC.

I personally believed the criticisms of the DLC missed the point. Yes, we wanted to change the party, because a party that lost 49 states twice in four elections had to be changed—radically—to survive. True, our membership at the outset was mostly white southerners, but white elected Democrats in the South were in danger of extinction. True, we focused on winning back white middle-class voters who had left our party in droves, but without them, we could not win back the White House, and without the White House we couldn't do anything to help Democratic constituencies. It was clear that playing identity politics was not a path back to power but a path to political oblivion in an electorate that, in 1985, was still about 90 percent white.

Most importantly, I was convinced that once we put together a new agenda of growth and opportunity, grounded in traditional party values, Democrats of all races, ethnic groups, and ideological persuasions would rally around our flag. To me, the way to create a diverse coalition was not to mandate it by quota, but to build it around shared principles and ideas. And we believed that our core principles served the aims of Democratic constituencies, though our policies may have been new and offered a different way to achieve them.

But in the spring of 1985, with a tiny staff and a small bank account, we were playing on the party's playing field, not ours, and we needed a smart strategy if we were going to survive even a few months.

The first step was to reduce the tension with the DNC. We had made a clear statement just by establishing the DLC as an independent group—we didn't need to rub it in. That's one reason why I made Dick Gephardt the DLC's first chairman. Of the principal DLC founders, Dick Gephardt had the best relationship with party leaders and his personality was the most conciliatory and least controversial in party circles. It was hard not to like Dick Gephardt, and having him as chairman would help smooth some of the rift.

I had known Dick Gephardt since 1961, when he was student body president at Northwestern University and I covered him as a cub reporter for the *Daily Northwestern*. We reconnected when he was elected to the House from his St. Louis district in 1976. With Jim Blanchard, he was a principal House sponsor of the Sunset Bill, and the biggest advocate of applying sunset to tax expenditures. One of Gillis Long's closest allies, Gephardt was elected to succeed him in December of 1984 as chairman of the House Democratic Caucus. So he was a logical, as well as strategic, choice to be first chairman of the DLC.

As in my first months with the caucus, I tried to avoid fights that we could not win or that would play into our critics' hands. At a meeting with members of the Coalition for a Democratic Majority (CDM), the group of centrist Democrats formed by Washington Senator Henry "Scoop" Jackson after 1972, I was urged to start a fight over the party rules requiring equal numbers of men and women delegates at Democratic Conventions. I politely demurred, arguing that the worst thing the DLC could do was take on a fight that both reinforced a negative stereotype about us and which we were sure to lose. Our purpose was to change our party so we could win the presidency, not tilt at windmills until we withered away.

To counter the diversity and exclusivity criticisms, we adopted a "big tent" strategy to actively recruit minorities and women into the DLC. Congresswoman Lindy Boggs of Louisiana, who would become a long-time member of the DLC governing board, proved particularly helpful in recruiting New Orleans Mayor Ernest "Dutch" Morial, a former head of the local NAACP, and encouraging her female colleagues in the House, like Connecticut's Barbara Kennelly (the daughter of a former DNC chairman), to join. Because most governors, senators, and members of Congress were white males, we decided to expand our membership to state and local officials, bringing in Atlanta Mayor Maynard Jackson, San Antonio Mayor Henry Cisneros, Texas State Treasurer and future Governor Ann Richards, and former Texas Congresswoman Barbara Jordan, the first black woman elected to the House from the South.

But to make real gains, we needed to create our own playing field. To do that, we decided to leave Washington and take a message of "change and hope" to Democrats across the country. Our first trip was on Friday, May 17, 1985, when nearly a dozen DLC members—including Gephardt, Nunn, Chiles, Jim Jones, and Congressman Jim Cooper of Tennessee—converged on Florida. The three-city swing through the state—we would visit Tallahassee, Tampa, and Gainesville in one day—was our inaugural venture outside of Washington and launched our strategy designed to put the DLC mark on the national political scene.

We got off to a rocky start. At our first event, a briefing for reporters, the breakfast fare included quiche and croissants, prompting a snide piece by Phil Gailey in the *New York Times*. At our next stop in Tallahassee, a legislative meeting in the State Capitol, State Representative Helen Gordon Davis of Tampa chastised us for our all male traveling party.

But the trip picked up from there, and we were able to deliver our message.

Over the next six months, groups of DLC members, dubbed "the cavalry" by Florida Governor Bob Graham, traveled to Texas, California, North Carolina, and Georgia, and Florida again, to carry our message of "change and hope." The tour had a straightforward goal: assure Democrats that change was on the way and urge them not to switch parties.

Our strategy was crafted in part to counter a Republican effort called Operation Open Door, a plan to convert 100,000 registered Democrats, nearly half of them in Florida, to the GOP. But more importantly, we were showcasing our biggest asset, an attractive group of emerging young leaders, several of whom might run for president. By taking this group on the road, we hoped to create enough stir in the country to get the national press corps located in Washington to take us seriously. We designed this strategy, just as we had in the House Democratic Caucus, to create our own playing field, one on which we would have a clear home field advantage. We believed very simply that we would generate enormous local press attention wherever we went, and, after a while, that attention would cause national political writers to take note.

Despite the shaky start in Florida, we demonstrated that, even with our small staff, we had the ability and ingenuity to pull off complex political trips—quite a feat in the days before cell phones, email, and Google maps. We were mobile and quick off the mark. That became our hallmark—and it was a clear contrast with the DNC policy council that was mired in its own procedures for months.

We really showed our mettle on our next trip: the Texas Blitz. About 20 DLC members met in Austin on July 1 and fanned out across the state for town hall meetings and press briefings in Houston, Dallas, San Antonio, El Paso, and Abilene. Our aim was simple: to get our message into six media markets in Texas in one day.

Two weeks before the trip I had met with Senator Lloyd Bentsen, the first DLC member on a national ticket when Governor Michael Dukakis picked him as his running mate in 1988, to tell him about our plans for the Texas Blitz. Bentsen looked me straight in the eye and said, "You can't pull this off. It's too much." I nervously assured him that we could. And we did.

Among the DLC stars we brought to Texas were Gephardt, Robb, Chiles, Babbitt, and Senator Jeff Bingaman of New Mexico. Mindful of our previous errors, we also brought Lindy Boggs and Beverly Byron, both members of the House. In Austin, we hooked up with the Texas luminaries of the party—Bentsen, House Majority Leader Jim Wright, Governor Mark White, Lieutenant Governor Bill Hobby, State Treasurer Ann Richards, San Antonio Mayor Henry Cisneros, and several members of the state's congressional delegation. Greeted by enthusiastic audiences at every event, DLC members proclaimed that they were ready to challenge the Republicans to a competition over which party had the best ideas for making America stronger.

Setting the tone, Gephardt said the DLC was exploring new ways to advance traditional Democratic commitments to growth and opportunity at home and strength abroad. "We're not interested in changing the Democratic Party's basic values, its traditional underpinnings," he told the packed press conference in Austin. "We are interested in changing its policies, its proposals, its ideas, its themes, its message—to be in tune with today."

At that same July 1 news conference, Babbitt invoked the spirit of Independence Day as he explained the DLC's mission. "We're revolutionaries," he said. "We believe the Democratic Party in the last several decades has been complacent. . . . We're out to refresh, revitalize, regenerate, carry on the revolutionary tradition."

Lambasting the Republicans for distorting what Democrats stand for, later that day Robb told an overflow crowd in Dallas: "We're tired of letting somebody else tell the American public what we're about. We've got some bright young leaders. We're prepared to fight for a whole agenda, to change our party to make it a party of economic opportunity."

The Texas Blitz went off without a hitch, and, just as we hoped, we got extensive press coverage all over the state. "Democratic team blitzes Texas in campaign to polish image," blared a headline in the *Dallas Morning News*.[7] "Democrats won't be written off—'We're revolutionaries,' Leadership Council tells local party" was the headline in the *Dallas Times Herald*.[8] We got similar coverage in Austin, Houston, and San Antonio, and positive editorials and political columns in nearly all of the state's major daily newspapers.

August is usually a dead time in Washington, with Congress in recess and most of the city on vacation. But August 1985 was anything but dead for the DLC. Midmonth, with Gephardt, Robb, Babbitt, and Missouri's Lieutenant Governor Harriett Woods leading the way, we took a three-day swing through California. It was an important and exciting trip.

At a fundraiser in San Francisco on Wednesday, August 14, sparks flew between Babbitt and San Francisco Mayor Dianne Feinstein. Trying not to offend what they assumed was a decidedly liberal crowd, Gephardt and Robb had given rather bland descriptions of the DLC and its purpose. One guest responded by asking exactly how the DLC was different than the old Democrats.

I could see Babbitt two tables away from me revving up to respond. He jumped to his feet and blurted out: "I'll tell you how we're different. We don't need these slush funds the federal government routinely hands out to mayors and governors." Sitting at the table next to Babbitt's, Feinstein shot back, "Name one slush fund." Babbitt proceeded to list several urban programs, including the community development block grant program, a favorite of mayors who wanted unrestricted federal aid, before Gephardt stepped in to stop the argument from escalating.

At a breakfast two days later in Santa Monica, the Arizona governor caused another stir, this time among the mostly elderly audience when he suggested that he thought it was time to begin means testing entitlements like Social Security and Medicare. I turned to Melissa Moss and joked that you could hear the pacemakers pause.

Babbitt's skirmish with Feinstein in San Francisco and his suggestion that we means test entitlements in Los Angeles served notice that the DLC was not afraid to take on Democratic orthodoxy, something that would become more apparent in the next 18 months.

We followed the California swing with a trip to North Carolina in October and another to Georgia in November. In North Carolina our strategy of going to the country to break into the national press hit pay dirt. On Sunday, November 10, 1985, the *Washington Post* ran a front-page story on the DLC written by Paul Taylor, their young, star political reporter.[9] Taylor's piece was datelined Raleigh, NC because he had accompanied us on our North Carolina swing three weeks earlier. Taylor was blown away by an overflow crowd of more than 300 waiting for us at a lunch at the Sheraton Hotel in Greensboro, organized by former Congressman Robin Britt. When we arrived late due to weather delays, the room was so packed that none of the traveling party, including Taylor, could find a seat inside. We had to force our way in.

Headlined "Democrats' New Centrists Preen for '88," Taylor's story delivered the message we could have only dreamed of just six months earlier:

> Welcome to the new-look Democratic Party—a party determined above all else to be "of the political center"—and say hello to a new generation of Democrats who are busy preening for 1988. . . .
>
> On his own, each of these '88 "mentionables" [referring to Gephardt, Biden, Nunn, and Chiles, who made the trip] would have some trouble filling a firehouse with potential voters outside his home base. So they've banded together, along with the likes of Govs. Bruce Babbitt of Arizona, Charles S. Robb of Virginia, Bill Clinton of Arkansas and Sen. Dale Bumpers (Ark.), into a sort of political road show—a touring company of like-minded presidential and vice presidential long shots.
>
> They call themselves the Democratic Leadership Council (DLC). . . . [O]ne year after the Democrats' 49-state presidential drubbing, these moderates seem poised to capture the soul of their beleaguered party. . . .[10]

With Taylor's piece, we had made our mark on the national political scene. We were, as we immodestly claimed, a new force in American politics. In just eight months, we had taken our road show to some of the most important states in American politics and our beyond-the-beltway strategy was working. We had shown that this upstart insurgency had both the capacity and the discipline to flourish in national politics.

We were successful for a number of reasons. First, the 1988 "mentionables" realized that if our party didn't change, none of them would ever be elected president. That gave them a powerful incentive to work together in the DLC to change the party even as they were planning their individual campaigns. And together they were a powerful sales force.

Second, DLC members, particularly members of Congress, like Buddy McKay and Bill Nelson of Florida, Martin Frost of Texas, and Mel Levine of California, provided the resources, mailing lists, and ground troops that made our forays possible. With a small staff of four, there was simply no way we could have done sweeps of states like Florida, Texas, California, North Carolina, and Georgia in a six month period without the assistance of their congressional offices. They gave us the capacity to execute a strategy that the DLC staff by itself could not have carried out.

Third, and perhaps most important, we maintained message discipline. While all of our members didn't agree on every policy detail, we kept a laserlike focus on the themes of change, hope, growth, and strength. We stayed away from controversial social issues that divided us and hammered away on the economy, competitiveness, and national security.

By the fall of 1985 it was clear we had not only survived our critical first year, but that we had burst onto the national political scene. Taylor made that clear when he called us the "new-look Democratic Party" and said that we seemed "poised to capture the soul" of our party.[11]

As Taylor wrote, despite the belief among many traditional Democrats that we would "not last past the summer," we had "flourished, shrewdly playing off the chemistry between new ideas and new presidential faces."[12]

SIX

BREAKING NEW GROUND
IN THE IDEAS WAR

1986

I t's one thing to burst on to the national political stage. Using our
greatest asset—the next generation of Democratic leaders that com-
prised our leadership—we had successfully established our presence in
1985.

But the luster we enjoyed wouldn't last forever. For one thing, the
novelty would wear off and what was new and fresh in 1985 would become old news in 1986. More importantly, within the next year, it was
likely that at least four of our leaders—Gephardt, Babbitt, Biden, and
Gore—would launch presidential campaigns. Allies in the DLC, they
would soon be adversaries on the presidential trail.

To sustain our gains, we needed to have something to say. For the
DLC, 1986 became a year of groundbreaking new ideas that challenged
Democratic orthodoxy. In many ways, our work in 1986 laid the foundation for the New Democrat agenda that, under Bill Clinton's leadership six years later, would lead our party back to the White House.

Our idea work had gotten off to a good start in September 1985
with the release of a report titled "Winning in the World Economy" that
had established the DLC as the pro-trade wing of the Democratic Party.
We had contracted with the prestigious Wharton School at the University of Pennsylvania to produce an Economic Competition Index that
measured why America was suffering a competitive decline as evidenced
by a large trade deficit.

Historically, Democrats had been the low-tariff free trade party and the Republicans, the isolationists and protectionists. But in the 1980s, under pressure from the unions, the Democrats were becoming increasingly protectionist. Our pro-trade stance clearly reinforced our message that we were different from the old Democrats. We took that stance because trade is an important and necessary element of an economic growth strategy. The competition from imports keeps prices down, and opening foreign markets to increase American exports of goods and services creates jobs at home. Because the index identified the overvalued dollar and high interest rates as the major reason for America's competitive decline, we argued that the Reagan administration's "borrow and spend" policies that resulted in big deficits were undermining America's economic strength. The *Washington Post*'s David Broder wrote about it in a column headlined: "A Welcome Attack of Sanity Has Hit Washington."[1]

In January 1986, Dick Gephardt, Bruce Babbitt, Chuck Robb, and Sam Nunn were joined by Governor Jim Hunt of North Carolina, Congressmen Bill Richardson of New Mexico, Mike Synar of Oklahoma, and about 40 donors from around the country at a retreat in Phoenix to discuss plans for the DLC's second year. There we made three important strategic decisions.

We decided that the DLC would not go away—that we would remain in business until there was a Democrat safely ensconced in the White House in 1989. Second, we reaffirmed our decision to remain independent from the DNC. And, third, we decided that we had a unique opportunity to lead the redefinition of the Democratic Party: Ted Kennedy's decision not to run for president in 1988, Tip O'Neill's retirement as speaker, and Walter Mondale's 1984 defeat would leave the door open for a new generation of Democratic leaders to occupy center stage in the national party.

"Strategists for the Democratic Leadership Council, encouraged by their first year success, have decided to expand the group's activities in 1986," the *National Journal* reported. "A self-styled 'catalyst for change' in the party and the nation, the council concluded during a Jan. 23–24 meeting in Phoenix that it has made strides in shifting the party's center of gravity toward the middle, both in terms of perception and reality. Its leaders were so pleased with their success that they plan more of the same." I told the *National Journal* that "we are perfectly poised to lead an effort to redefine the party from traditional Democratic orthodoxy."[2]

Our opportunity was underscored when four DLC-ers, including Chuck Robb, were among the five Democrats selected to deliver the

Democratic response to President Reagan's 1986 State of the Union Address. It was our moment to make a move.

Gephardt was about to give up the DLC chairmanship to begin his presidential campaign, and in order to take full advantage of our moment, I needed to convince Robb to take the job. We needed someone with the courage to take on party orthodoxy. Robb was our man. He was disciplined, a straight shooter, and fearless about taking on the necessary political fights.

Elected lieutenant governor of Virginia in 1977 and then governor in 1981, Robb was personally credited with turning around the state's Democratic Party, ending 12 years of Republican dominance. He would have been overwhelmingly reelected in 1985, but Virginia law precludes a governor from serving consecutive terms. The election of Democrats to the top three state jobs—Gerry Baliles as governor, Doug Wilder as lieutenant governor, and Mary Sue Terry as attorney general—was widely viewed as an endorsement of Robb's leadership. That Wilder, an African American, and Terry, a woman, were elected to statewide office in Virginia, the center of the massive resistance movement during the civil rights era, added to the Robb mystique.

When I offered Robb the DLC chairmanship, he reacted favorably, but I wasn't about to take any chances. On February 9, 1986, I wrote him a long memorandum to allay any concerns he had and to make a strong argument about why he should take the job.

I told him that his taking the chairmanship would be good for him because having completed his term as governor, the DLC would be his vehicle for staying in the public arena, and it would be good for the DLC because as its chairman, he would give the DLC a presence everywhere he went. Unlike members of the House or Senate who had to work within their congressional caucuses, Robb would answer to no one but himself when proposing controversial ideas. That would give us enormous freedom as we set out on the mission of shaping a policy agenda.

I pointed out that the chairmanship would be good for him because it would provide a rationale for traveling around the country—other than running for president—and a place to engage his political allies in Virginia and elsewhere. Most important, the DLC would give him an institutional base for doing something he wanted to do: change the message of the Democratic Party.

Before Robb accepted, he wanted assurances that the DLC would broaden its base to involve more minorities, women, and even liberals. I assured him that Bill Gray, Barbara Kennelly, Bill Richardson, and

California Congressman Howard Berman, a well-respected liberal, all now had active roles in the DLC.

Robb agreed to assume the chairmanship at the beginning of April 1986. Gray would become a DLC co-chair and both Kennelly and Lindy Boggs would join our governing board. We didn't wait for Robb and the new team to formally assume their roles to move ahead. March 1986 was an important month for the DLC on both the political and idea fronts.

In early March, Senator Lawton Chiles and Congressman Buddy McKay announced the first DLC state chapter in Florida. State chapters were a way to involve state and local elected officials who wanted to identify with DLC. By 1992, we would form more than two dozen chapters, and many chapter leaders would play key roles in the Clinton campaign in their states. Later, with the advent of the internet, we disbanded most of them because we could connect with state and local officials directly from Washington without the hassle of managing state organizations.

At a DLC forum in Dallas on March 14, Sam Nunn and Les Aspin, the two most important Democrats on defense issues, assailed the Reagan administration's credibility on the military, serving notice that the DLC was ready to take on the party's perceived weakness on national security. That forum laid a key marker for the DLC. "Council officials billed today's event as the beginning of its campaign to reestablish Democratic credibility on this troublesome issue by focusing on what they consider to be their most credible spokesmen on national security and military issues," wrote Phil Gailey in the *New York Times*.[3] The forum spurred a full-page feature in the March 31, 1986 issue of *Time,* including pictures of Nunn, Aspin, Gephardt, and Robb, titled "Rising Stars from the Sunbelt: The Democratic Leadership Council is redefining the party."[4]

To kick off his chairmanship, Robb gave a series of more than a dozen major speeches that outlined our big ideas.

Will Marshall and I often worked late into the night at the DLC office crafting those speeches. Marshall would write a draft, then he and I would go over it. When we were satisfied with the message, I'd deliver it to Robb for his review and approval at his home along the Potomac River in McLean, Virginia. Most of the time, Robb and I would spend a couple of hours editing the speech. He always added key insights. When she was home, Lynda Bird Johnson, Robb's wife and Lyndon Johnson's daughter, would occasionally come downstairs to the room where we were working and join in the speech review. Lynda had excellent political judgment, having learned politics at her father's knee. "Daddy would have done it this way," she would say when she suggested a particular change.

In his first speech as chair of the DLC at the National Press Club, Robb argued that a sea change was taking place in American politics. "The New Deal consensus which dominated American politics for 50 years has run its course," he began.

> A new political era is taking shape in which ideas are the currency of politics . . . and Democrats won't begin to win national elections again until we're competitive in the battle of ideas. Since the late 1970s, the Republicans have been on the intellectual offensive. They've appropriated themes that used to belong to the Democrats: keeping our economy healthy and our defense strong. Democrats need to reclaim these bedrock issues.

He continued that in an effort to regain the political initiative, a number of elected Democrats had created the Democratic Leadership Council as a vehicle for a new generation of Democrats whose political views were shaped by the social movements of the 1960s, the rampant inflation of the 1970s, and the Vietnam War.

> Our generation has seen liberalism—once the moving spirit of American progress—grow dogmatic and resistant to change. We've seen government programs conceived in a spirit of innovation somehow become permanent fixtures. We've seen our party become more responsive to the most vocal pressure groups than to ordinary citizens with no special ax to grind. . . .
>
> We want our guiding principles to be clear in everything we do. Since Mr. Jefferson our party's fundamental purpose has been to assure American citizens the freedom and opportunity to rise to their full potential.

Robb ended the speech with a call for national service—the idea that would become the cornerstone for New Democrats and the New Democrat movement. "To reclaim our heritage as the party of national purpose, we need to issue the call for a renewed commitment to the ideal of citizenship in America."

Robb's speech set the political context and the framework for the speeches to follow. Over the next several months, he would go to distinguished forums such as the Commonwealth Club in San Francisco, the Federal City Club in Washington, the Detroit Economic Club, and the World Affairs Council in San Antonio, to deliver groundbreaking speeches on economic innovation, competitiveness, national security, and the ethic of citizenship.

No single speech broke more new ground or garnered more attention than his second speech calling for a whole new social policy, delivered on April 12, 1986, at the retrospective on the Johnson presidency and the Great Society at Hofstra University on Long Island. Robb called for an overhaul of the welfare system that would enable it to end dependency and bring poor Americans, particularly the predominantly African American communities in the inner cities, into the nation's economic mainstream.

Robb cited the striking accomplishments of the Great Society, including winning civil and voting rights for African Americans, nearly eliminating malnutrition, sharply reducing infant mortality, making health care affordable for the poor and elderly, lifting 12 million people out of poverty, and substantially reducing poverty among the elderly. The real legacy of Johnson's Great Society, Robb said, was its bold spirit, not its programs—its willingness to experiment, to risk new departures, to seize the initiative. He called on Democrats to invoke that spirit again to "confront a status quo that should be as repugnant and intolerable to us as the social conditions of the '60s were to most Americans." The "new social dilemma," he described,

> is the rise of a dependent, demoralized, and self-perpetuating underclass in our cities—several million Americans who are drifting farther and farther from the economic and social mainstream of our nation. For the first time in our history, the bottom segment of our society has become immobile. In our city centers, millions of people, mostly black, are trapped in a tragic cycle of deprivation, disorder and dependency. They are headed toward a permanent status as wards of the state, without jobs or hope or any meaningful sense of membership in American society.

To deal with that, Robb called for a new social policy:

> Over the long haul, the cost of tolerating the status quo—in both a financial and a moral sense—will be far greater than the cost of doing something about it. I believe this nation needs to undertake a

fundamental restructuring of our public welfare system. For me, the issue is not just cost. In fact, as an acknowledged fiscal conservative, I'd be willing to spend as much or even more than we do today if I could be confident that the money would go into a system that really works.

We need a whole new approach to social policy. We need a social policy that fosters upward mobility, not one that freezes people in dependence and despair. We need a social policy that rewards self-discipline and hard work, not one that penalizes individual initiative. We need a social policy that encourages families to stay together, not one that pulls them apart. We need a social policy that instills basic values, not one that simply yields to the laws of the street. Above all, we need a social policy designed to restore America's poor and dispossessed to full citizenship—to both the benefits and the obligations that citizenship entails.

Had Robb just said that, the speech would have been noteworthy. Throughout the early 1980s—and particularly after the 1984 landslide defeat—Democrats, with the sole exception of Senator Daniel Patrick Moynihan of New York, had shied away from talking about poverty. The idea of a major Democratic leader other than Moynihan calling, in essence, for a new war on poverty was significant.

But Robb did not stop there. He went where few white politicians had dared to tread, challenging Americans to tackle the root causes of problems in the underserved urban population and "to come to grips with some uncomfortable truths. And we've got to end the conspiracy of silence that has inhibited frank public discussion of the new obstacles to black progress."

For too long, now, public debate on social policy has turned on the question of how deeply we cut social programs. But that argument misses the point.

Drastically scaling back or dismantling public welfare programs—as some conservatives have suggested—is really no solution at all. Laissez-faire may be good economic policy but it is terrible social policy.

Yet we can't afford to perpetuate or simply expand a welfare system which clearly isn't working well enough and which, in fact, seems to be subsidizing the spread of self-destructive behavior in poor communities.

The prerequisite for any successful social policy has to be healthy economic growth. This isn't the time to get caught up in distributional politics—it's time to make the economic pie grow . . . while racial discrimination has by no means vanished from our society, it's time to shift the primary focus from racism—the traditional enemy without— to self-defeating patterns of behavior—the new enemy within. It's time to do what a number of black leaders have started to do: focus on the causes and possible remedies to the epidemic of teenage pregnancy in poor communities . . . the disintegration of families . . . rising dropout rates and widespread illiteracy . . . and to appalling rates of crime and violence and imprisonment.

If we don't break the cycle of joblessness and dependency, the social ills which fester in our cities will eventually affect those who ignore them in comfort today. Our entire country will pay—as indeed we are already paying—a heavy price in both social alienation and lost productive potential. . . .

Today—and this is truly astonishing—murder is the leading cause of death for young black men. And if the trend toward out-of-wedlock births continues, by the turn of the century nearly 70 percent of all black families will be headed by single women.

By doing nothing in the face of these realities, the federal government has created a de facto social policy of welfare dependency for women and prison for men. We've all heard about the growth of welfare dependency, but it is also true that the number of inmates in federal and state prisons has increased since 1980.

A policy that relies primarily on prisons to handle social problems is costly, callous, and ultimately futile.

Robb outlined a series of principles and ideas to break the cycle of dependency, including deficit reduction, which he saw as critical to gaining the political support for new social initiatives. "The political support for new social initiatives is not likely to materialize in the shadow of giant deficits," Robb said. "That's why, for Democrats, reducing the deficit is more important than preserving individual programs. If some old programs must be cut or killed to make way for new ones, so be it. But we're not going to be able muster the political will to make a fresh start against dependence and poverty until we get our fiscal house in order."

In the spring of 1986, few Democratic politicians had the courage to challenge party orthodoxy on poverty and race. But as the next day's *New York Times* reported, Robb was able to do so, both because of his family ties to President Johnson and because, as governor of Virginia, he had an exemplary record of bringing African Americans and women into the government in a state that had once served as the capital of the Confederacy. In an editorial two weeks later, the *New York Times* gave Robb credit for his political courage: "Former Gov. Charles Robb of Virginia offers this challenge to fellow Democrats: End the 'conspiracy of silence' and start a frank discussion of 'new obstacles to black progress.' It would be an undertaking both risky and promising, but the Democrats are well advised to try it. . . . His central challenge is correct. Civil Rights and welfare programs alone are not enough for the most disadvantaged of our citizens. The Democratic Party ought to be leading the search for new ideas. And Americans of every persuasion ought to join in."[5]

I got particular pleasure out of the Robb speech. I was sick and tired of liberal Democrats attacking the DLC for trying to move the party to the right. Fighting poverty was a liberal cause, and as a veteran of the War on Poverty, I was deeply devoted to it, but liberals were afraid to broach it. Like Robb and Muskie before him, I believed the approaches we were pursuing in the DLC were essential to saving liberalism from its excesses.

For the DLC, the impact of that speech was dramatic. It won us the active support of Barbara Jordan and led to our cosponsoring a major forum on welfare and poverty in New York City with New York Governor Mario Cuomo.

At a June 11 dinner in Austin during a three-day Texas swing, I found myself seated next to Barbara Jordan.

The silver-tongued Jordan first burst on the national scene in 1974 when, as a member of the House Judiciary Committee during the Nixon impeachment hearings, she gave a riveting speech calling for Nixon's impeachment. Two years later, she gave the keynote address at the Democratic National Convention in New York that nominated Jimmy Carter. In 1992, Jordan would give her second keynote address at a Democratic Convention in New York—this one nominating Bill Clinton. Suffering from multiple sclerosis, she served in the House for just six years, giving up her seat in 1979 but leaving a deep impact on the political landscape.

That night in Austin, I began a friendship with Barbara Jordan that would last until her death a decade later. She told me that she wanted to become involved in the DLC, that she had been waiting for years to see a white politician with the courage to address the underlying issues in predominantly black inner-city communities as Chuck Robb had. A firm believer in personal responsibility, she believed that self-help needed to be a key element of any antipoverty strategy.

Barbara Jordan's support was a critical milestone for the DLC; she gave us a new degree of credibility. Because our position on fighting poverty was not the prevailing party view, our critics argued that we were insensitive to our critical black constituency. With Barbara Jordan embracing our position, it was much more difficult to make that argument.

Later in June, Governor Cuomo invited the DLC to hold a policy forum in Manhattan. Robb set the tone: "I believe we need to launch a new, targeted offensive against joblessness, dependence, and poverty, an offensive that confronts the self-defeating patterns of behavior that are now endemic in many [of] our central cities. Yet it is clear that we can't afford to simply expand, or even perpetuate, a welfare system that clearly isn't working well enough and may be subsidizing the spread of self-destructive behavior in our poor communities."

The most striking takeaway from the forum was that, as the *New York Times* reported, "there appeared to be widespread agreement that the poor must be encouraged to help themselves break the cycle of poverty, dependency, and self-destructive behavior within their communities. At the same time, a consensus emerged that government must find ways to help those who help themselves."[6]

To me, the forum was important not so much for what was said as for the fact that it took place. For one of the party's leading liberals, Cuomo, to invite the DLC to put on a forum in New York attested to our growing importance. It drew top political reporters from several of the country's leading newspapers, another full-page piece in *Time,* and a positive editorial in the *Wall Street Journal.* And the symbolism of having Cuomo, Robb, and Sam Nunn appear together was not lost on the press. Larry Eichel of the *Philadelphia Enquirer* wrote: "'That's the ticket!' exclaimed one panelist, Rep. Barbara Kennelly of Connecticut, as Cuomo posed for pictures with Robb on one side and Nunn on the other. It was not clear which ticket she had in mind."[7]

We were clearly on a roll. But that did not deter criticism from the party's left. In a column in the *Washington Post* entitled "Democrats Should Be, Well, to the Left" and in his TRB column in the *New Republic,* Michael Kinsley ridiculed the DLC for wanting the Democrats to be "a force for advancing the common interest, for spurring growth, creating jobs and opportunity and defending freedom." While saying he found our "growth and strength" agenda unobjectionable, he wrote: "But what is the point of trying to rebuild a party on such unobjectionable themes? First, it probably won't work. If these issues were once thought of as Democratic, the Republicans 'stole them fair and square,' to borrow from Senator S.I. Hayakawa. It will be a long time before growth and strength will be perceived as reasons to vote Democratic." Kinsley then said essentially that the Democrats should move to the left, though the specific ideas he touted, such as cutting the payroll tax, had already been raised by Robb in his National Press Club speech.[8]

To me, Kinsley's argument was so ludicrous that it didn't even deserve a response. If we ceded growth and strength to the Republicans, we'd never win the White House back.

However, I thought differently about an attack in the July 6 *New York Times* by the distinguished historian, Arthur Schlesinger Jr., Roosevelt's and Kennedy's biographer. Schlesinger, who won a Pulitzer Prize for his work on Andrew Jackson and served as a special assistant to JFK, had been a key player in the Americans for Democratic Action's decision to back Truman's anticommunist agenda against Henry Wallace in 1948.[9]

Schlesinger attacked "faint-hearted" Democrats, "who find expression in quasi-Reaganite formations like the Democratic Leadership Council" for "me-tooism" toward the Reagan administration, which he called "an infection within the Democratic Party." Citing support among House Democrats for the Nicaraguan Contras and Democratic support for the Bradley-Gephardt tax reform bill for what he said was a "rejection of progressivity," Schlesinger wrote, "Faint-hearted Democrats feel that President Reagan knows a secret and if they could only learn that secret they could be as popular as he is."[10]

He implied that we believed "Democrats should demonstrate their enthusiasm" for Reagan's misguided defense and domestic policies, including cutting back social programs, deregulation, abandoning racial minorities, worshipping at the shrine of the free market and "dumping FDR's New Deal and Harry S. Truman's Fair Deal and John F. Kennedy's New Frontier and Lyndon B. Johnson's Great Society into the ash heap of history."[11]

Schlesinger's impassioned critique was one we had heard before—and continued to hear even through the Clinton presidency. But we could not allow such a harsh critique in a newspaper of record to go unanswered. So I responded for the DLC with a letter the *Times* published two weeks later. Ordinarily letters to the editor in the *New York Times* were edited down to a few sentences. But in this case, the *Times* printed my column-length response:

[Schlesinger's] arguments were not new—but they were wrong. They have long been made by the stand-patters in our party, who yearn for a return to the pre-Reagan status quo at home and advocate a neo-isolationism abroad. The Democratic Leadership Council rejects sentimental adherence to past policies as the best way to promote Democratic ideas and principles in the future.

The real Democratic tradition—the thread that runs through the presidencies of Roosevelt, Truman, and Kennedy—is characterized by innovative policies that engendered broad prosperity and expanded opportunity for millions of Americans at home; by an unbending commitment to civil rights and social justice, and by vigorous opposition to totalitarian tyranny abroad.

To uphold that tradition, we Democrats need to stand on our principles. We cannot be constrained by policies that no longer work and labels that no longer apply.

The new generation of Democrats in the Democratic Leadership Council and in other forums is attempting to revive our party's progressive tradition. They are worthy heirs to a proud Democratic legacy, a legacy that Mr. Schlesinger has played a large role in building.[12]

In July at the Commonwealth Club in San Francisco, Robb delivered another paradigm-shattering speech—this time laying out a new agenda for economic change. During the 1932 campaign, Franklin Roosevelt gave one of his greatest speeches on the relationship between business and government at the Commonwealth Club. It was in that speech that Roosevelt uttered words that would become a lodestar for the DLC: "New conditions impose new requirements on government and those who conduct government." From that simple proposition came the innovations of the New Deal.

Using Roosevelt's words as a launching pad, Robb in his speech said that America was in the midst of major changes to its economic and political life.

America today faces an historic opportunity: to become preeminent in the new economic order of information and technology just as we dominated the industrial era of steam and steel. Few societies have successfully undergone such a transformation: usually, new and more dynamic societies arise and eclipse nations that have developed a deeply-rooted bias in favor of the status quo . . . and against the uncertainties of disruptions of economic change.

To the extent we try to block or retard economic change, we condemn our people to diminishing opportunities and our society to certain decline. Our job is not to put our finger in the dike, but to help our society adjust swiftly and smoothly to the wrenching effects of inevitable change. Just as Roosevelt assailed the economic royalists whose rapacity stood in the way of both individual opportunity and national progress, we need to attack the new obstacles to hope and opportunity and upward mobility for all our people: sluggish productivity growth . . . institutional inertia and rigidity . . . and a disquieting loss of competitive prowess.

Robb argued that, "to win against tough competitors in the world economy, all of us—in government, industry and the workforce—need to learn new ways of doing business." And he suggested three bold ideas for doing just that: tying pensions of business executives to their companies' performance after they've left; linking worker pay to performance; and making increases in productivity or GNP—rather than inflation— the benchmark for entitlement growth and wage settlements. As Carl Irving wrote in the *San Francisco Examiner,* "Here's something new and different from Democrats."[13]

Actually, I was nervous about how other DLC members would react to ideas like tying pay to performance and adjusting the formula for increasing entitlements. Both were pretty radical departures from traditional Democratic orthodoxies. A few days later I had a chance to find out. Having read Robb's Commonwealth Club speech, Peter Kilborn, an economics reporter for the *New York Times* called me to say that he wanted to do an article about the Democrats' new thinking on the economy. To accompany the piece, he wanted a photo of several DLC members working on the ideas. Much to my surprise, members were eager to be in the picture. Robb, it turned out, was unavailable for the photo shoot. But Biden, Gore, Jim Wright, Gephardt, Kennelly, Nunn, and Chiles all appeared in the front-page photo implicitly endorsing Robb's radical ideas.[14]

The article entitled "Democrats' Ideas on the Economy Shift: Many in Top Posts Differ with Party's Longtime Policies" was terrific for the DLC. "Many leading Democrats, including some Presidential aspirants, are reaching for new themes in economic and industrial policy that depart sharply from those the party has stressed for decades," Kilborn wrote. "Most of the effort is concentrated within the Democratic Leadership Council, an organization of 140 elected Democratic officeholders."[15]

On Tuesday, September 16, 1986, at a press conference in the Cannon House Office Building, Robb, along with the party's most credible spokesmen on national security—Nunn, Aspin, and Gore—released the DLC's manifesto on national defense called "Defending America: Building a New Foundation for National Strength." Three years before the fall of the Berlin Wall, the Cold War was still going strong, and by reasserting Democratic leadership on defense issues, "Defending America" put us right in the middle of the national security debate.

As Will Marshall, who worked with Nunn, Aspin, and Gore to write the paper, said in a strategy memorandum, the statement provided a political opportunity to dispel the party's antidefense image, put Republicans on the defensive on military policy, and showed that the DLC—and, by extension, the new breed of pragmatic and progressive Democrats it represented—was at the cutting edge of change and political innovation.

The document included a blistering attack of Reagan's defense policies, charging that his administration's rapid military buildup had been a bad bargain for America. We simply hadn't gotten what we paid for. We argued that to meet the security threats of the 1980s and beyond, we needed to make fundamental changes to the planning, financing, organization, and deployment of our armed forces.

The report identified three new national security threats: the rapid Soviet nuclear and conventional weapons buildup, the rise of unconventional warfare such as terrorism and guerilla insurgency, and the risk of political instability stemming from economic turmoil and collapse.

The paper presented a series of policy alternatives described by the *Washington Post*: "Among them: developing more 'smart weapons' and proceeding with the mobile Midgetman missile; purchasing more equipment 'off the shelf'; reconsidering the Strategic Defense Initiative if the Soviets meet certain conditions; pressing Japan and Western Europe to assume more of the allied defense burden; giving field commanders greater authority; and cutting military headquarters staff by more than 17,000. In what is likely to be one of the most sensitive recommendations, the report calls for a program of universal national service—civilian and military—to meet staffing needs and 'to rekindle a sense of citizenship.'"[16]

A week later, when the DNC's policy commission came out with its national security report, the *New York Times* quoted an unidentified Democratic Party official as saying "it resembled in many ways the statements that have been issued by the moderate-to-conservative Democratic Leadership Council."[17]

"Defending America" also provided a national security framework for Democratic candidates in the 1986 Senate races. That point wasn't lost on the Reagan administration. In a memorandum to Secretary of Defense Caspar Weinberger, Assistant Defense Secretary John Duncan concluded that "the DLC has done its homework in an incredibly astute way." Calling "Defending America" a "serious, highly-politicized critique of the Reagan defense program" and "a slick, articulate presentation that distorts in a most convincing way," Duncan concluded: "Any intelligent Democrat (barring knee-jerk liberals) will immediately see the political utility of the DLC's approach. The themes in Defending America will inevitably surface in key campaigns this fall."

Having broken new ground on economic, social, and national security policy, Robb, in a speech before the Federal City Council in Washington on September 30, expanded on the "ethic of citizenship," which he said "entails obligations as well as rights" and "keeps our social fabric from unraveling." That speech did not get the attention that his social policy and economic speeches did, but it was the clearest articulation yet of the theme of civic responsibility that would be a fundamental principle of the New Democrat movement for the next decade and a half—and clearly separate New Democrats from the Republicans.

> More than other nations, the strength of our social compact depends on the quality of our citizenship. Americans don't have a common racial, ethnic, religious or cultural identity. We're bound not by blood but by instinct and intellect—by our national commitment to a set of political precepts about freedom and equality. Since the first enduring English colony was planted in my home state of Virginia, Americans have understood and accepted their obligation to contribute to the commonwealth.
>
> Frankly, it bothers me that today, on matters of pressing national concern, we seem to ask so little of our citizens. That's a failure of political leadership—and both parties have been guilty: . . . the Republicans with their promises that we can have economic growth without pain, strength without sacrifice, and compassion without cost; . . . [a]nd Democrats with a politics of entitlement that speaks of the obligations of our country to our people, but not of our people to our country.
>
> I think we ought to stop selling the American people short. They know that our nation's progress has been built on hard work and

shared sacrifice. And they know that America is truly a union, not just a place where millions of individuals act out their private destinies.

Then Robb outlined three steps we could take to awaken the spirit of citizenship. First, leaders needed to resolve the deficit dilemma in order to have the moral authority to "inspire citizens to make sacrifices for the common good." Second, we needed to put a greater emphasis in our social policy on "a sense of mutual and reciprocal obligation." Third, he advocated that we "add some form of universal national service to the obligations of citizenship." As Robb put it, "I don't think it's too much to ask that each young American render his or her country a period of military or civilian service."

At 6 a.m. Tuesday, October 14, we were scheduled to depart Dulles Airport for a three-day, four-city National Issues Blitz, anchored by Robb and Nunn, intended to inject our ideas into the fall campaign. A contingent of DLC members would conduct issues forums in Tampa, St. Louis, Denver, and Pittsburgh—coincidentally in states of hotly contested Senate races. Our plan was to have Robb, Nunn, and Representative Cathy Long of Louisiana, Gillis Long's widow, on the entire trip, and to have other DLC members join them at the various locations. Because most of the forums were on national security, Nunn was the single key player on the trip.

The day before was Yom Kippur, and at about 8 p.m., just after I had broken my fast, my telephone rang. It was Sam Nunn. "Al, I've got some bad news for you," he said. "I can't go on the trip." The Reykjavik Summit between President Reagan and Soviet Leader Mikhail Gorbachev had collapsed in disagreement a day earlier and the president had called an urgent meeting at the White House for the next morning, exactly the time our trip was to begin. Nunn had to be there, and he wasn't sure he'd be able to join us at any point later in the week. That was not what I wanted to hear less than twelve hours before we were supposed to take off.

Nunn was the party's most respected voice on national security, and I had to find a replacement. I called Al Gore at home and pleaded with him to replace Nunn. With so little notice, Gore said he could not do the whole trip, but that he would fly to Tampa with us for the first event. The three-day trip emphasized the DLC's importance on the national political scene—a point that was underscored three weeks later when the

Democrats won back control of the Senate. Seven of the eleven newly elected Democratic senators were members of the DLC.

In the late afternoon on Wednesday, December 11, 1986, a special Amtrak train with nearly 400 DLC members and supporters as well as about 100 members of the political press corps rumbled out of Washington's Union Station. The train was headed to Williamsburg, Virginia, the site of the DLC's first-ever national issues conference.

The mood on the train was, in the words of Robin Toner of the *New York Times,* "ebullient from the start."[18] In one car, Nunn, about to become chairman of the Senate Armed Services Committee, was being pressed by reporters about his presidential ambitions. In another, House Armed Services Committee chairman Les Aspin was holding court. Chuck Robb and newly elected Louisiana Senator John Breaux wandered up and down the train, greeting members of Congress who were aboard.

At the conference, more than 65 DLC members sat around a hollow square, surrounded by tables of supporters and press, discussing economic, social, and national security policies.

For the DLC, the conference in historic Williamsburg was both a celebration and a statement. It was a celebration of our success in the twenty months since the DLC was formed and of the Democrats winning back the Senate. And, it was a statement that the DLC had become the center of intellectual ferment and "the place to be" in the Democratic Party.

Conference speakers included not just the DLC regulars—Robb, Nunn, Gephardt, and Babbitt—but also the incoming leadership of the Congress—Speaker-to-be Jim Wright and Majority Leader-to-be Robert C. Byrd—and the incoming chairs of both the House and Senate Budget Committees, Bill Gray and Lawton Chiles. Most impressive of all was Barbara Jordan, who, confined to a wheelchair, had made the trip up from Austin to deliver her message on responsibility, that poor people on welfare had an obligation to help themselves.

The conference was swarming with press. C-SPAN televised it live. The television networks sent crews, and ABC's Charlie Gibson did a live interview from Williamsburg with Chuck Robb on *Good Morning America.* Nearly every major newspaper sent its top political reporter; the *New York Times* sent two.

Our fast rise to prominence in the party was not lost on the press. *Business Week* wrote: "Initially derided as a splinter group, the DLC has in many ways eclipsed even the Democratic National Committee in the party's effort to refine its political message and broaden its appeal. . . . The DLC membership list includes 8 of the 16 new standing committee chairmen in the Senate."[19]

"A funny thing happened to the Democratic Leadership Council, which was started two years ago by people who were unhappy with the Democratic Party," wrote the *Chicago Tribune*. "It has become the Democratic Party."[20]

And Robert A. Rankin, a member of the editorial board of the *Philadelphia Enquirer* succinctly stated, "To the degree the DLC shapes the thinking of the broader Democratic Party, the party will benefit—and so ultimately will the nation."[21]

SEVEN

THE ILLUSION OF POWER

1987–1988

"All power is illusory," Bob Strauss told me when I started the DLC. "You make them think you have power, and you have power."

Through our travels, the Robb speeches and policy conferences, and especially the Williamsburg conference, the DLC had created the illusion of power. We were viewed as a new force in politics, redefining the Democratic Party. Not bad for a disparate group of elected officials with a miniscule budget and none of the levers of party power. We weren't even allowed by law to support candidates.

But as 1986 slipped into 1987, and the 1988 presidential campaign began to take shape, that illusion of power and influence would become harder and harder to project. This posed a twofold dilemma. First, as an entrepreneurial organization with no formal party responsibilities, we had to figure out our next act. At the close of the Williamsburg conference, reporters asked what was next for the DLC. My answer was that I wasn't sure, but that we'd figure it out. No one would have asked that question of the chairman of the DNC or of the congressional or senatorial campaign committees—they had formal responsibilities that had to be carried out.

Second, and most important, the DLC success in the first two years had been achieved by creating our own playing field. We controlled our trips and idea forums. We controlled the content of the Robb speeches and our policy papers. We controlled what happened at Williamsburg. We played by our own rules. As we got into the presidential race, that, too, would change. The nominating process was definitely not our turf.

Activists and interest groups, particularly organized labor, were still the dominant influences in the primaries and caucuses. And the voters who actually went to the polls in Democratic primaries were more liberal than rank-and-file Democrats.

In 1984, according to a *New York Times* survey, half of the delegates to the Democratic Convention self-identified as liberals, about twice the percentage of Democrats nationwide. In short, the nominating process was a powerful magnet that drew candidates to the left—and even candidates who were members of the DLC were likely to be affected. Despite all we had accomplished in our first two years, there was a real danger that by the time of the 1988 election, the Democratic Party would look very much like it did in 1984. And, as outsiders during the campaign, the DLC could do very little to affect that.

So for the DLC, our challenge was to remain relevant as the presidential campaign got into full swing. Our very existence was at stake. We were a movement to change and redefine the Democratic Party so that it could win back the White House, and we were determined to stick it out until we succeeded. But we knew that if we faded into irrelevance during the campaign, our support and our money would dry up, and we could very well be forced out of existence.

Although as Democrats we hoped our candidate would be successful in 1988, we knew deep down that our effort had just begun. We had injected interesting themes and ideas into the debate, but hard work was needed to develop those ideas and hone them into a politically potent message. Even among DLC members, only a few had incorporated our approach into their day-to-day politics. While a handful of DLC members might get in the race, the odds against one of them winning the nomination, let alone the White House, were extremely long.

I was confident that we were on the right path, that with the DLC message and approach and the right candidate who truly believed it, we would win the support of the American people. But political movements take time, especially idea-based political movements. So the challenge we faced in 1987 and 1988 was to develop a survival strategy—a strategy to stay alive to fight another day. We had to put Bob Strauss's lesson to work in droves. We had to create the illusion of power to remain relevant in the political world.

At the beginning of 1987, the leadership inside the DLC spent a lot of time figuring out how we could influence the direction and the message of the campaign.

To be sure, we continued the things that worked so well in 1985 and 1986. Robb, for example, did three major speeches in March 1987. And in April we launched a DLC chapter in Louisiana. But the impact just wasn't the same. The national political press corps that flocked to Williamsburg was now focused on Gary Hart, Dick Gephardt, Mike Dukakis, Jesse Jackson, Joe Biden, Bruce Babbitt, and Paul Simon—the announced or likely candidates.

It was clear that to remain relevant we needed to become part of the campaign story. The clearest way would have been to have a candidate who was identified as the DLC candidate. Gore eventually got in, but not until much later in the race. Gephardt, Babbitt, and Biden were in the race from the beginning and had all traveled with the DLC in 1985 and 1986—but none carried the DLC imprimatur as clearly as Robb or Nunn would have.

I don't think Robb ever gave serious thought to running. I once told him that a lot of people thought that for him the golden ring would never be closer than in 1988. His immediate response was "You tell them, it's not close enough for me to grab." Instead, Robb spent most of the year pushing Nunn to run for president.

In January and February 1987, Nunn faced considerable pressure, particularly from southern Democrats, to jump into the race. He was scheduled to speak to 3,000 of his strongest supporters at the Jefferson-Jackson Day dinner in Atlanta, Georgia on Friday, February 20. I knew a Nunn candidacy was unlikely, but I also believed that if he issued a definitive statement that he would not run, it would diminish the influence of the DLC. Just the slightest possibility that Nunn would be a candidate at some time later in the race would keep the press from ignoring us altogether.

I sent a memorandum to Nunn the weekend before the speech, urging him to leave the door cracked open just a little when announcing that he would not establish an exploratory committee to pursue the presidency in 1988. I actually advised Nunn to make the announcement in a national forum like the National Press Club in Washington and not disappoint his supporters in Atlanta.

Nunn took the first part of my advice, but not the second. He announced that he would not create an exploratory committee at the Jefferson-Jackson dinner; it would not have been in character for Nunn to leave his supporters with the impression that he might announce such a committee after he had decided against it. While he did leave open a slight possibility that he might reconsider that decision later in the year, he never really had the fire in the belly for a run. "When I look in the mirror in the morning, I see a chairman of the Armed Services Committee, not a president," Nunn said when he called me in late August to tell me he would not run.

The truth is that Nunn made the right decision. He would have had a difficult time surviving the nominating process. With a very conservative voting record in the Senate, liberal activists would have savaged him in the primaries. And, while he had built close relationships with black leaders like Maynard Jackson, Andrew Young, and John Lewis, Nunn had sought the endorsement of George Wallace his first Senate campaign, something that would have drawn heavy fire if he joined the race.

With Nunn out of the race and Robb never in it, we set about to find a new handle to wedge our way into the presidential race and to make the DLC players for the next two years. Meanwhile, I thought it was important to continue to press both our political analysis and our substantive idea agenda. I wanted us to influence the campaign from the outside as best we could, though I was realistic that, with no identified DLC candidate, our impact would be limited. But pressing our case was important to put us in a position to pick up the pieces if Democrats suffered another debacle in 1988, which in 1987 already seemed a strong possibility. We needed to be ready to fight another fight in the 1992 cycle.

We decided on a four-pronged strategy. We would inject ourselves into the primary process by hosting a summit meeting of elected officials from more than a dozen southern and border states who scheduled their primaries on the same day—Super Tuesday, March 8, 1988—an event that would draw most of the candidates and the political press to us.

Second, we would host at least three candidate debates in key southern states on issues in our wheelhouse: national security, social policy, and economic growth. Like the summit, the debates would draw the candidates and the press to DLC events.

Third, we would develop the national service idea and try to make it and the themes it embodied—opportunity, responsibility and community—an idea that would clearly be identified with the DLC when, and if, the candidates talked about it. And, lastly, we—particularly Robb, Nunn, and I—would remain active commentators during the 1988 race, taking advantage of every opportunity the campaign afforded to press our argument that the party needed a new strategy and a new message to appeal to swing voters if we were to end our presidential losing streak.

Super Tuesday would be biggest day of the primary season. By scheduling their primaries on the same day, governors and legislators in 14 southern and border states believed they could draw the candidates to the South where they would have to face more moderate and conservative voters, the very voters who were traditionally Democratic but had deserted the party in most recent presidential elections. The DLC didn't create Super Tuesday, but because most of the Super Tuesday advocates were active in the DLC, most of the press thought it was our idea.

That made me uncomfortable: I worried about the law of unintended consequences. I was skeptical that we could convince moderate and conservative white voters in the South to vote in the Democratic presidential primaries, especially with a contested race on the Republican side. If those voters did not vote in the Democratic primaries, the outcome of Super Tuesday would be much different from what its supporters anticipated. If only blacks and liberal activists, who had dominated the southern primaries in 1980 and 1984, came out in large numbers again in 1988, Super Tuesday would simply boost a Jesse Jackson candidacy and reinforce the results of earlier contests in Iowa and New Hampshire, not change the dynamics of the race. Moreover, since Massachusetts, Rhode Island, and several western states had also scheduled their contests on Super Tuesday, I worried that the results outside the South might be the big story of the night, particularly since the New England results would be reported early in the evening.

But Super Tuesday was a reality—and we couldn't do anything about it. We had to try to make it work as its creators envisioned. Our solution was the Super Tuesday Summit. The Summit would include discussions about how to stir up interest and turnout on Super Tuesday and about issues we wanted the candidates to address. We believed the summit would get enormous attention.

In the weeks leading up to the meeting, the race took a dramatic shift. Gary Hart, the front-runner, dropped out in scandal, and Al Gore entered it. Gore's entry meant the race had a southern moderate. Of course, Jesse Jackson of South Carolina was a southerner but he represented the most liberal part of the party. Some political pundits began to raise some of the same questions I had about the efficacy of Super Tuesday. Rhodes Cook wrote in a cover story in the May 9 issue of *Congressional Quarterly,* "For the candidates and for the 'New South' Democrats whose brainchild it is, Super Tuesday may be trouble."[1]

On the evening of June 21, 1987, more than 300 elected officials and party supporters gathered with about 100 political reporters at the Marriott Marquis Hotel in Atlanta for the opening reception of the DLC's Super Tuesday Summit. Among the speakers were four presidential candidates: Michael Dukakis, Jesse Jackson, Dick Gephardt, and Al Gore, and potential candidate Bill Clinton. A fifth candidate, Joe Biden, participated in the discussions the next day.

This was Clinton's first DLC event, and he didn't miss another one for nearly a decade. I had thought for some time Clinton would be a good fit for the DLC, so I asked Bruce Lindsey, Clinton's confidante and former law partner who I knew from when we worked together on Capitol Hill, to invite him. Clinton was in his fourth term as governor of Arkansas. Chastened by a defeat in his first reelection campaign in 1980, he won back the statehouse in 1982 by campaigning as a moderate and quickly gained a reputation as one of the nation's most innovative governors. He had broad appeal in all factions of the Democratic Party.

Clinton spoke only briefly at a reception, but he was an immediate hit, urging Democrats to find a candidate who "will unite those with means and the dispossessed, the urban and the rural." It was "the only address that seemed to draw applause from both groups," wrote *San Francisco Examiner*'s Carl Irving. "Clinton added that southerners 'are not ashamed to be together, black and white. That's the way we live and grow here.'"[2]

For the DLC, the Super Tuesday Summit achieved its goals and then some. It put us at the center of the political world and, for two days at least, focused the political discussion on our terms—how Democrats needed to broaden their appeal and not just cater to interest groups—to reverse their four-decade decline in presidential elections. It gave us a chance to lay out our political arguments and discuss our idea agenda in front of a national political audience. As a bonus, it connected us with Bill Clinton, who would soon become the leader of our movement.

There were two other unexpected benefits for the DLC as well. The summit drew a diverse group of participants, including many of the nation's most important black leaders such as Andrew Young, Maynard Jackson, John Lewis, Bill Gray, and Jesse Jackson, demonstrating that the DLC was no longer the "southern white boys' caucus." And, with blacks and conservative Democrats agreeing, it validated our political premise that to win presidential elections, Democrats needed to win *both* black and white votes. In a sense, it showed that the DLC could, perhaps better than any other entity in the party, bring together liberals and the moderate and conservative Democrats who had been drifting away from our party in recent presidential elections.

I had no idea at the time, but Tuesday, July 14, 1987, turned out to be an important day for the DLC and the New Democrat movement. That day, in Little Rock, Arkansas, Bill Clinton announced that he would not seek the Democratic presidential nomination in 1988. I had just met Clinton a month earlier at the summit in Atlanta, and I wasn't among his friends and supporters in Little Rock for his announcement. The day before, I was giving a speech in Jackson, Mississippi. I had hoped to meet with former Mississippi Governor Bill Winter while I was there, but was told he was in Little Rock and would likely assume a major role in Clinton's presidential campaign, which would be announced in a couple of days. So I adjusted my speech in Jackson to add Clinton to the list of DLC members running. Much to my surprise, when I called my office the next day from the Cincinnati airport between planes, I had received a number of press calls asking me to comment on Clinton's withdrawal.

Clinton is such a skilled politician that I have no doubt that he would have made a formidable candidate in the 1988 race. But had he run then, he probably would not have become involved in the DLC. Once he decided against running in 1988, I was determined to get him more engaged. In August Robb was scheduled to see Clinton while he was in Little Rock for a speech. I asked Robb to broach the subject of a future DLC chairmanship with Clinton while he was there. Clinton expressed some interest, and I began to talk to him on a regular basis throughout the rest of 1987 and 1988.

In the run-up to Super Tuesday, the DLC sponsored three presidential debates, each with a different issue focus: national security in Miami, social policy at Tulane University in New Orleans, and the economy at the College of William and Mary in Williamsburg. All were part of our strategic plan to keep us near the center of the campaign and to influence it as best we could.

The first debate, at the University of Miami on October 5, 1987, on national security policy, was of particular strategic importance given the party's lingering perceived weakness on national security issues, which we believed would be underscored in Iowa where peace groups tended to dominate the debate. One of those groups, known as STARPAC (an acronym for Stop the Arms Race Now Political Action Committee), had scheduled their own debate in Iowa for Sunday, September 27, eight days before ours. By having our debate in hawkish Miami, we hoped to counteract the tendency of candidates to take positions on defense and national security issues in Iowa that would plague them in the general election. The *Washington Post* got the point in a September 27 editorial: "The juxtaposition [of the STARPAC and DLC debates] gives candidates an incentive to come up with a consistent [foreign policy] approach that will sell in the first contests in the dovish North and on Super Tuesday in the hawkish South. It's a good test that everybody, dove *and* hawk, should be watching."[3]

In 1987, when the only cable news channel was a fledgling CNN, we had to put together our own network for the Miami debate to assure television coverage. We rented satellite time and arranged for Florida Public Television to telecast the debate. We then secured an agreement with the public broadcasting stations in the major markets in Florida to carry it and encouraged PBS stations outside of Florida to televise it either live or by tape-delay.

To the viewing audience in the hall or television, the debate went off smoothly. But that was only due to the incredible professionalism and skill of moderator Ted Koppel. The debate began at 6:30 p.m. and was scheduled to go for 90 minutes. A few minutes after the debate began, I got a message that Florida Public Television had been informed that we had only secured the satellite for an hour—and that at 7:30 the satellite would be broadcasting another program.

I immediately dispatched Will Marshall to call the satellite company and plead our case—no easy task since it was after business hours—while I slipped a note to Koppel explaining the situation. I told Koppel that with a hall full of reporters, we wanted the debate in the hall to proceed as planned. Koppel artfully arranged his questions so that if we did go off the air, television viewers would believe the debate had come to its planned end, even as it continued in the hall. Luckily, just before 7:30, Will reached the satellite company, which agreed to keep us on the air for the final 30 minutes. I informed Koppel and once again he adroitly changed course. When I watched a tape of the debate the next day, had I not known about the satellite problem, I would have thought the debate proceeded exactly as planned.

Like the Super Tuesday Summit, the national security debate was covered by nearly every major national political reporter. By forcing the candidates to address security issues outside of Iowa, it reminded them that they needed to play to an audience broader than peace activists.

Gore especially stood out by taking a tougher stance than his adversaries. "Mr. Gore attempted to set himself apart from the field on foreign policy matters, a troublesome issue for the Democratic Party, which has been perceived as weak on national security issues in recent elections," wrote Paul West in the *Baltimore Sun*.[4]

To underscore our political premise underlying the debate—that to win the White House Democrats needed to reach voters who had deserted the party in 1980 and 1984—we contracted with pollster Stan Greenberg to survey swing voters who watched the debate. Greenberg polled 495 swing voters, defined as voters who had voted for Reagan in 1984 and for a Democrat for Senate in 1986, in Atlanta, Charlotte, and Jacksonville before the debate. He circled back after the debate to 295 of them who had watched it on television.

The poll allowed us to reinforce our argument that those swing voters were the key to victory in 1988. The poll showed that while swing voters thought better of the Democratic candidates after watching the debate, we had a long way to go to win their confidence on the most important issues. By a 28 point margin, the swing voters thought Republicans did better than Democrats in assuring the nation will be respected around the world, and by 30 points, they thought Republicans did a better job at keeping the country prosperous.

Our second debate on social policy was at Tulane on November 2. The debate itself was uneventful, but the lead up to it was not. I spent most of that day in Federal District Court in New Orleans, defending the DLC's decision to keep David Duke, the white supremacist from Metairie, Louisiana, who was a fringe candidate for president, from participating in the debate.

Our third debate on economic policy at William and Mary, was a featured event of the DLC's second Williamsburg conference. It was eight days before Super Tuesday and the dynamics of the race had already changed dramatically. Gephardt, campaigning as a protectionist and economic populist, won the Iowa caucus. As expected, Dukakis, from Massachusetts, won the New Hampshire primary. Gore didn't really compete in either Iowa or New Hampshire, holding his fire for Super Tuesday. After separating himself from the field on national security issues at our Miami debate, Gore hoped to fill the "Sam Nunn void" and sweep the South on Super Tuesday.

The DLC stood scrupulously neutral with Gephardt, Gore, and Babbitt in the race. For me personally, it was a difficult time. All three were my friends, and all three wanted my help and DLC support. Babbitt trailed badly and never made much of a showing in either Iowa or New Hampshire; he dropped out shortly after New Hampshire. The day after he quit the race, the ever-resilient Babbitt, with aides Elaine Kamarck and Mike McCurry, came bounding into my office. "I tried your ideas," Babbitt said. "You were just four years too early," I responded without missing a beat.

Gephardt and Gore were essentially both going after the same voters, and the tension between them and their campaigns became palpable. I felt caught in the middle. My natural inclination would have been to help Gephardt. He was my old friend, my close ally at the House Democratic Caucus, and the first chairman of the DLC. In August 1985, anticipating his run, I had written him a long memo suggesting he use his DLC chairmanship, as Clinton would do in 1992, as a central part of his presidential strategy. But Gephardt was convinced that he needed to run a more conventional race for the nomination, and he had taken a number of positions, particularly his protectionist stand on trade, that were different from the DLC's and made me uneasy.

Gore, on the other hand, had done all he could to be identified with the DLC on national security, one of our defining issues. But while Gore took a distinctive a position on national security and, much to our liking, he skipped the Iowa caucus, he never was willing to step out with cutting-edge ideas on the economy, something Will Marshall and I had suggested to him in a long memo that he had requested. Still, because of his position on national security and his staying out of Iowa, the press assumed he was the DLC candidate.

Gore's strategy depended entirely on which candidates made it to the South on Super Tuesday. It was clear that his competition would include Dukakis, by virtue of his New Hampshire win, and Jackson, with his strong base of black voters in the region. It was likely that one more candidate would survive until Super Tuesday, the candidate who came in second in New Hampshire, either Gephardt or Paul Simon, a liberal senator from Illinois. If Simon had edged out Gephardt for second in New Hampshire, the Super Tuesday field would have been Dukakis and Simon competing for liberal voters, Jackson going after blacks, and Gore having clean shot at moderate and conservative Democrats. Unfortunately for Gore, Gephardt beat Simon by three points—about 3,000 votes in tiny New Hampshire. That meant Gephardt continued south where he battled Gore for the moderate and conservative votes, while liberal votes went to Dukakis and black votes to Jackson.

So by the time of our third debate, Gore and Gephardt were in a pitched battle to appeal to the DLC voters. And the debate may have been the most lively of any of the two dozen debates in the entire primary season. With C-SPAN televising it live, the debate once again brought the political world to a DLC venue.

Politically, the debates were a great success for the DLC precisely because they did bring so much attention to our forum. But financially, they nearly drove us out of business. I made a serious miscalculation. I assumed that donors—especially corporate donors—would be eager to sponsor the debates, just as they had our first Williamsburg Conference. Wrong. At a policy conference—like Williamsburg—lobbyists, corporate representatives, and other donors could spend a day or two mingling with several dozen senators and members of Congress. They were happy to contribute for that.

But I quickly learned that they saw no reason to sponsor the debates as the candidates had no time to mingle with donors. Candidates flew in for the debate and, unless they had a campaign event of their own, they flew right back out to the campaign trail. In addition, in the fall of 1987, with the big names like Cuomo, Nunn, and Clinton not running and Hart having dropped out, the press pejoratively referred to the field as the "seven dwarfs." Without face time with the candidates and with little probability that the Democratic candidate would win, donors happily put their money elsewhere.

That third debate got the headlines, but, for those attending the Williamsburg conference, Bill Clinton stole the show.

"The best received speech at the two-day conference was delivered by Arkansas Governor Bill Clinton," wrote Donald Kimelman, the *Philadelphia Inquirer*'s deputy editorial page editor. "He talked about the need for a 'special compact within the inner city' to head off a looming national labor shortage in the year 1995. Government would do more in the areas of education, crime prevention, and housing, while corporations would promise to provide jobs and training. But the poor would have to do their part as well—mainly by being willing to work and learn."[5]

In his book *My Life*, Clinton said, "The most important political speech for my political future was one called 'Democratic Capitalism,' which I delivered to the Democratic Leadership Council in Williamsburg, Virginia, on February 29. From then on I got more active in the DLC, because I thought it was the only group committed to developing the new ideas Democrats needed both to win elections and do right by the country."

On the night of his speech, after we returned from the debate, Clinton joined Melissa Moss, a small group of DLC supporters, and me for a drink at the bar of the Williamsburg Inn. In the middle of our conversation, he turned to me and said, "You know I really like that national service idea that Sam Nunn, Chuck Robb, and Dave McCurdy were talking about. The idea of young kids volunteering to fight poverty in the Mississippi Delta and earning a college scholarship for their work makes real sense." That night Clinton first embraced an idea that a few years later would be a cornerstone of his presidency.

The next morning, Robb passed the DLC gavel to Sam Nunn, who became our new chairman. Robb would announce his candidacy for the Senate a few weeks later. At the same time, Clinton joined the governing board, the first formal leadership role he assumed in the DLC.

Nunn's chairmanship during the 1988 campaign would prove strategically important to the DLC. When it became clear that we would not have a DLC member as nominee for president, I decided that it was important for the organization to maintain its influence by having a DLC chairman who was "the most important Democrat not on the national ticket." Nunn, because of his reputation on national security issues, fit that bill perfectly.

Michael Dukakis, the 1988 Democratic nominee, had no experience in foreign or national security policy and badly needed validation as a potential commander-in-chief. Nunn was the single most important validator in the party on national security issues. The Dukakis campaign badly wanted Nunn to speak on security issues at the Democratic National Convention later that summer in Atlanta, Nunn's home base. Nunn resisted. "I don't want to speak at the convention. I'd rather play golf," Nunn told Gordon Giffin, one of Nunn's top political confidants and eventual U.S. ambassador to Canada during Clinton's second term, and me.

Gordon and I hammered Nunn to speak at the convention. We told him that his speech would be nationally televised—and that he should not pass up that opportunity. Finally, he relented.

Nunn spent days working on his speech. He took his responsibilities seriously and always prepared thoroughly for even the most routine events. Nunn was scheduled to speak on July 19, 1988, the same night Jesse Jackson addressed the convention. Nunn delivered his speech and then went back to his hotel room where his wife, Colleen, had been watching the convention on television. "Sam, when are you going to speak?" Colleen asked him. The networks had ignored Nunn and focused only on Jackson that night. Nunn's speech had gone untelevised, though it would have been much more helpful than Jackson's to Dukakis. Four years later, Giffin and I paid the price when we tried to convince him to second Clinton's nomination at the 1992 convention in New York. This time, Nunn would not relent.

Truth be told, nothing Nunn or anyone else could have done would have validated Dukakis on national security issues. The candidate himself made sure of that in September when his campaign arranged for a photo opportunity in an Abrams tank at a General Dynamics plant near Detroit. Dukakis looked so ridiculous in the picture that "Dukakis in the tank" became a campaign joke, and the George H. W. Bush campaign used the photo in their ads to make the point that Dukakis was unfit to be commander-in-chief.

Dukakis's nomination was assured on Super Tuesday. Gore did win four border states, and, by locking in the black vote, Jackson won four states in the Deep South. But Dukakis was the big winner. By maximizing his support in liberal enclaves, he won the two biggest prizes in the South—Florida and Texas—and he won his home state as well as other contests outside the South. While Gore continued in the race for another month, Super Tuesday realistically narrowed the race to Dukakis and Jackson, with Dukakis the inevitable winner.

Super Tuesday confirmed my biggest fears. The biggest beneficiaries were Dukakis and Jackson.

Still, by forcing the candidates to go to the South to discuss economic, social, and national security issues, the DLC did help diminish the influence of the interest groups. While Dukakis was clearly to the left of the DLC, he was a technocrat, not an ideologue, and certainly not a visionary. The most remembered line of his acceptance speech told it all: "This election is about competence, not ideology." His platform sent the same message—it was short and bland with few specifics. In many ways, he was the candidate of a party that had begun but not completed a transition. Dukakis sent the message that, unlike Mondale, he was not an interest group liberal, but he never really told the voters what he was.

I made that point over and over again in interviews before and during the convention. Dennis Farney of the *Wall Street Journal* captured the essence of my message: "Mr. Dukakis has avoided making detailed promises to the gaggle of Democratic pressure groups, thus sidestepping the 'pandering' charge that helped sink Mondale in 1984 and would be poison to suburban voters this year. The great accomplishment of the party over the last four years, says the Democratic Leadership Council's

Mr. From, is that it now speaks to the electorate as a whole. Trouble is, it still isn't quite sure what to say. 'We've erased the graffiti from the wall,' says Mr. From. 'Now we have to paint the mural.'"[6]

Unfortunately, Dukakis never did paint the mural—but the Bush campaign painted it for him. By the time the Republicans had finished, voters saw Dukakis as the same kind of soft on crime, weak on patriotism and defense Democrat that they had been voting against for 20 years. Dukakis held a 17-point lead after the Democratic convention, but wound up losing 40 states as 1988 turned into another Republican landslide.

At the DLC, we did our best to help Dukakis paint the mural. In May, we released a short book written by Will Marshall called *Citizenship and National Service: A Blueprint for Civic Enterprise*. Like the GI Bill, our proposal tied college benefits to service. Based heavily on the work of Northwestern University professor Charlie Moskos, the DLC proposal awarded young Americans a $10,000 stipend for higher education, job training, or a down payment on a home for every year they devoted to voluntary military or civilian service. It embodied the principles and values at the heart of the New Democrat movement—opportunity, responsibility, and community—and it soon became one of the defining ideas of our politics.

The national service idea appealed to the patriotic instincts of Americans across the political spectrum, and newspapers across the country endorsed it. But we could not convince Dukakis to support it.

In August, after the two party conventions, the Bush campaign launched a brutal attack on Dukakis that questioned his patriotism. The attack focused on Dukakis's veto of a 1977 bill during his first term as governor that would have fined teachers who did not lead their classes in reciting the Pledge of Allegiance to the flag. Rather than answer those charges, the Dukakis campaign went dark, and Bush continued to pound away on the patriotism issue. Just before Labor Day, I talked to John Sasso, Dukakis's chief political operative, and urged that Dukakis define patriotism as John Kennedy had—as giving something back to your country. I urged that Dukakis propose the DLC's national service plan to underscore his point. I believed that national service would give him a chance to flip the patriotism issue in his favor. Sasso seemed interested and asked me for a memo laying out my idea, which Will Marshall and I did the next day.

Citizenship, we wrote, "is the best answer to the Republican canard that Democrats are 'soft on patriotism.' It's easy to stand up and recite the Pledge of Allegiance—real patriotism means a willingness to sacrifice and give something back to your country. *Democrats need to redefine patriotism in terms of civic duty.* . . . The theme of civic participation and responsibility will be most effective if it is moored to a concrete proposal like voluntary national service."

In late September, Gene Sperling, then a young aide in the Dukakis campaign, called me to say Dukakis was interested in endorsing national service the day after his first debate with Bush, scheduled for September 25 in Winston Salem, North Carolina. The endorsement never came. Dukakis did well in that debate—and the campaign decided he should try to build momentum out of that rather than back a new idea.

Finally, Vice President Bush picked up the idea and proposed a meager volunteer service plan of his own, causing the *New York Times* to editorialize: "Youth service programs foster feelings of community and citizenship. It is baffling that Mr. Bush's Democratic opponent, Gov. Michael Dukakis, has not come forward with a proposal of his own, particularly since the Democratic Leadership Council urged one with great fanfare earlier this year. On this issue, Mr. Bush rightly deserves to be called the front-runner."[7]

David Broder made the point more harshly in his column in the *Washington Post*: "Dukakis has ignored what may well be a recurrent impulse for community service. When the Democratic Leadership Council last spring proposed a national service plan for young people, who would be rewarded with assistance for their own education or home buying, Dukakis gave it a cold shoulder. He left it to George Bush to propose last week an appealing but modest plan that would send young volunteers from affluent suburbs to help tutor and assist center-city youths, whose hopeless lives Bush has said 'haunt' his conscience."[8]

Eventually, Dukakis did endorse the DLC's national service plan— on the day after the election in his post-election press conference. I had noticed that on election night Dukakis had ended his concession speech with a call for young people to give something back to their country, rhetoric that sounded like it was right out of the memo Will and I had sent him. The next day at his press conference he raised the DLC's national service plan as the kind of ambitious idea that all Democrats could and should support.

The first four years of the DLC were a decidedly mixed bag. We had burst on to the national political scene. We had injected some interesting ideas—like national service—into the debate. And we had demonstrated that we had the imagination and resilience to defy our critics and survive, even without a DLC candidate. But we failed in our main missions. We did not fundamentally change our party, and the Democratic candidate was once again routed in the presidential election. In many ways, despite everything we did to change the dynamic, the outcome of the 1988 election was eerily identical to the outcomes in 1980 and 1984. But early in my political career, I learned that there is opportunity in every defeat. And, in the 1988 landslide loss, I saw a real opportunity for the DLC.

To me the election outcome made our mission for the next presidential cycle crystal clear. We had to paint the mural.

EIGHT

THE ROAD BACK,
PHASE 1—
REALITY THERAPY

1989

In the aftermath of the 1988 presidential election, it didn't take a genius to figure out that the American people weren't buying what the Democrats were selling. If Democrats wanted to begin winning national elections again, we needed to stand for ideas and beliefs that the American people would support.

We had learned a hard lesson in the last presidential cycle. For all the good things we did between 1985 and the end of 1987, when we got into the presidential year of 1988, it was much like the presidential years of previous cycles. Those of us who wanted to see a different kind of Democratic Party were disappointed.

To bring about real change in the Democratic Party, the DLC had to become a national political movement. That required two things.

First, we needed an intellectual center, because without a candidate to rally around, we needed a set of compelling ideas. Just as it was clear that we needed to paint the mural, it was also clear that we needed to beef up our capacity to paint it. We needed more substantive help. We needed a political think tank with the capacity to develop politically potent, substantive ideas that our elected officials and political supporters could embrace.

In November 1987, when I first sensed that we would likely lose in 1988, in a confidential memo to Chuck Robb and Senator Sam Nunn, I proposed that we create our own policy institute that would be affiliated with but be legally separate from the DLC.

I liked the idea of setting up a policy institute separate from the DLC for two reasons. First, I explained, "the only way we are going to generate the amount of new ideas and high quality policy analysis I believe we should is to put together a small staff that does nothing else. Second, while I would expect the DLC to endorse most of the ideas it developed, a separate institute would give us a way to develop and test real cutting-edge ideas, even some that may be too politically hot for the DLC to embrace at first blush."

Throughout 1988, we developed plans for the think tank. Will Marshall, who would move over to run it day to day, wrote at least half a dozen drafts of a prospectus. I courted and recruited the legendary hedge fund operator Michael Steinhardt to be its chairman and most important financial backer. I would be vice-chairman and chief executive officer. In January 1989, we created the Progressive Policy Institute (PPI).

The second thing that we needed was to recognize that all knowledge did not reside in Washington. To reach out across the country for ideas and support, we had already begun organizing state DLC chapters. And by the middle of 1992, we had a presence in every state and DLC chapters in half of them, with more than 750 elected officials and thousands of rank and file members.

PPI and state chapters gave the DLC critical weapons for the battle to change our party. But we still needed a battle plan.

So we looked at the results of the last six presidential elections to determine why the Democrats had lost.

We discovered that we were losing because middle-class voters, voters at the heart of the electorate, had voted Republican in 1988 by a 5–4 margin. The reason was that they did not trust Democrats to handle the issues they cared about most. In a *Time* magazine survey a week before the election, voters said that Republicans would do a better job than Democrats of maintaining a strong defense by 65–22; of keeping the economy strong by 55–33; of keeping inflation under control by 51–29; and, of curbing crime by 49–32. Those were the issues that drove presidential elections, and until the perception on them changed, Democrats simply were not going to be competitive.

Armed with this knowledge, we launched a four-part strategy to change the Democratic Party.

Phase one was reality therapy. We believed that Democrats needed to face the reality of why we had lost three presidential elections in a row by landslides so they would not repeat their mistakes for a fourth straight time. So we would tell them.

Second, we had to articulate a clear philosophy, a simple philosophical statement that told voters what we stood for.

Phase three was the development of substantive ideas that made up a governing agenda. That's why we needed the PPI.

But even having the philosophy, and the governing agenda, in hand, we still stood to be disappointed in the 1992 election as we were in 1988 if we didn't have a candidate espousing the DLC philosophy as the nominee. Like it or not, a political party is defined by its presidential candidate. So our philosophy and ideas had to pass the market test, and this was phase four of our strategy. In our system, a market test can only come in the presidential primaries, so we needed to find a candidate.

On Tuesday morning, January 24, 1989, I met Bill Galston for breakfast at my favorite haunt on Capitol Hill. William A. Galston was a professor at the School of Public Affairs at the University of Maryland. He had been issues director of the Mondale campaign in 1984 and would serve as a domestic policy advisor in the first Clinton term. Galston looked every bit the professor. A small, slight, wiry man with glasses and a mass of curly hair, you would have never thought he had served in the Marine Corps in the Vietnam era. Most important, Galston was one of the smartest political analysts in Washington.

Before our breakfast, I barely knew Bill Galston, and I was suspicious of his politics because of his role in the Mondale campaign. I quickly learned that Galston was not only a New Democrat but that he had done a crisp and cogent analysis of the true plight of the Democratic Party after the 1988 election.

Confirming what I had long believed, he told me that over the past two decades the American people had come to see Democrats as inattentive to their economic interests, indifferent if not hostile to their moral sentiments, and ineffective in defense of their national security.

"It is these perceptions, rooted in the history of the past generation, that predisposed crucial portions of the electorate to believe the charges George Bush leveled against Michael Dukakis last year," Galston said. "For too long, we have ignored our fundamental problem. We focused on fundraising and technology, media and momentum, personality and tactics—on everything but what matters most. Rather than facing reality, we have embraced the politics of evasion. The result has been repeated defeat. And if we do not listen, and learn, and change, we will keep on losing."

But Galston didn't stop there. He listed seven myths that Democrats believed and kept them from facing reality in presidential elections—and one by one he debunked them.

Myth 1: Non-voters are the problem and higher turnout is the solution.
Reality: If everyone had voted, Bush would have still won—by a larger margin.

Myth 2: Our nonvoters are the problem, and selective mobilization is the solution.
Reality: Such a mobilization would help, but it isn't enough to get the job done. If blacks and Hispanics had voted at the same rate as whites, Dukakis would have still lost by more than four million votes. If the poor had voted at the same rate as the non-poor, Dukakis would have lost by more than five million votes.

Myth 3: Our ability to compete has been damaged by the rise of upscale professional and white-collar voters.
Reality: Upper income voters are no less likely to support the Democratic nominee than they were in 1976. The most significant change has occurred in the heart of the middle class—voters with family incomes between $25,000 and $50,000—40 percent of the total electorate. Fifty-one percent voted for Carter and only 43 percent supported Dukakis. If only middle- or lower-class voters, those with family incomes of $50,000 or less, had voted in the 1988 election, George Bush still would have won.

Myth 4: The party's most significant losses since 1976 have occurred among white Protestants, for whom Jimmy Carter had a special appeal.
Reality: While there has been a huge swing among southern White Protestants, nationally the percentage swing among Catholics has been larger than among Protestants—and by some measures twice as large.

Myth 5: Because the party's nominees have feared the liberal label, the centrist timidity of their general election campaigns has turned off core Democratic supporters.
Reality: Dukakis got 82 percent of the liberal vote versus only 74 percent for Carter.

Myth 6: Democratic presidential nominees have been losing because the electorate has become significantly more conservative.

Reality: There had been little ideological change over the past four elections. In 1976, 20 percent of voters called themselves liberals. In 1988, that figure had dropped just two points to 18 percent. In 1976, 31 percent called themselves conservatives. In 1988, just two percent more—33 percent—identified as conservatives. The real difference was that voters perceived the Democrats as more liberal.

Myth 7: The gender gap has worked increasingly in favor of Democratic presidential nominees.

Reality: Dukakis was supported by, at most, the same percentage of women as was Carter, and by some measure a slightly lower percentage. Dukakis's support among men was 9 points lower than Carter's 42 percent. The gender gap is not the product of a surge of Democratic support among women, but rather the erosion of Democratic support among men.

In short, Galston concluded that the Democratic Party had been losing ground among voters, not nonvoters; among the middle class, not the rich or the poor; among Catholics as well as Protestants; among nonliberals, not liberals; among whites, not minorities; among men, not women. Yes, intensified mobilization among groups that still support us is important, he said, but the gains from such an effort cannot by themselves compensate for the broader erosion of support we experienced. The only alternative he saw for the Democratic Party to rebuild a presidential majority was to regain competitiveness among the kind of voters it had lost in the past generation.

Galston's analysis was exactly the reality therapy I believed Democrats needed to hear. After every defeat, the party honchos parroted the same excuses, and in the next election, we went out and repeated our mistakes. Galston had debunked Democratic excuses one by one. I immediately pounced on it. I told Galston I would make him famous. I asked Galston to present his analysis on the first panel at the DLC's annual conference scheduled for March 9–11 in Philadelphia, the political panel that I hoped would establish the context for the entire conference.

The Philadelphia annual conference was our first major event in the North—our first two conferences had been in Williamsburg, Virginia, our Super Tuesday Summit, in Atlanta, and our debates in Miami, New Orleans, and Williamsburg. In the late afternoon of Thursday, March

9, about 300 DLC supporters and press, including about 70 elected officials, boarded a train to Philly.

Like Williamsburg, the Philadelphia Conference attracted a cavalcade of stars. New faces like Virginia Lieutenant Governor Doug Wilder and newly elected DNC chairman Ron Brown joined DLC regulars like Nunn, Robb, and Gephardt. Both the new Senate Majority Leader George Mitchell and Speaker Jim Wright spoke. So did Jesse Jackson. Senator Lloyd Bentsen, viewed as the titular head of the party after Dukakis's defeat, gave the keynote. Bill Clinton highlighted the second day of the conference with a riveting speech on education reform. Even a Benjamin Franklin impersonator graced the conference.

But Galston's presentation was the highlight of the first day—and it set off a spat between Chuck Robb and Jesse Jackson that made headlines across the country. Both Robb and Jackson were on the first panel that responded to Galston's analysis. The panel discussion itself was quite tame. But at the conclusion of the panel, when both were pressing their case in front of a gaggle of reporters, the sparks flew.

Robb, building on Galston's presentation, argued that Democrats needed to adopt strategies that could maintain support among the party's poor and minority base and, at the same time, reach out to white working- and middle-class voters who had been defecting in droves to the Republicans in recent elections. Jackson took the opposite position: the course to victory was to fervently energize the base.

Standing next to Jackson amid the reporters, Robb started out by praising Jackson's skill as a political messenger. Then he suggested Jackson was delivering the wrong message. Jackson, Robb said, "encouraged the public perception that the Democrats want to divide the country between the haves and have-nots—a perception that we are bringing together all who have a greater need, and pitting them in some way against those who are currently successful. The public perception that we're dividing the country is not conducive to the electoral sense we are looking for."

As print reporters from across the room sensed something was happening and rushed to join the gaggle, and radio and television reporters pushed their long-handled boom mikes in front of the two combatants, Jackson shot back: "We cannot be all things to all people. We have to decide which side of history we are on. If we are all things to all people, we become rather ill-defined, indecisive—kind of like warm spit."

That question of whether the road to victory depended on mobilizing the party's base or on regaining lost ground among working- and middle-class whites—the party's central dilemma—dominated the conference. The truth was that Democrats needed to do both, and no one had advocated abandoning the base. But if we focused only on the base and didn't expand our appeal to the middle class, we would be bound to repeat our recent electoral failures. For the most part, the conference participants, including Ron Brown, agreed about that.

Lloyd Bentsen said it best: "Where the two [approaches] conflict, as they sometimes do, I feel we have to reach out. When you've decided your house is too small, it's all very well to do some shoring up and strengthening of the foundation. But at some point you've got to build where nothing had existed before."

The issue was a question of political strategy. As Elaine Kamarck told E. J. Dionne of the *New York Times:* "There has been confusion between the party's moral imperatives and its political imperatives. Of course we should register black voters. Of course, we should empower poor people. But to say that will do the job is nonsense."[1]

The chasm between the DLC and Jesse Jackson was not just on political strategy, but also on ideas. We believed the liberal redistributive and antidefense policies he espoused caused middle-class voters to question our commitment to economic growth, opportunity, and the defense of the country. In Williamsburg in 1986, Barbara Jordan pointedly warned Jackson not to "frighten everybody off." He did not heed that warning in 1988, and we did not want a repeat performance in 1992. Jackson had run a strong race for the nomination in 1988, finishing second in delegates and increasingly became the strongest voice for the old liberalism in the Democratic Party. Left unchallenged, as he largely was in the 1988 race, he threatened to define the party again as we headed into a new presidential cycle.

With Galston's analysis and the Philadelphia Conference, we had begun to administer a little reality therapy to the Democratic Party. For the first time in my political memory, the top leaders of the Democratic Party had confronted the party's central strategic dilemma. Clearly, we didn't solve it in Philadelphia, but we did confront it. And that was something that Democrats had been too reluctant to do, either publicly or privately, for a very long time. Confronting it was a critical first step to dealing with it.

Writing for *USA Today,* Richard Benedetto understood what occurred: "Moderate Democrats meeting [in Philadelphia] over the weekend, tired of losing presidential elections, sent a clear message to the Rev. Jesse Jackson. If you decide to run for president in 1992, you won't get the kid glove treatment from your Democratic opponents. Unlike 1988, expect to be fully engaged in debate by Democrats on the issues."[2] And under his byline with Gannett News Service, Benedetto wrote:

'The debate on Jackson's ideas has already started,' noted Florida's Sen. Bob Graham yesterday. And it started Friday at the annual gathering of the Democratic Leadership Council, a group of conservative and moderate Democratic officials, primarily from the South and West, who believe the party's liberal image has been a major reason it lost five of the last six presidential elections.[3]

Over the summer of 1989, Galston joined forces with Elaine Kamarck to expand on his analysis and produce a well-documented, academically credible political study. A protégé of famed political scientist Nelson Polsby at the University of California where she earned her doctorate, Kamarck was an experienced political operative and among the party's leading experts on nominating process rules. She had worked at the DNC and on three presidential campaigns. Like Galston, she had impeccable academic credentials, and she was as charismatic as Galston was professorial. Together they were a formidable team.

Their study "The Politics of Evasion: Democrats and the Presidency" was powerful and compelling. It quickly became a seminal document in the New Democrat movement. The authors included the points Galston had raised at his first meeting with me: We had ignored our fundamental problems, focused on other matters than reality, and embraced the politics of evasion. The Democrats, they wrote, "have manufactured excuses for their presidential disasters—excuses built on faulty data and false assumptions, excuses designed to avoid the tough questions. In place of reality, they have offered wishful thinking; in place of analysis, myth. This systematic denial of reality—the politics of evasion—continues unabated today." Their study explored "three pervasive themes in the politics of evasion":

The first is the belief that Democrats have failed because they have strayed from the true and pure faith of their ancestors—we call this the myth of Liberal Fundamentalism. The second is the belief that Democrats need not alter public perceptions of their party but can regain the presidency by getting current nonparticipants to vote—we call this the Myth of Mobilization. The third is the belief that there is nothing fundamentally wrong with the Democratic Party: there is no realignment going on, and the proof is that Democrats still control the majority of offices below the presidency. We call this the Myth of the Congressional Bastion."

They described a choice of two basic strategies. The passive one was for the party "to hunker down, change nothing, and wait for some catastrophe—deep recession, failed war, or a breach of the Constitution—to deliver victory." The active strategy would

> address the party's weaknesses directly. Thus the next nominee must be fully credible as commander-in-chief of our armed forces and as the prime steward of our foreign policy; he must squarely reflect the moral sentiments of average Americans; and he must offer a progressive economic message, based on the values of upward mobility and individual effort, that can unite the interest of those already in the middle class with those struggling to get there. Finally, he must recast the basic commitments of the Democratic Party in themes and programs that can bring support from a sustainable majority.

Galston and Kamarck's analysis indicated Republican weaknesses that offered some hope for the task facing the Democrats.

> The Republicans have not solidified their hold on a governing majority. For all their successes at the presidential level, success at other levels is coming only gradually. For all the positive opinions voters have of Republicans, they are still perceived as the party of the rich. For all the gains they have made in party identification, there are still large numbers of independent voters in the electorate. The Democratic Party can recapture the middle without losing its soul.
>
> The Republican Party was transformed into a governing party during the 1970s because it was willing to endure a frank internal debate on political fundamentals. If Democrats hope to turn around their fortunes in the 1990s, they must put aside the politics of evasion and embark on a comparable course.

Galston and Kamarck's conclusion was a perfect summation of the DLC point of view and laid out in clear terms the need for the strategy on which we had embarked. After the 1988 election, we decided that *we* would paint the mural, that we would forge a public philosophy and governing agenda for the 1992 nominee that would demonstrate to voters that our candidate was different from the Democrats they had been voting against for a quarter century.

Now we were ready to begin shaping that new message in a DLC process, on DLC turf. Over the next two years, the DLC would be the venue for redefining the Democratic Party.

NINE

CLINTON

A little after four o'clock on the afternoon of April 6, 1989, I walked into the office of Governor Bill Clinton on the second floor of the Arkansas State Capitol in Little Rock.

"I've got a deal for you," I told Bill Clinton after a few minutes of political chitchat. "If you agree to become chairman of the DLC, we'll pay for your travel around the country, we'll work together on an agenda, and I think you'll be president one day and we'll both be important." With that simple proposition, Clinton agreed to become chairman of the Democratic Leadership Council, and our partnership was born. With Clinton as its leader, the New Democrat movement that sprung from the DLC over the next decade would change the course of the Democratic Party in the United States and of progressive center-left parties around the world.

The idea of forging a new agenda for 1992 particularly appealed to him. I'm convinced that after he decided against entering the presidential race in 1988, he concluded that the most important thing about running for that office was knowing what you're going to do for the American people.

We talked for a few more minutes about what our agenda might include. We agreed that the Democratic Party had to modernize and reestablish its sense of national purpose, and that it was important for the party to get on the right side of the security issue. Then he called in a couple of members of the Arkansas legislature to meet me and suggested I join him and a few of his staff members for a drink at a local hangout.

Ever since Clinton had told Chuck Robb in 1987 that he was open to taking the DLC chairmanship, he was my first choice to succeed Sam Nunn. After hearing the response to his speech the year before in Williamsburg and watching him captivate the audience the previous month at the DLC meeting in Philadelphia, I was convinced that he was the best political talent I had ever seen.

In Philadelphia the night before his speech, we talked for a couple of hours in the hotel lobby with other conference attendees dropping in and out of our conversation. As at the Williamsburg Inn bar, I had the chance to watch firsthand his remarkable person-to-person political skill.

But political skill was just one of several reasons I was so determined to make Clinton the next DLC chairman. He was a reform governor and understood the importance of innovative ideas to political success. As he would say in his inaugural speech as DLC chairman, "In the end, any political resurgence for the Democrats depends on the intellectual resurgence of our party. There's far too much talk about personality in politics and far too little about what we're going to say and do to make sense to the American people." Clinton loved to talk about ideas, and he had a striking ability to explain the most complicated concepts clearly.

He was not afraid to challenge old orthodoxies. In the early 1980s, long before I knew him, he and Hillary Clinton pushed cutting-edge education reforms, like pay for performance and public school choice, against the opposition of the powerful Arkansas Education Association. Speaking about education in his Philadelphia speech, Clinton said the Democratic Party was "good at doing more. We are not so good at doing things differently, and doing them better, particularly when we have to attack the established ideas and forces which have been good to us and close to us. We are prone, I think, to programmatic solutions as against those which change structure, reassert basic values or make individual connections with children."

Most important, Clinton believed in the DLC philosophy—in the basic bargain of opportunity and responsibility. In his speech on Democratic capitalism in Williamsburg, he demonstrated that he understood the importance of both the private economy and the growth of small business, which he called the backbone of the economy. He recognized the role of government in making sure every American has the opportunity and the tools to get ahead.

Clinton was a leader among governors in calling for welfare reform and personal responsibility measures, including requiring kids to stay in school to get a driver's license and fining parents who missed their kids' parent-teacher conferences. In Philadelphia, he told us that Democrats needed "to embody these ideas the DLC has been talking about all these years: the social contract, no rights without a responsibility; family preservation; more market mechanisms and government school choice; more accountability, and becoming internationally competitive."

Though Clinton came from a conservative state and knew how to communicate with the moderate and conservative voters Democrats needed to win back, he was also well regarded among liberals—and so would help the DLC broaden its appeal in all but the most extreme left parts of the party. Appealing to a broader spectrum of the Democratic Party was important for the DLC, and for me personally. Though the political shorthand had always referred to the DLC as moderate or conservative Democrats, our ideas were really about modernizing liberalism and defining a new progressive center for our party, not simply pushing it further to the right. Coming from the center-left of the party, I was tired of having the DLC labeled as conservative. I decided to call our think tank the Progressive Policy Institute because I thought it would be harder for reporters to label it as the "conservative Progressive Policy Institute."

Finally, Clinton would strengthen our support outside of the nation's capital, and as a presidential possibility, he would attract national press.

During most of 1988, Clinton and I had talked regularly on the telephone, strengthening our relationship. At the convention in July, Dukakis asked Clinton to give his nominating speech. Convention speeches are always difficult because the crowd is usually not paying attention, but this speech was a disaster for Clinton. It was long and was made even longer because the crowd screamed every time he mentioned Dukakis's name. The result: It was widely panned. To bounce back, the ever-resilient Clinton went on Johnny Carson's *The Tonight Show* the next week, told a few self-deprecating jokes and then played the saxophone with the band. I knew Clinton was down after the speech, and I sent him a handwritten note: "It doesn't matter how long you speak or how well you play the sax, just so you're still part of our team. Just in case you need a reminder, you've got an awful lot of admirers—and none greater than your friends at the DLC."

In offering him the chairmanship, I had gotten a little ahead of myself. When I made my April 1989 trip to Little Rock, I knew Robb was favorably inclined toward a Clinton chairmanship, but Nunn, who was planning to step down as chairman of the DLC by the fall, was not as convinced. He was concerned that Clinton would be too liberal. That was a complaint Nunn heard from a number of his Senate colleagues when he talked to them about Clinton assuming the chair.

Nunn raised those objections when the DLC board, including Nunn, Robb, Jim Jones, and me, met on July 21 to pick the next chairman—three months after I had offered the job to Clinton. I told the board that a number of members had expressed an interest in the chairmanship including Clinton, Virginia Governor Gerry Baliles, Florida Senator Bob Graham, and Tennessee Senator Jim Sasser. But, assuming we could work out the logistics—and I was sure we could—I preferred Clinton.

Robb argued strongly for Clinton. Nunn, who argued Clinton might run for president and not give the DLC enough attention, finally agreed. As we walked together back to the Russell Senate Office Building after the meeting, Robb said to me: "If Clinton spends the next four years running for president on our stuff, we'll be all the better for it."

Once the board agreed, I thought it would be a simple matter to schedule an official transfer of the position. Clinton had told me he would take the chairmanship in Little Rock, but we still had to set a date for him to assume the gavel. One possibility was to have Nunn pass the gavel to Clinton at a Washington issues conference we had planned for November, a few days after the election. But as I soon learned, with my friend Bill Clinton nothing is ever simple or easy.

He did come to the November 13 conference and once again was a big hit, but he said he wasn't quite ready for the transfer to occur. And so it would be for the next four months. He would repeatedly tell me that he was going to take the job, but he was trying to decide whether to seek another term as governor in 1990 and that decision could impact when he could take over the DLC. So 1989 turned into 1990, and Clinton had yet to take up the reins.

Nunn was getting antsy and kept pressing me to get a date from Clinton. He had met with Clinton in December of 1989 and Clinton had assured him, too, that he would take the chairmanship. The obvious time to make the change was at our national conference scheduled for New Orleans on March 22, 1990. But I had no guarantee from Clinton. Finally, in frustration on February 23, a month out from New Orleans,

I wrote a "personal and confidential" memo to Clinton and personally handed it to him at the Hyatt Hotel on Capitol Hill where he was attending the annual meeting of the National Governors Association. My message was blunt:

> We are getting past crunch time on the DLC chairmanship. There are a number of strategic and procedural decisions we simply have to make before the end of the day today so that we can put them into place by the New Orleans Conference.
>
> I realize your personal situation is complex, but at the DLC, we've run out of time. If you can't make a 100 percent commitment to take the DLC chairmanship this week, I have to recruit someone else.

I wrote that he was my choice and that Chuck Robb and I "put our necks on the line to get board approval," but that was the previous July and we were still hanging.

> Sam Nunn has taken his meeting with you in December and your statements to me in early January as a commitment that you would take the chairmanship, and is expecting to pass the gavel to you in New Orleans. But every signal I've gotten from you in the last month indicates you're still up in the air. That ambivalence is a killer for us as we prepare for New Orleans.
>
> I believe you are the right person for the DLC job—and the DLC job is the right job for you. We have the opportunity to redefine the Democratic Party during the next two years. If our efforts lead to a presidential candidacy—whether for you or someone else—we can take over the party, as well.
>
> We are poised to expand the DLC effort exponentially. But our New Orleans Conference is a critical juncture—and if we are to turn the DLC effort into a full-blown political movement, New Orleans is the best launching pad we are likely to have this year. We're a month out, and we simply need to put some things in place now or we will lose that opportunity.

Clinton looked at the memo and then said, "If I don't run for reelection, then I'm going to have to make at least $100,000 a year." A hundred thousand a year probably seemed like a lot of money for Clinton in 1990; his gubernatorial salary was just $35,000 a year—among the lowest of all governors. And if he left the governor's mansion—he used to quip that he spent most of his life in public housing—he would have had to pay for a place to live for the first time since he was out of office in 1981 and 1982. I told Clinton that I'd be delighted to pay him $100,000 a year to be a full-time chairman of the DLC.

After going back and forth about whether to run for a fifth term as governor, he was scheduled to make an announcement on March 3. Craig Smith, Clinton's aide who often traveled with him on DLC trips, called me in the middle of Clinton's announcement speech to tell me Clinton was not running for reelection. He called me back a few minutes later and said he was indeed running. "He talked himself into running in the middle of his speech," Craig told me.

After months of pondering, Clinton decided to run for re-election as governor and become chairman of the DLC. Nearly a year after our Little Rock meeting, at the DLC's Annual Conference in New Orleans on Saturday, March 24, 1990, Bill Clinton became the DLC's fourth chairman. Calling Clinton a "rising star in three decades," Sam Nunn passed him the gavel. Nunn quipped that when the DLC was created "we were viewed as a rump group. Now we're viewed as the brains of the party. In just five years, we've moved from one end of the donkey to the other."

Under Bill Clinton's leadership, the DLC would cement that image and redefine the Democratic Party along the way.

TEN

THE ROAD BACK, PHASE 2— NEW ORLEANS

1990

The theme for the DLC's 1990 New Orleans Conference was "A Turning Point for Democrats"—and it was that for the DLC, as well. In New Orleans we took on the challenge of redefining the Democratic Party before the 1992 election.

During 1989, we had added important tools for our effort.

First, in June we publicly launched the Progressive Policy Institute (PPI) that gave us the capacity to develop and popularize innovative, paradigm-breaking ideas that could sustain a political movement. We also moved into new headquarters on the House side of Capitol Hill just three blocks from the Capitol. That was significant because the new office was large enough to house both the DLC and PPI, allowing us to better coordinate the political and intellectual arms of our effort.

Then in October, we launched our own bimonthly magazine, *The Mainstream Democrat,* giving us an important tool in the pre-internet era for communicating with our supporters around the country. I hired Bruce Reed to be DLC policy director and editor of the magazine. Bruce, who had been Al Gore's speechwriter, is one of the smartest, most unassuming people I've ever met, and he would go on to become domestic policy advisor for President Clinton and chief of staff for Vice President Joe Biden.

I had laid out an ambitious strategy for the DLC in a November 3, 1989 memorandum to Clinton, Nunn, Robb, and Senator John Breaux of Louisiana, our main host in New Orleans. That strategy was premised on making New Orleans a cut above our previous annual conferences by releasing a mainstream Democratic credo and by launching a national effort to organize DLC state chapters. A sharply honed credo could articulate the basic philosophy, serve as a rallying point for our movement, and contain the main message Democrats could take to the electorate in 1992.

I consider the November 3 memorandum one of the most important I've ever written. I had consulted with four of the best strategists in the Democratic Party before writing it: Bob Beckel, Tom Donilon, Joe O'Neill, and Elaine Kamarck. Many of the elements in the strategy were not new, but the memo was the first time I had pulled everything together, and it projected a sense of determination, even a degree of militancy, that I had never before suggested.

"Make no mistake about it," I wrote, "what we hope to accomplish with the DLC is a bloodless revolution in our party. It is not unlike what the conservatives accomplished in the Republican Party during the 1960s and 1970s."

I wanted the New Orleans Conference to be larger than Williamsburg and Philadelphia; my target was to bring between 100 and 150 elected officials to New Orleans. I asked Clinton, Nunn, Robb, Breaux, and the other elected DLC members to recruit their colleagues to become active in the DLC and come to New Orleans.

In the memo, I emphasized that undertaking this strategy would mean changes for the DLC both operationally and politically. Operationally, it would mean adding a new dimension: political organization. Politically, it meant drawing lines, which to that point, we had not done. If we wrote a credo with real edge, we could face heat from some DLC members who might not like the positions we took. And, some might even want to disassociate from the DLC. "I suspect defections will be few compared to the supporters we will attract," I wrote in the memo. "Some defections will strengthen our case, but we need to be careful that we don't lose support we need to maintain our political credibility."

Finally, if we carried out our strategy successfully, we would likely be accused of trying to build a parallel party, and we would have to resist efforts by party leaders to co-opt us, lest "we suffer the same fate we did in the last cycle—where for three years we set much of the tone of the party's message, but in the presidential year, the liberal fundamentalists came out of the woodwork and reasserted control of the party and its message."

In fact, in my mind, we *were* trying to create a parallel party. Or, at least, create a new playing field. We had two years to forge a new message for the party, a philosophy and governing agenda that made it clear we were different from the Democrats that Americans had been voting against in recent presidential elections. Then, our candidate—if one emerged—could test it in the primaries in 1992. It would be hard enough to do on our own playing field—we certainly could not do it in existing party forums.

The clearest way to show that New Democrats were in fact different was to promote bold ideas that challenged old orthodoxies. We were off to a good start with our national service plan. It was certainly bold and defined a new public ethic for the party by tying college aid to service. Sam Nunn in the Senate and Dave McCurdy in the House introduced legislation embodying the DLC's plan.

The national service plan got plenty of attention because it was controversial. The original DLC plan and the Nunn bill provided sub-sistence wages during service and generous vouchers for each year of completed service: $10,000 a year for civilian service and $12,000 a year for a minimum of two years of military service. But the plan replaced all other kinds of college aid with national service. In other words, to receive any kind of college aid, a young person would have to serve his or her country.

"This is a truly bold idea which converts entitlements into earned benefits," wrote columnist Mark Shields in the *Washington Post*. "Just like the GI Bill, after which it is modeled, the national service act links opportunity to obligation. . . . Democrats may still grow misty-eyed when they hear the call from JFK's inaugural address to 'ask not what your country can do for you; ask what you can do for your country,' but in recent election years, the party's appeal has been tailored to each clump of voters with its own agenda and postage meter: You want it? You got it!"[1]

National service ran into tough sledding in Congress. The military component was jettisoned in favor of the existing Montgomery GI Bill, which provided education benefits for men and women in the armed forces.

The higher education lobby came down hard against tying aid to service. They enlisted the black colleges in their cause by arguing that requiring service for college aid was discriminatory against poor people since rich youngsters who did not need federal aid would not have to serve. We argued that tying service to aid would give policy makers a rationale for increasing aid and that for most of the 1980s the amount of aid for poor students going to college was declining relative to the cost of college, in part because many Americans thought that we asked nothing of those who received assistance. In the end, and not unexpectedly, we lost that battle. Still, due to the persistence of Sam Nunn and Ted Kennedy, an advocate for civilian service, Congress did pass a pilot program to test the service idea.

Of course, we would have liked Congress to have passed a full-blown service plan in 1989, but our idea had penetrated the national debate. Congressional action on a pilot program notwithstanding, we continued to make national service a cornerstone of the DLC message. For our goal of redefining our party, it was much more important to send a message to the electorate than to prove we could survive the congressional meat grinder.

Over the months leading up to the conference in New Orleans, PPI developed and promoted a series of innovative policy ideas. These ideas included individual development accounts for low-income people, community policing and the police corps, and youth apprenticeships for non-college-bound youth. All of these plus national service and the expanded Earned Income Tax Credit (EITC) would be integrated into the New Democrat credo in New Orleans.

PPI started with a bang. Its first paper, released in mid-June 1989, tackled one of the Democratic Party's sacred cows: the minimum wage. In it, Rob Shapiro, the PPI vice president for economic studies, argued that expanding the EITC was a better, more effective, and less costly way to help the working poor than increasing the minimum wage.

Not surprisingly, the paper, coming from a Democratic-leaning think tank, created quite a stir. Shapiro had circulated a draft to several colleagues asking for comments. One of them sent a copy to Senator Ted Kennedy. Kennedy tried to get us to bury it, a request I politely but resolutely refused. I did, however, decide to hold it until the congressional Democrats failed to override a presidential veto of an increase in the minimum wage.

When President Bush vetoed the minimum wage increase there was no public outcry and the Democrats got no political benefit for supporting the increase. The bottom line was that the country and economy had changed, and the minimum wage, so important in the New Deal, had ceased to be an effective way to help the working poor. Shapiro's plan for expanding the EITC was exactly the kind of paradigm-shifting idea we wanted to define the DLC. It was a new way to further a traditional Democratic goal: that any American who worked full time, year around, should be able to support a family above the poverty line. For years, raising the minimum wage to help the working poor was Democratic orthodoxy. But Shapiro's analysis revealed the discomforting fact that 85 percent of those who stood to benefit from an increase in the minimum wage were not poor; fully half were second and third earners in families with incomes twice the poverty level.

As Shapiro wrote in an op-ed on July 3, 1989, in the *Washington Post,* Democrats with long memories could not imagine the "the minimum wage, practically invented by Franklin Roosevelt to help 'one-third of our population [who are] ill-nourished, ill-clad, and ill-housed,' could ever hurt poor people." They had to face up to "evidence that in the 1980s, an increased minimum wage often takes from the poor to help the middle class." The reason: Poor people who did not benefit from an increase would still have to pay the higher prices resulting from businesses increasing their prices to cover higher labor costs.[2]

Shapiro's paper got the attention of the *Baltimore Sun*'s Paul West. Calling the Democrats "brain dead," he said, "One exception to the Democratic torpor has been the debut of a new Washington think tank, the Progressive Policy Institute, which says it wants to steal the 'intellectual initiative' away from the conservative Republicans. The institute drafted a study that dared to conclude that traditional Democratic adherence to raising the minimum wage harmed the poor, since those who stood to benefit most from higher minimum wages were second or third earners in middle class families. Traditional liberals, led by allies of Sen. Edward M. Kennedy, D-MA, howled in anger, scolding the institute privately for producing an analysis that, they said, would hurt the party politically."[3]

I was convinced that the DLC was the only organization in the party that could undertake an overhaul of the Democratic message. The DNC certainly was not capable of producing anything close to a mainstream political message. Neither were Democrats on Capitol Hill, who spoke with too many voices and were too reactive to the president, the committee chairs, and their day-to-day business. Moreover, the congressional agenda tended to be dominated by discrete interest groups who were never hesitant to push their own concerns, even when they delivered the wrong political message for Democrats.

In late September, in a *Washington Post* column headed "The Democrats Need a Policy Voice," David Broder confirmed the need for this process to occur outside the Democratic Party proper. He pointed to the policy review project undertaken by the British Labour Party to change its most politically damaging policies after it lost its third straight election in 1987. "The Democrats have lost three in a row, too," Broder wrote. "But they have no machinery for asking themselves where they went wrong or for figuring out what they might say differently. They have no policy voice. . . . To find their voice, the Democrats must create a mechanism that does not now exist."[4]

We had created that mechanism and our goal was to put it on display in New Orleans.

Honing the credo was the most important component of our strategy, and that exercise took more than six months.

As part of the run-up to New Orleans, we hosted a one-day issues conference on November 13 at the Hyatt Regency on Capitol Hill. Most of the attention at that Washington event focused on the appearance of newly elected Virginia Governor Doug Wilder, his first major public appearance since his election. Wilder had run on a DLC-like theme of "The New Mainstream," and his appearance at our mini-conference, after pointedly stiffing us four years earlier following his election as lieutenant governor, underscored to the media the new respect that the DLC commanded.

Wilder's appearance aside, our November mini-conference featured policy experts from all parts of the party who offered serious input as we drafted the credo. Robb, in his keynote speech, talked about the principles in our draft credo. Clinton outlined a path to educational excellence. Competitiveness expert Joel Kotkin offered a new economic strategy. David Osborne, government reinvention expert, and local D.C. activist Kimi Gray proposed a fundamental shift in social policy.

Nunn and New York Congressman Stephen Solarz suggested the path for American foreign policy in the post-cold war era. Our panels included Albert Shanker, the president of the American Federation of Teachers; Keith Geiger, president of the National Education Association; Dr. Robert Spillane, superintendent of schools in Fairfax County, Virginia; Jeff Faux, president of the liberal Economic Policy Institute; and Ralph Neas, executive director of the Leadership Conference on Civil Rights.

The New Orleans Conference on March 22–25, 1990 was by any measure a major success. But when our weary crew arrived back in Washington late Sunday afternoon, we did not appreciate the historic role that it played in the New Democrat movement. In retrospect, it was the turning point for Democrats and for the DLC that we had hoped it would be.

Twelve years earlier, with their party out of power and out of ideas, a group of Republicans had gotten together at the Tidewater Inn on Maryland's Eastern Shore and adopted a series of resolutions redefining their party that helped them reclaim the White House in 1980 and dominate the national debate throughout the 1980s. We wanted New Orleans to achieve the same results for our party—and, in the end, it did just that. Our credo, "The New Orleans Declaration," became a seminal document for New Democrats, and as Clinton would say at Hyde Park near the end of his second term: "The New Orleans Declaration is largely responsible for the success we have enjoyed in the last eight years because it gave us a platform on which to stand, and a framework from which to work."

About 700 people, including about 200 members of the press and more than 130 federal, state, and local elected officials, attended the conference sessions on Friday and Saturday. We configured the room like the House of Representatives with the presiding officer located in the front of the room and speakers addressing the conference from one of two lecterns located in a simulated well.

As in Philadelphia, Senator Lloyd Bentsen keynoted the conference. It turned out the DLC and DNC were meeting at the same time, creating a little stir in the press, but, nonetheless, DNC Chairman Ron Brown flew in to give a major speech. Other major speakers included Nunn, Robb, Breaux, Wilder, Blanchard, Gephardt, Gray, McCurdy, Kennelly, Boggs, Michigan Congressman Sandy Levin, and Gore, who had recently argued in a *Mainstream Democrat* piece that "[m]arket forces are the fairest, most efficient way to encourage environmentally sound behavior," an idea also endorsed in the Declaration.

One of the idea centerpieces of the conference was a payroll tax cut presented by Senator Daniel Patrick Moynihan of New York. Like national service and the EITC, cutting the payroll tax was a break from Democratic orthodoxy that said you never mess with Social Security. Conference attendees were greeted with a freshly printed edition of *Mainstream Democrat* with a cover story by Moynihan headed "The Tax on Work." A payroll tax cut also was endorsed in the New Orleans

Declaration. Jesse Jackson addressed the conference on Saturday morning shortly before Nunn turned the gavel over to Clinton. The theme of his speech was "delighted to be united." Jackson claimed that the DLC had moved to his positions on taxes, cutting military spending, and a host of other economic and cultural issues. None of that was true; Jackson and the DLC differed on most important issues, and his speech was not well received by many DLC supporters. When asked by reporters about Jackson's speech, Clinton quipped: "Jackson and I are both southern Baptists . . . and our church permits a lot of interpretation of common documents."[5]

Clinton gave the closing speech of the conference. True to the strategy I had laid out in November, he announced that the DLC would launch an effort to organize state chapters. He also announced that, using the New Orleans Declaration as a starting point, we would spend the next year traveling around the country gathering ideas that would help us flesh out the declaration into a governing agenda to be presented at our next annual conference.

In a memo to Clinton three days before the conference began, I had suggested that "the thrust of your speech ought to be that the intellectual renewal of the party is necessary if we are going to achieve the political renewal. In other words, if we stand for the right things, our political support will build." He hammered home that message with a flourish.

Pointing to the success of the Republicans' Tidewater Conference, Clinton said:

> That's what we've tried to begin doing here in New Orleans. Everyone here hopes the 1990s will see a political renaissance for the national Democratic Party. Every one of us knows we can't reach our goals until we elect a Democratic president. But at least I believe we will never restore our party's strength with self-seeking obsession about the next presidential election. In the end, any political resurgence for the Democrats depends on the intellectual resurgence of our party. There's far too much talk about personality in politics and far too little about what we're going to say and do to make sense to the American people.

He continued hitting that theme:

> When I entered politics, I was even more thin skinned than I am now, and every time I read something bad about myself in the newspaper,

I went into a deep funk. And one day, my wife, who is a lot smarter than I am, said, "I don't know why these bad press reviews upset you so much. Your biggest problem is that most people get up every day and go about their business, and you don't even cross their minds. You think about that . . . the real tragedy is that most people in this country go about their business every day and we don't ever cross their minds." Because they don't know what we stand for, they don't know who we are, and they don't know what we are trying to do.

And so help me, I believe that that is what we ought to spend the rest of 1990 working on and we should forget about who is going to run for president and whether that person can win in '92. If we stand for something that makes sense and if people can identify with it and participate in it, this party is going to do just fine. And if we don't, then all this talk about the presidential election amounts to nothing more or less than sitting around waiting for something bad to happen to George Bush. And that's wrong and un-American. We need to worry about what we're going to do and what we're going to stand for and why that makes a difference to the American people.

After talking about education reform and saying he took the DLC chairmanship to make the DLC the idea wing and the action wing of the party, he returned to the essential message:

If you want to be a Democrat, it seems to me, you've got to believe in a few basic things. If you want also to be relevant to the emerging century: one, you have to believe that there's a role for government in solving common problems. Two, you have to believe that when a government does something with individuals that themselves are disabled or irresponsible or incapacitated, you must attempt to empower those individuals and/or to impose responsibility on them.

The earned income tax credit for the working poor is an empowerment issue. School choice is an empowerment issue. Welfare reform is a responsibility issue. Yeah, we will give you a check, but not unless you promise and follow through on the promise to pursue a path to independence through education, training, and taking a job if it's offered. We need to find more issues like that because there are too many problems, given the dramatic change in the relationship of children and child-rearing in this country, that cannot be solved by unilateral attempts by the government to help people without either empowerment or to demand the responsibility.

In closing, he sent the crowd out of the room on an emotional high by connecting our work with the lives of ordinary people, as only Clinton could do. He told of a visit he and his wife, Hillary, made to a Los Angeles school where he talked with a dozen 11-year-olds. The kids' number one fear was "of being shot going to and from school by crack-crazed kids who were shooting for the hell of it. Their number two fear was that by the time they were 13, boys or girls, they'd have to join a gang and start using crack or they were going to get beat up." Clinton asked the children about their families and learned from one girl who lived with foster parents that her natural parents were drug abusers. Then he asked the kids if they thought they should turn in their parents if they were addicted to drugs if they knew their parents would not be put in jail the first time, but would be given the opportunity for treatment, and all but two raise their hands. Clinton continued,

> Now, it's a long way from a kid who can remember holding his great-grandfather's hand to a child who will never have a picture of a grandparent in the house and thinks he or she ought to turn their parents in because they can't fulfill the most basic responsibilities. . . .
>
> That's what we are fighting for. That's what this whole thing is about. Never let our work be rooted in who gets elected president or governor or anything else. People don't know what we stand for and what we care about. If we go tell them and we do things, the Democratic Party's future is secure.

The New Orleans conference got an enormous amount of press coverage, most of it about Jackson's speech and our reaction to it, about the array of stars who traveled to New Orleans to appear with the DLC, and about the DLC's role in trying to push the party to the center.

Our New Orleans Declaration was the real legacy of the 1990 DLC Annual Conference although it received only passing mention in the press. Perhaps this was an indication that the most significant and historic events are often not recognized in the day-to-day press coverage.

The process for drafting the Declaration was not pretty. We went through after draft after draft. At one review session in the U.S. Capitol, Sam Nunn and Speaker Tom Foley got into a shouting match over the use of the word "statist" to describe a Democratic approach in an early draft. As the conference approached, the draft became so bloated with comments added by members, it was virtually unintelligible—and certainly not definitional. At one point Nunn accused us of turning it into pabulum.

So we did the only sensible thing: We pitched it. And, with the skilled hands of Will Marshall and Bruce Reed, we wrote the final version from scratch. It was short, concise, expressed our principles and ten goals that we thought could be the foundation of a New Democrat agenda. We showed our new draft to Nunn and Clinton who responded positively. They agreed that this final version said something important.

We got all 11 members of our governing board to sign the introduction which expressed our purpose for issuing the declaration:

> With this New Orleans Declaration, members of the Democratic Leadership Council reaffirm our commitment to the fundamental values and principles that have traditionally guided our party—and can unite it again today.
>
> This Declaration carries forth the best of our Democratic tradition: Jefferson's belief in individual liberty and responsibility; Jackson's credo of equal opportunity for all, and special privilege for none; Roosevelt's thirst for innovation; Truman's faith in the uncommon sense of common men and women; Kennedy's summons to civic duty and public service; Johnson's passion for social justice; and, Carter's commitment to human rights. . . .
>
> We believe the New Orleans Declaration represents a turning point for Democrats. It declares our intent to transcend our differences, set forth our principles, and forge a broad national agenda to restore America's economic strength, expand opportunity for every citizen, and promote freedom and democracy in the world.
>
> Even in an era often dominated by 30 second sound bites and by campaign consultants and large television buys, we believe ideas count. The New Orleans Declaration is a clear statement of the ideals in which we believe and ideas that will further them.
>
> The specific proposals we offer in the New Orleans Declaration do not attempt to address every national need or solve every national problem. Nor do they represent the official policy of the Democratic Party, or even of every member of the Democratic Leadership Council. Taken together, however, they form a coherent and innovative approach for strengthening our country, reinforcing mainstream values, and enabling millions of our citizens to realize America's true promise of equal and expanding opportunity—a blueprint for change that most Democrats can embrace.

We view this New Orleans Declaration not as our final word, but rather as a fresh point of departure for a vigorous national debate on how to lead America forward in the 1990s. We believe this Declaration will help put the DLC in the vanguard of this debate.

The first section of the New Orleans Declaration entitled Where We Stand articulated 15 core beliefs of the New Democrat movement:

We believe the promise of America is equal opportunity, not equal outcomes.

We believe the Democratic Party's fundamental mission is to expand opportunity, not government.

We believe in the politics of inclusion. Our party has historically been the means by which aspiring Americans from every background have achieved equal rights and full citizenship.

We believe that America must remain energetically engaged in the worldwide struggle for individual liberty, human rights, and prosperity, not retreat from the world.

We believe that the U.S. must maintain a strong and capable defense, which reflects dramatic changes in the world, but which recognizes that the collapse of communism does not mean the end of danger.

We believe that economic growth is the prerequisite to expanding opportunity for everyone. The free market, regulated in the public interest, is the best engine of general prosperity.

We believe the right way to rebuild America's economic security is to invest in the skills and ingenuity of our people, and to expand trade, not restrict it.

We believe that all claims on government are not equal. Our leaders must reject demands that are less worthy, and hold to clear governing priorities.

We believe a progressive tax system is the only fair way to pay for government.

We believe in preventing crime and punishing criminals, not in explaining away their behavior.

We believe the purpose of social welfare is to bring the poor into the nation's economic mainstream, not to maintain them in dependence.

We believe in the protection of civil rights and the broad movement of minorities into America's economic and cultural mainstream, not racial, gender or ethnic separatism. We will not tolerate another decade in which the only civil rights movement is backward.

We believe government should respect individual liberty and stay out of our private lives and personal decisions.

We believe in the moral and cultural values that most Americans share: liberty of conscience, individual responsibility, tolerance of difference, the imperative of work, the need for faith, and the importance of family.

Finally, we believe that American citizenship entails responsibility as well as rights, and we mean to ask our citizens to give something back to their communities and their country.

The Where We Stand section was followed by ten policy goals for the country with this introduction: "As we enter the 1990s, we believe Democrats must be the architects of national purposes, not just the mechanics of government policy."

The goals we advocated were: a series of ideas and public investments to promote growth and rebuild American economic security; bold school reforms, including giving parents a choice of the schools their kids attend; youth apprenticeship; national service; the police corps, an ROTC program for police officers; environmental security, including market-based solutions that would make polluters pay the cost of their pollution; a guaranteed working wage grounded in an increased EITC; individual development accounts, modeled after IRAs, for poor people; an emerging democracy initiative to promote democratic capitalism and democratic values in the world; and, a plan to pay for progress that included getting the deficit under control and a cut in the regressive payroll tax.

In his closing speech to the conference, Clinton lamented that "this New Orleans Declaration has not been given enough attention in the public." A decade later, after two successful terms as president, Clinton would reflect on the New Orleans Declaration for the pivotal role it played in shaping his own agenda. But to get there, Clinton and I, joined frequently by other DLC leaders, set off on an arduous year of trips, speeches, and DLC chapter openings across the country, all designed to establish the New Orleans Declaration as a platform for a new kind of Democrat.

Al From advising Ed Muskie during markup of the Congressional Budget Reform Act in 1973, Committee Chairman Sam Ervin is on the far right.
CREDIT: *Photo by Bill Goodwin*

Al From with Gillis Long (L) and Tim Wirth (R) at Democratic Caucus event in 1981.
CREDIT: *Photo courtesy of Gillis Long and Tim Wirth*

Al From hugging daughter Sarah on election night 1992 in DLC Suite in Little Rock as Bill Clinton wins in Ohio to be elected 42nd president of the United States. Ginger From is in the background and friend David Dunn is on the left.

The $3 million photo. Al From walking down the steps in the Arkansas Capitol on November 5, 1992 with President-elect Bill Clinton and Bruce Lindsey (R). Photo ran on front page of the Washington Post the morning invites to a DLC fundraiser hit the streets.
CREDIT: Timothy A. Clary/AFP/Getty Images

Ginger and Al on the podium before Clinton's swearing in at 1993 inauguration.

Future son-in-law Mark Rouse, daughter Ginny, Clinton, daughter Sarah, Ginger, and Al at surprise fiftieth birthday party Clinton's threw for Al in the State Dining Room at the White House in 1993.
CREDIT: Photos by Elisa Morris Photography

Al with First Lady Hillary Rodham Clinton at White House birthday party.
CREDIT: *Photos by Elisa Morris Photography*

Al with Vice President Al Gore at White House birthday party. John Breaux is on right.
CREDIT: *Photos by Elisa Morris Photography*

Al with Clinton and Breaux at DLC event in New Orleans in 1993 where Clinton announced his national service program. Will Marshall is in background.
CREDIT: *Photos by Elisa Morris Photography*

John Breaux, Al, Mack McLarty, Clinton, and David Gergen on way to Clinton speech at 1993 DLC Conference in Washington.
CREDIT: *Photos by Elisa Morris Photography*

Al (second from right) running with Clinton at Fort McNair before DLC conference in 1996.
CREDIT: *White House Photograph*

Al on Air Force One in 1999 with (L to R) Clinton, trip director Kirk Hanlin, Small Business Administrator Aida Alvarez, Transportation Secretary Rodney Slater, and Education Secretary Richard Riley.
CREDIT: *White House Photograph*

Al with Third Way Leaders (L to R) Tony Blair, Clinton, Gerhard Schroeder, Wim Kok, and Massimo D'Alema before DLC Third Way forum at the National Press Club in Washington, D.C., in 1999. CREDIT: ©Jason Miccolo Johnson

Al From, Bill Clinton and Tony Blair at the Press Club in 1999. CREDIT: ©Jason Miccolo Johnson

Al with former DLC Chairmen (L to R) Dick Gephardt, Chuck Robb, Sam Nunn, Al, John Breaux, Dave McCurdy, Joe Lieberman, and Tom Vilsack at Al's DLC retirement dinner in June 2009. (Former DLC Chairmen not pictured: Bill Clinton, Evan Bayh, Harold Ford, Jr.)
CREDIT: *Photo: GeorgeLong.com*

Al with Clinton and John Breaux at Al's 2009 DLC retirement party. Chuck Robb is in the background.
CREDIT: *Photo: GeorgeLong.com*

ELEVEN

THE ROAD TO CLEVELAND

1991

The 14-month journey from New Orleans to the DLC's 1991 Conference in Cleveland was hectic and arduous. We operated at a campaign pace. Whether it was Clinton, Nunn, McCurdy, Breaux, me, or others, DLC members were constantly on the road, visiting more than half the states and establishing fledgling DLC chapters in 20 of them, testing out ideas that were generated mostly by our Progressive Policy Institute (PPI)—all with the purpose of building the core of a political infrastructure and shaping an agenda that a New Democrat candidate could carry to the White House.

I had laid out the strategy for that journey in a memorandum to Bill Clinton on April 15, 1989, three weeks after our New Orleans Conference. My memo said that we needed to develop a galvanizing message and an organizational structure around the country, so that at the right time we could "translate support for our ideas into political muscle inside the Democratic Party and in the nominating process. The bottom line is this: If a candidate from our movement doesn't win the Democratic presidential nomination in 1992 or 1996, or if the nominee doesn't adopt our message, we will have failed."

The cornerstones of that strategy were seeking ideas around the country "to expand the New Orleans Declaration into a platform that could be ratified at our next annual conference" and launching "an ambitious organizational effort, with the goal of establishing DLC chapters in 25 states in the next 12 months."

The road to Cleveland was not without obstacles. In New Orleans, Jesse Jackson may have been "delighted to be united," but two weeks later in a speech before the Minister's Action Coordinating Council at the First Baptist Church in Washington, Jackson resumed his attacks on the DLC by calling our New Orleans Declaration statement—"we believe the promise of America is equal opportunity, not equal outcomes"—a perversion of the Democratic tradition.

That question of equal opportunity versus equal outcomes was a major philosophical divide between new and old Democrats. It also divided American liberals from European social democrats. As the great political sociologist Seymour Martin Lipset explained in a paper he wrote for PPI, the American ethic was equal opportunity—assuring every American had the tools to get as far as his or her talents would allow—while the European ethic was equality with large social welfare benefits to bring about equal outcomes.[1]

Most of the press coverage out of the New Orleans conference was favorable, yet some was not. Margaret Carlson wrote a particularly snotty column titled "The Neoliberal Blues" in the April 2, 1990 issue of *Time*. She implied that the New Orleans Conference resembled a "meeting of accountants," accused us of promoting mechanical "Mr. Goodwrench programs," and said our stars like Clinton, Nunn, Robb, Breaux, and Bentsen were "dizzy with turning points, raw with fresh starts, wide awake with new days dawning." She was particularly tough on Clinton, calling him a "perfect front man for an organization that celebrates the work ethic of the common man while relying almost entirely on the Fortune 500 for operating funds." Finally, she said with its "teeny, tiny programs . . . the DLC is rewriting the lyrics of the 1960s song: 'Ask not what you can do for your country but what educational vouchers, economic nationalism and savings incentives can do for you.'"[2]

Carlson proved to be wrong on almost every point. We never supported school vouchers or economic nationalism. In fact, we were pilloried by many Democrats for promoting trade. And she was dead wrong about implying we had been bought by our corporate funders. We did raise a lot of corporate money, but there were never any quid pro quos, implicit or explicit. When creating the structure of the DLC, I had purposely created a firewall between those who gave money and those who made organizational decisions. I took it as a point of pride to always use the money I raised to achieve DLC goals, not the agenda of the donors.

I never enjoyed raising money, but it's hard to pay scholars to develop ideas or travel around the country with nothing in the bank. And, travel around the country we did.

In April 1989 Sam Nunn and I traveled to Columbia, South Carolina, where, with former Governor Dick Riley, we launched a South Carolina DLC chapter. In May Representatives Dave McCurdy of Oklahoma and Louise Slaughter of New York and I launched the Minnesota chapter in Minneapolis. Later that summer, I went to Boston to join State Representative Dick Moore in establishing a chapter in Massachusetts.

In June Clinton and I traveled to California to set up a chapter in Los Angeles, under the leadership of two rising superstars—John Emerson, who had gained prominence for managing Gary Hart's California primary victory over Walter Mondale, and Cynthia McLain-Hill, a dynamic, young African American attorney who had built a statewide network of support.

Clinton's trip to California was a prototype of the campaign-like travel he would do for the DLC over the next fourteen months. After a Sunday filled with meetings and a working dinner, we were up for a 7:30 a.m. breakfast on Monday morning at our hotel with about 20 local politicos and activists. By 9 a.m. we were heading to McDonnell-Douglas in Long Beach for a fundraising meeting, and by 11:30 a.m. we were at a short private meeting at the Pacific Club in Newport Beach with a small group of Orange County business leaders. Then we walked down the hall at the Pacific Club for a luncheon fundraiser.

We slipped out of the lunch at 1:45 p.m. and raced to a 2:10 p.m. flight to San Francisco. When we landed, we headed straight into the city for a 4:15 p.m. editorial board meeting with the *San Francisco Chronicle.* After that, we had about an hour to grab a cup of coffee and make some phone calls—in those days before cell phones, we traveled with a lot of dimes to feed pay phones—before we battled rush hour traffic on U.S. 101 toward Silicon Valley.

We made it to Los Altos Hills by 7:30 p.m. for an event with prospective donors hosted by Los Altos Hills Mayor Toni Casey. At about 10:30 p.m.—15 hours after our day began—we headed back to the Hyatt Hotel in Palo Alto.

The next morning it was up at 7:15 a.m. to do the whole dance over again.

That California trip would be the last DLC trip Clinton would take until after he was safely reelected as Arkansas governor. Two weeks earlier, Clinton had a closer than expected Democratic primary. He was never in danger of losing, but his opponent won nearly 40 percent of the vote, and it was clear that the Republicans would go all out to beat him in the fall.

During our California trip Clinton was worried, as he should have been, about his reelection, and we decided that he should forego more DLC travel over the summer and get back to campaigning in Arkansas. My message to him was straightforward: You're not going to be worth anything on the national scene if you get your clock cleaned in Arkansas.

While Clinton was taking care of business in Arkansas, the DLC kept busy. The PPI cranked out policy papers on individual development accounts, youth apprenticeship, the police corps, community policing, racial quotas, and a number of other issues. I continued on the road, hitting Texas, Massachusetts, West Virginia, California again, Michigan, and New York City several times.

In July 1990 we launched the Mainstream Forum under the leadership of Dave McCurdy as a way to use the televised House proceedings to deliver our message. Under House rules, members can reserve up to an hour a day to speak on the House floor on any topic they choose after the body concludes its regular business. A decade earlier, Newt Gingrich used that forum to build support for conservative ideas and for his successful effort to wrestle the GOP leadership away from Bob Michel. Our goal was to use speeches by Mainstream Forum members at least one day a week to promote our New Democrat ideas. McCurdy enlisted a number of DLC stalwarts including Mike Espy of Mississippi, David Price of North Carolina, and Tim Penney of Minnesota—all of whom would lead their state chapters.

But while the Mainstream Forum got off to a fine start, it never really became the message machine we had hoped. It got quickly consumed by internal House matters—like getting members' bills scheduled—and after a few months, members tired of going to the floor to make speeches.

On July 9, Deb Smulyan, the DLC executive director, and I made a site visit to Cleveland, which was bidding to host our 1991 annual conference. Cleveland, hailed by the local press as the "Comeback City," had just elected Michael White, a dynamic 39-year-old African American, as mayor. We were interested in holding our convention in the Midwest where Democrats needed a big comeback of their own. Mayor White and local business leaders pledged to raise $600,000 for us if we came to their city.

In September, Mike White joined us in Williamsburg for a DLC Board of Advisors retreat. Clinton made the trip to Williamsburg, his first appearance at a DLC event since his California trip and the only one he would make until after his gubernatorial reelection.

In October, I was back on the road, organizing chapters, working the press, and recruiting supporters. On Thursday, October 18, I was in Dallas courting a story in the *Dallas Morning News* and the next day I was in Austin, where we organized the Texas chapter. Then, after returning to Washington for the weekend, I was back in the air on Monday morning, this time off to Nashville, Kansas City, and Independence, before heading back to Washington.

Clinton won reelection comfortably, taking nearly 58 percent of the vote. But the exit polls on Election Day were showing a tighter race and Bruce Lindsey was still nervous about the outcome when he called me at home as the polls were closing. Clinton himself was concerned enough about the Republican challenge that he promised the people of Arkansas that he would not run for president in 1992 if they returned him to the statehouse.

Three days after the election, on Friday, November 9, I was in Little Rock to plan Clinton's DLC activities for the next seven months.

At 8 a.m. that morning, I arrived at the Governor's Mansion for breakfast with Clinton. I always enjoyed those morning meetings at the mansion. We'd sit in a den on the first floor at a large round table in one corner of the room as the prison trustees who staffed the mansion would pile on the bacon and eggs. This morning, they put a big plate of bacon in the middle of the table and constantly replenished it as Clinton and I wolfed it down while he regaled me with stories of the campaign.

About half an hour later, my staffer Deb Smulyan and Clinton's staffer Craig Smith joined us and we got down to business. We decided to make full use of November and December before Clinton had to be back in Little Rock in January for a biennial session of the State Legislature. Clinton would travel to Minneapolis and New York City before Thanksgiving, and then, after a quick trip to Washington in early December, would do a six state swing to set up DLC chapters in the South.

On November 27, Chuck Robb and I traveled to Cleveland where, with Mayor White at his side, Robb announced that Cleveland would be the site of our 1991 convention.

As we entered December, Sam Nunn was constantly in the headlines. He was leading the Democratic response to the president's build-up in the

Persian Gulf in the months preceding the 1991 Gulf War. A *Washington Post* profile by David Broder entitled "Sen. Nunn: Democrats' Shadow Commander" stated he was cautiously exploring the possibility of running for president in 1992.[3]

Nunn was a favorite of many DLC-ers and a number of major Democratic donors in New York. Nunn had scheduled a day of meetings with a star-studded cast of donors in that city for Wednesday, December 5, 1990, and he asked me to join him for those meetings.

The day before my trip to New York with Nunn, Bruce Reed sent me a memorandum arguing for a Nunn-Clinton ticket in 1992. He made a compelling case. "Almost every successful candidate for the Democratic nomination in recent years has won by running in a whole new way," he wrote. "There are many different routes to the nomination, but one of the most compelling strategies for 1992 is one that has never been tried: two like-minded candidates running from the start as a ticket. It worked for Lawton Chiles and Buddy MacKay in Florida, and it might just work nationally."

Then he laid out the arguments for our dream ticket: "A bold stroke like this will demonstrate to the American people that for once, Democrats have their act in order. By naming his vice president right off the bat (and ideally, laying out his governing agenda), Nunn would demonstrate confidence, leadership, and a sense of where he's going. *The only way to avoid being destroyed by the dynamics of the nominating process is to set the agenda.*"

Moreover, he argued, two candidates would be better than one because they could double the amount of campaigning and nearly double the amount of press attention they would get. And, choosing a vice presidential candidate earlier would spare him the preconvention "special interest and constituency jockeying" that so hurt Mondale and Dukakis.

As to what Clinton would bring to a Nunn ticket, Bruce wrote: "As the most experienced Democratic governor, Clinton is a natural counterpart to the most trusted Democrat in Washington. Nobody can deliver a message of peace through strength as well as Sam Nunn; nobody delivers a message of getting America moving again better than Bill Clinton."

While we were in New York, I handed of copy of Bruce's memo to Nunn. He reacted positively.

The next morning in Washington, I met Clinton for breakfast and slipped him a copy of Bruce's memo, too. He smiled and said he liked it, though I'm sure he was thinking that a Clinton-Nunn ticket would be better.

After breakfast, Clinton and I headed over to the Rayburn Office Building for a Board of Advisors meeting. After that meeting, Clinton, Nunn, Robb, and I repaired to a small anteroom to make some decisions about what precisely we wanted to accomplish and exactly how we would proceed over the next six months. Most important, we decided that by the time we arrived in Cleveland, we wanted to have an agenda with which a New Democrat candidate could win the White House in 1992.

To get there, we would continue our heavy travel around the country, setting up chapters where we could, but most importantly gathering ideas and input on turning the New Orleans Declaration into a full-fledged platform. Clinton and Nunn agreed to do the heavy lifting, with a caveat: Clinton's six-state southern trip would get us off to a fast start, but while Clinton was tied up with his 1991 legislative session, Nunn would pick up more of the burden.

But as so often happens in politics and in life, things did not go as planned. In early January Nunn led the opposition to the resolution authorizing the Gulf War. He believed that a commander-in-chief should not send a young man or woman into harm's way unless he could look the parents in the eye and say I've tried everything else and there is no other way. In this case, Nunn believed that Bush had not passed that test and that additional sanctions against Saddam Hussein should be implemented before we went to war to drive Iraq out of Kuwait. The resolution authorizing the war passed the Senate by five votes on Saturday, January 12, and President Bush signed it two days later. On January 17 Operation Desert Storm began, and the U.S.-led coalition commanded by General Norman Schwarzkopf quickly drove the Iraqis out of Kuwait.

For Nunn, the political reaction to his vote was harsh, particularly in Georgia. Republicans accused him of voting against the war to aid a potential presidential campaign. A sign went up on a Georgia highway calling him "Saddam's Best Friend," and his approval ratings in the state, while remaining high, dropped significantly. On the evening of Martin Luther King Day, January 21, Nunn called me at home and told me that he would do any DLC travel that he had already committed to, but I was not to schedule any trips not already set. I could tell from his voice that he had lost his stomach for politicking. By the end of January it was clear that if there was a DLC candidate in 1992—and it was still far from a sure thing—it would be Clinton.

Clinton's December swing went exceedingly well. Starting on Saturday, December 8, in a five day swing, we kicked off DLC chapters in Alabama, Kentucky, North Carolina, Mississippi, and Texas, and slipped in an event with the South Carolina chapter along the way.

Our travel was always arduous, but never boring. To get to our events, we often had to take commercial flights with difficult connections or find small private planes, on which we could fly as long as there were two pilots. Whenever possible, Clinton wanted to overnight back in Little Rock—he was still governor—and I always wanted to get home for weekends to see my family. Sometimes that was hard. With our Alabama event stretching well into Saturday night, for example, I could not get a flight back to Washington until Sunday morning, where I had just eight hours on the ground—barely enough time to get home—before I had to be back in the air to Louisville for an early breakfast on Monday morning.

On Monday, December 10, during our breakfast in Louisville, Mayor Jerry Abramson mentioned that the University of Kentucky was playing the University of North Carolina that night in Chapel Hill. Our schedule called for us to arrive in Raleigh that night about 45 minutes before game time. Clinton looked at me without hesitating and said, "Let's go to the game."

We landed in Raleigh, just in time to head to the game, where on instructions from the state police, we parked right outside the Dean Dome. After the game, our car was gone. The campus police had towed it. Clinton and I and the rest of our traveling party walked a couple of blocks to the campus police station where we waited more than two hours until our car was returned.

The rest of the trip was less adventurous. We kicked off DLC chapters in Mississippi and Texas before Clinton headed to Little Rock to launch an Arkansas chapter.

Clinton's trips didn't go unnoticed. In his December 12 syndicated column, the *Washington Post*'s David Broder wrote about our Southern swing. A group with the kind of local political and financial base that the DLC was trying to put together in most major states "obviously would be well positioned to play presidential politics," Broder wrote, "and Clinton said he is hopeful that 'one or more people' will espouse the DLC approach in the 1992 primaries."

Broder noted that possible DLC candidates would be Bentsen, Gore, and Gephardt. "Clinton often is mentioned as a potential presidential candidate but promised Arkansas voters in his reelection campaign this year that he would serve out a full four-year term. 'I am far more interested in building a movement than helping myself,' he said."[4]

The DLC chapters were more of a grass tops than a grassroots effort. We enlisted key Democratic office holders and other politically influential leaders into our chapters, but a small organization like the DLC—in the pre-internet days—didn't have the manpower or financial resources for a real grassroots organizing effort. Nonetheless, in large part because Linda Moore, our political director, was so good at identifying the best people to run the chapters, our chapter leaders in almost every state would play a significant role in the campaign once Clinton became a candidate.

In the first four months of 1991, we undertook an intensive effort to continue to shape our message, work the local and regional press, and establish ten additional chapters. In the last week of January, I did a hectic swing with Moore through six western states, meeting with key political reporters, important politicos and elected officials, and potential chapter organizers in Phoenix, Salt Lake City, Salem (Oregon), Billings, Cheyenne, and Denver. By the time Moore and I touched down at Washington Dulles Airport on Friday afternoon, February 1, we had established operating chapters in Oregon, Montana, Wyoming, and Colorado.

In March Clinton's legislative session ended and he was able to get back on the road. On March 10 he flew to Detroit to launch the Michigan chapter, and in April traveled to Oregon, Wyoming, Colorado, California, Louisiana, New Mexico, and Ohio to launch or boost DLC chapters.

While Sam Nunn and Governor Zel Miller launched a Georgia chapter in Atlanta, I went to Indianapolis and Phoenix to formally launch chapters, and to Iowa and New Mexico to lay the groundwork for chapters in both states. Iowa, normally a hotbed of early presidential election activity, was virtually deserted with no announced candidates and the likelihood of favorite son Senator Tom Harkin getting into the race. It was so deserted, in fact, that David Yepsen, the well-respected political writer for the *Des Moines Register,* showed up early to meet me for a 7:30 a.m. breakfast.

During our Detroit trip I got the first inkling that Clinton was seriously thinking about running for president in 1992. He had not returned a couple of my calls the previous week as his legislative session was coming to a close, and I was irked. Before the trip, I had sent him a strong memo that said we needed to talk about his commitment to the DLC and suggested that since it looked unlikely that the Democrats would have their act together in time for 1992, we ought to be thinking about a five-year strategy that looked ahead to 1996.

As was often the case, we really didn't get a chance to talk until the end of the trip—about 5 a.m. on Monday morning as we were sitting in the lobby of the Radisson Hotel in Southfield waiting for a car to pick him up to take him to the airport for an early flight back to Little Rock. "I've been thinking that maybe I ought to make a run in 1992," he said. "That way we could get our ideas out there, and even if I lost but I ran a respectable race, people would be more receptive to our ideas the next time." Though I thought we were on the right track and making real progress in developing a winning message, with President Bush basking in the aftermath of the spectacularly successful Gulf War, I was skeptical that even a candidate as skilled as Bill Clinton could win in 1992. I'm sure that Clinton did not share my skepticism.

On Monday, April 21, before a kick-off rally for the Louisiana DLC, Clinton and I sat down for a long interview with Adam Nagourney of *USA Today*, an important national political reporter who had traveled to Baton Rouge to see the DLC in action outside Washington. When Nagourney's story appeared the next morning, it created quite a stir.[5]

It was a favorable story for the DLC. Nagourney wrote that in a "display of political muscle," the DLC was expanding that week into five states—Louisiana, New Mexico, Georgia, Florida, and Ohio— and that just six years after we began, "DLC leaders said they're positioned to be a major influence in 1992." Clinton compared the DLC to the insurgent campaign that helped Ronald Reagan take over the Republican Party. Nagourney quoted Clinton as saying, "I'd like us to be what people think of when they think of the Democratic National Committee."[6]

That last quote was a misquote—our tape revealed that Clinton had said "Democratic national party" not "Democratic National Committee"—but it angered DNC Chairman Ron Brown, whom Clinton had supported. Tensions were already high because a *Newsweek* article a week earlier had said we were challenging liberals for control of the party and had quoted Clinton saying "we want our ideas to be what people think about when they think about the Democratic Party."

"We win the White House by being a unified party," Brown told Nagourney. "All of my time and energy is spent on that, without commenting on anything they [the DLC] say or do. I know there are a few in the party who want an intraparty fight. I think that would weaken rather than strengthen us."

I'm sure I was one of the people Brown was referring to when he said "some in the party wanted an intraparty fight." I profoundly disagreed with the idea that what the Democratic Party needed was unity. I saw unity as the wrong goal—like rearranging the chairs on the deck of the *Titanic*. Three straight presidential elections had shown that party unity was not our problem. We needed to attract more voters. Clinton had made the right point in the *Newsweek* article: "A lot of people don't think Democrats can be trusted with their national security or their tax money. We need to change that if we want to win a presidential election."[7] To me, if changing that perception meant an intraparty fight, so be it.

Brown's reference to me may have been veiled but his reference to Clinton was not. "Well, maybe the DLC wants to come up with a candidate," he told the *Atlanta Constitution*. "Too bad it can't be Bill Clinton, since he's already announced to the people of Arkansas that he will not be a candidate in 1992."[8] His pique passed and he welcomed the Clinton candidacy when Clinton announced an exploratory committee four months later.

I also infuriated Jesse Jackson by telling Basil Talbott of the *Chicago Sun Times* that Jackson and Senator George McGovern, who was also making noises about running again in 1992, would not be invited to make major speeches at the Cleveland Conference because "we are trying to change the party, and Jackson and McGovern represent the ideological approach to government we are trying to change."[9] I said that Jackson and McGovern represented the left wing of our party that people had come to judge as inattentive to their economic needs and weak on defense—the old style politics, tired liberalism. We, in contrast, I told him, were the new choice—progressive, radical centrist. I had made my point, but in retrospect I could probably have made it less stridently.

The decision to deny Jackson a major speech had not been mine alone. Nunn, Clinton, and I had discussed it a couple of months earlier. We decided to invite him to participate in the convention, but not to give a big speech.

Jackson called our decision a major slight and responded to Talbott's piece by attacking me in the press and sending letters to Clinton,

Nunn, Robb, Bentsen, and other DLC leaders asking whether I spoke for them. He also urged black leaders to boycott our convention. For the next three weeks, I felt more heat than I had ever felt—before or since. I had told Clinton when he took the chairmanship that I would be willing to take the heat for tough choices so that he would not have to, but I never expected it to get so hot.

Day after day, stories appeared in papers across the country about the DLC's snub of Jackson, most of them blaming me. With the help of my press secretary, Catherine Ann "Kiki" Moore, I tried to respond so that the focus would be on me and not on the elected officials. The story wouldn't go away.

Clinton and the DLC leaders nervously backed me up. They all said they didn't agree with my comments, but they didn't capitulate and offer Jackson a speech. Clinton responded to Jackson's letter with a letter that said in the past the DLC's annual convention had featured a large number of speeches highlighting the talent and views of party leaders, citing his speeches at the previous two conferences as examples. He then said that this year we decided to limit the speeches and have more discussion, and that an invitation for Jackson to participate had been mailed to him earlier. In his letter, Clinton reiterated that invitation for Jackson to come and participate in the discussion.

As to my comments, Clinton wrote: "Regarding the recent press accounts, any remarks that could be interpreted as being exclusionary or divisive are inconsistent with my goals and vision for the organization. I am working to expand the DLC to include all Democrats who are working to develop a message that a majority of Americans will support, consistent with the basic values of our party and committed to the kind of dramatic change we have to make to preserve America's leadership and to keep the American dream alive for all people."

But Clinton, who always likes to avoid conflict, was not happy that we were in such a public fight with Jackson, and he let me know that in no uncertain terms. One day my phone rang and I picked it up just to hear Clinton on the other end shouting, "I'm so damn mad at you that I can't talk to you today" and slamming down the phone. But through it all, he stood by the decision and by me. In response to specific questions, Clinton told reporters I was not speaking for him with my comments to Talbott, but he always defended my motives and integrity.

In essence, Clinton and the other DLC leaders followed the advice of an April 22 editorial in the *Baltimore Sun*. Citing my comments, the editorial board said that, in denying Jackson a speaking role, they hoped

I was speaking for DLC leadership, but that they also hoped the DLC leaders would deny that I was speaking for them. "[T]he party needs to change direction," the *Sun* wrote. "It has to get away from the disastrous politics of the left advocated by Messrs. McGovern and Jackson."[10]

By May the time had come for the Cleveland conference. The night before, Clinton came to the DLC offices where almost all of the DLC and PPI staff was stuffing packets for the convention participants. I had brought Sarah, my 12-year-old daughter, to help.

When Clinton arrived, my wife, Ginger, and I were outside the conference room where Sarah and the staff were hard at work. I mentioned to Clinton that Sarah had been very upset by the press stories about me and Jesse Jackson, and she was particularly upset by an attack Bill Gray (the House majority whip from Pennsylvania) had made against me in *USA Today* because, at our Philadelphia conference two years earlier, Gray had personally escorted her around Independence Hall.

Clinton asked Sarah to come out of the room, and he, in his very special way, said to her that he knew she was upset by what she was reading about me in the newspapers—just like Chelsea was upset when she read unfavorable pieces about him. "Bill Gray is our friend," he told Sarah. "But right now we're trying to change things and he's very angry. Change is never easy, but he'll be our friend again."

The main business at the Cleveland Conference was to approve the "New Choice Resolutions" and when we arrived on the afternoon of Sunday, May 5, we went right to work, dividing the convention participants into working groups on the main topics of the resolutions: Defining America's New Role in the World; Restoring America's Competitive Edge; Meeting the Global Economic Challenge; Strengthening the Family; Making Public Education Work; and Beyond Welfare—New Paths to Opportunity.

We had worked long and hard to shape our New Choice. We had developed ideas at PPI, presented the themes and ideas in the *Mainstream Democrat* and in meetings and forums across the country. Clinton, Bruce Reed, Will Marshall, and I worked it over and over until we were satisfied. We built it on the foundation of the New Orleans Declaration, but this time our message had more political edge. We began the introduction with a tough attack on the Republicans and the Bush Administration:

After more than ten years of Republican rule in Washington, America's economy has been devastated. Today the Republican borrow and spend policies offer a hollow promise of opportunity for the ordinary men and women of America. Our social fabric has been torn by increasing tensions of class and race. More and more, America's schools don't teach our children well, America's streets are filled with crime, and our government costs too much and does too little.

For years, the Republicans have consistently chosen private gain over public responsibilities, put self-interest ahead of the common good, and clung to a doctrine of every man for himself in a nation that pledged long ago to go up and down together.

A reckless Republican fiscal policy has plunged the federal government into insolvency, burdened working families with one of the least progressive tax systems on earth, and paralyzed national initiative and progressive government.

So long as millions of America's families lack basic health insurance, so long as American workers aren't getting the skills they need to keep the best jobs here in America, so long as some Americans still suffer from discrimination while a Republican administration plays politics with civil rights, so long as 18 nations do a better job of bringing healthy babies into the world than we do—this country needs a strong Democratic Party more than ever.

But we also made it clear that neither party had sufficient answers and we didn't let our party off the hook:

When most Americans look at politics nowadays, they see too many old answers and choices that offer no choice at all. The old ideologies on the right and the left are no longer sufficient to realize the aspirations of the American people, and both political parties will be left behind unless they put forth new answers and new institutions for a new era.

In the minds of too many Americans, the Democratic Party has stood for government programs that don't work, special interests before the interests of ordinary people, and a reluctance to assert American values at home and abroad. The New Deal policies that built and united the middle class no longer command its loyalty.

Our party's challenge today is to discard the orthodoxies of the past and make government a champion of national purpose and not a captive of narrow interests, a creator of opportunity and not an obstacle to it.

America needs a new choice, and we believe that only Democrats can provide it. We have gathered from every state and region to show that Democrats everywhere want to set a new course for our party and our country.

We concluded the introduction with the core beliefs that would define the New Choice, a choice we defined as "a new public philosophy, not a new set of programs" that was "built on a set of common beliefs and broad national purposes, not on promises to disparate interest groups." We noted that this philosophy "looks for leadership not from Washington but from states and communities that have been laboratories of innovation."

Among our core beliefs were that "the mission of government is to expand opportunity, not bureaucracy," and that "America must lead the march of nations toward democracy and free enterprise, not retreat from the world." We reaffirmed "the Democratic Party's historic commitment to secure civil, equal, and human rights," and opposed "discrimination of any kind—including quotas." We stated our commitment to "make our economy an engine of growth and opportunity again, with a government that helps to create wealth, not just redistribute it, and seeks to expand trade, not restrict it," in order to create a "national strategy to compete for the best jobs in the world." We called for a "more progressive tax system, and a government that spends more on the future, not the present or the past." We declared our support for environmental stewardship, that government should be a "caretaker of our natural resources and seek to protect and manage natural resources for future generations." We said that "the role of government is to guarantee equal opportunity, not mandate equal outcomes" and that "our society has a moral duty to experiment with fundamentally new approaches to liberate the poor from poverty and dependence by promoting work, family, and independence." Finally, we stated our belief in "government that stays true to America's moral and cultural values," such as individual liberty, opportunity, and responsibility.

"Our purpose," we said, "is not to seek the middle of the road but to build a new road that leads beyond right and left to move America forward. The industrial age is over; the old isms and the old ways don't work anymore. Today, and in the months to come, we will put forth new answers and a new way of thinking which are based on the principle of inclusion and work for the greatest public good. We invite the American people to join our cause."

We followed that introduction with 17 pages of specific policy proposals, many of which challenged the standard Democratic orthodoxy. We called for the DLC cornerstone ideas like national service, welfare reform, a payroll tax cut, the police corps, community policing, and an expanded Earned Income Tax Credit. We also came out for a new idea in education reform—"giving entities other than school districts the opportunity to operate public schools." That idea would come to be called charter schools. In addition, we supported alternative certification for teachers and a system of youth apprenticeships for non-college-bound kids.

At a time when Democratic Congressional leaders opposed it, we endorsed the Brady Bill and a seven-day waiting period for the purchase of handguns. Despite opposition from organized labor, we endorsed fast-track negotiating authority for consideration of the North American Free Trade Agreement. We called for maintaining a strong, technologically advanced national defense and, in line with the tough-minded internationalism of Roosevelt, Truman, and Kennedy, endorsed America's energetic engagement in the world, arguing that some things were worth fighting for, like liberty, justice, and human decency.

We called for a new budget policy that limited spending increases to the growth rate of per capita income in the previous year. To bolster families, we called for increasing the personal exemption for middle- and low-income families with children under five. We supported tougher child support enforcement and holding parents responsible for keeping kids in school and monitoring their progress. We backed the Family Leave Act and called for comprehensive reform of the nation's health-care system.

We also called for a reaffirmation of the nation's commitment to civil rights and, while opposing quotas, we sought affirmative action and developmental programs to assure that opportunities are in fact equal.

Finally, to give low-income Americans a stake in their society and a chance to build personal assets, we proposed individual development accounts and a system of microenterprise loans to help poor people in urban and rural areas going into small businesses.

We introduced the New Choice resolutions at the Cleveland Conference and throughout both days of our annual meeting we discussed them before approving them by consensus. Our critics accused us of letting donors and lobbyists vote on the resolutions—and they had a point. In theory everybody present had a vote, and allowing that was bad judgment on my part. I really didn't think about it too much because I was sure we could control the outcome. Nonetheless, it looked bad, and I should not have let it happen.

Clinton kicked off the Cleveland Conference with a rousing keynote and Gore was the closing speaker on the second day—the role Clinton had played in New Orleans.

Clinton's keynote was short, crisp, and passionate. Bruce Reed had spent considerable time working with Clinton on a draft in the week preceding the convention. On Sunday night, before his Monday morning speech, Clinton said he wanted to work on it and asked me to get him somebody to type his final draft. He spent all night working on it. At 7 a.m. on Monday morning, we went to his room and he gave us a draft. Bruce and I looked it over, said it looked good. Clinton then proceeded to toss the draft aside, wrote nine or ten words of notes on a piece of paper, and went out and delivered the speech of his life.

Clinton was electrifying, working the crowd into a frenzy. He was interrupted by applause a dozen times, no small feat for a 20-minute speech first thing in the morning in front of a crowd of politicos and Washington lobbyists, who had probably been drinking most of the previous night. Clinton himself was not really a morning person, and I expect that his speech was much improved because he had stayed up all night working on it.

In the speech, Clinton started out by saying that he disagreed with those who said our party was dead and with the latest issue of the *New Republic* whose cover read "Democratic Coma." He then offered a critique of the Republicans that paralleled that in the New Choice resolutions. Clinton praised the job that Ron Brown had done as party chair to keep the party together and help members of congress and governors, like himself, get elected in tough circumstances.

But, he said that "if we want to be a national party, we have to do a lot more. We have got to have a message that touches everybody, that makes sense to everybody, that goes beyond the stale orthodoxies of left and right, one that resonates with the real concerns of ordinary Americans, with their hopes and their fears. That is what we are here in Cleveland to do."

"The Republican burden," he continued, "is their record of denial, evasion, and neglect. But our burden is to give people a new choice, rooted in old values, a new choice that is simple, that offers opportunity, demands responsibility, gives citizens more say, provides them responsive government—all because we recognize that we are a community, we are all in this together, and we are going up or down together."

With that statement, Clinton injected into the political lexicon three themes—opportunity, responsibility, and community—that would come to define the New Democrat movement in the United States and the Third Way movement across the globe for the next decade.

He then proceeded to define opportunity and responsibility, talking about the ideas in the New Choice that embodied those themes.

> Our New Choice plainly rejects the old ideologies and the false choices they impose. Our agenda isn't liberal or conservative. It is both, and it is different. It rejects the Republicans' attack on our party and the Democrats' previous unwillingness to consider new alternatives.
>
> People don't care about the idle rhetoric that has paralyzed American politics. They want a new choice and they deserve a new choice and we ought to give it to them. I want my child to grow up in the America I did. I don't want her to be part of the first generation of Americans to do worse than their parents did. I don't want her to be part of a country that's coming apart instead of coming together. That is what the New Choice is all about. That is what we are here to do. We're not out to save the Democratic Party. We're out to save the United States of America.

The Cleveland Conference was a game-changing event. The ideas in the New Choice challenged Democratic orthodoxy and left many in the traditional party nervous, uncomfortable, and even angry. Outside the conference hall, the United Auto Workers distributed leaflets expressing their opposition to our position on NAFTA. The teachers' unions were upset that we invited Polly Williams, the school voucher proponent from Wisconsin, to participate. A group of liberal Democrats—the Coalition for Democratic Values organized by Ohio Senator Howard Metzenbaum to oppose the DLC—met in a counter-conference in Des Moines that same weekend. Jesse Jackson came to Cleveland to lead two days of protest to our meeting.

Even some of our stalwarts like Gephardt, Kennelly, and Gray, who participated in our conference, were unhappy with us. When I got back from Cleveland, a group of moderate and conservative House members told me that Clinton and I were damaging their relationships with some interest group leaders. I responded that we were forging a message that could win us back the White House, and, in the end, all would be well.

The end result was that the way we ran the conference drew lines. And, as I had predicted in the November 3, 1989 memorandum that first laid out our strategy, some of our friends were coming down on the other side.

Unlike previous DLC conferences, Cleveland was not a sounding board for all factions of the Democratic Party. We had a mission: to send a message that there was a New Democratic Party with a new message and new messengers. And I was determined that we not deter from that mission. Cleveland was our turf; it was packed with DLC supporters from across the country. We had built our own playing field so that we could determine the outcome. And we intended to play our game on our field. A year and a half later when Bill Clinton, the keynote speaker, and Al Gore, the closing speaker, were elected president and vice president of the United States, the wisdom for our taking that tough course was vindicated.

I was standing in the back of the hall near the press risers when Bill Clinton finished his keynote address. Bob Beckel, the veteran political consultant, turned to me and said, "That's the best political speech I've heard in more than a decade."

Clinton knew he had hit a home run. In his memoir, he called the Cleveland speech "one of the most effective and important I ever made. It captured the essence of what I had learned in seventeen years of politics and what millions of Americans were thinking. It became the blueprint for my campaign message, helping to change the public focus from President Bush's victory in the Gulf War to what we had to do to build a better future. By embracing ideas and values that were both liberal and conservative, it made voters who had not supported Democratic presidential candidates in years listen to our message. And by the rousing reception it received, the speech established me as perhaps the leading spokesman for the course I passionately believed America should embrace."[11]

Clinton's speech was clearly the highlight of the conference and it catapulted him into the spotlight as a potential presidential candidate. He had given our movement what it had sorely lacked: a passionate spokesman for our mainstream message.

On the flight back to Washington, I sat next to Chris Matthews, then Washington bureau chief for the *San Francisco Examiner*. I had known Matthews from the days when we both worked for Ed Muskie and then for the House leadership. Matthews's column that appeared on May 9 said it all: "After years of silence, moderates and conservatives in the Democratic Party have found both a forum, the fast-growing council, and a voice: Arkansas's Bill Clinton."[12]

I might have taken issue with Matthews's portrayal of the DLC as the "Democratic right," but the essential message of his column was correct. We came out of Cleveland with a message powerful enough to win back the White House and with a potential candidate passionate enough to carry that message. We had the message and the messenger. The final part of our strategy was to market test both in the Democratic presidential primaries.

TWELVE

THE PRE-CAMPAIGN

1991

In the May 1991 issue we changed the name of our magazine from the *Mainstream Democrat* to the *New Democrat*. Announcing the change, editor Bruce Reed wrote on the inside cover: "Our mission has not changed: to rouse, inspire, goad, provoke, and incite Democrats to chart a new course for our party and the country. . . . But frankly, we think some people misunderstood the message we were trying to convey. We like the name *New Democrat* because it leaves no doubt as to our purpose. We're not trying to move the Democratic Party to the center; we want to move it forward."

Three weeks after Cleveland, on May 29, Reed, Linda Moore, Deb Smulyan, and I met with Bill Clinton in the Governor's Mansion in Little Rock to discuss our strategy for the summer. DLC supporters were ablaze with excitement. They wanted Clinton to run for president.

Reed and Moore, who had been through the 1988 campaign with Gore and Gephardt, respectively, wrote memos listing the tough questions he'd have to answer before he decided to take the plunge. I believed the chances were good that he would run, and I wanted to focus on the 100 days we had left before Clinton would have to resign the DLC chairmanship to begin the campaign. I didn't mince words.

"With Cleveland behind us, we need to move quickly to take full advantage of the momentum we gained there and to lay as much groundwork as possible for a 1992 presidential run by you or another DLC type candidate," I wrote in a memo I handed him during our meeting.

Our goals for the summer should be twofold: (a) to make this move-ment so hot that a candidate coming from it will have momentum get-ting into the race, and (b) to get you into the states that will be most useful to you should you choose to run for President.

For you, the next 100 days are crucial. You're hot property now, and you need to take full advantage of that. You need to be prepared to launch a full-scale campaign by the end of the summer. Whatever you decide, you should use the next three months to build the DLC movement and your own political stature at the same time. As I've said before, the DLC gives you the opportunity to turn Arkansas into a mega-state. This summer is the time to take advantage of it.

Linda asked him for five 2- or 3-day blocks on weekdays for trips to California, Texas, and key primary states. He agreed. The trips would include the typical elements of campaign trips—meetings with support-ers, usually at chapter events, meetings with donors, and a heavy dose of editorial board and press meetings. But we decided that these trips would include something else: events to put the spotlight on ideas in the New Choice resolutions that we talked about in Cleveland, events that would show our ideas in action.

Even before we hit the road for the DLC, battle lines began to be drawn. In early June, in an interview with the *Washington Post*'s Da-vid Broder, Mario Cuomo denounced the DLC and our call for "a new mainstream" in Cleveland. "I don't like those people at the DLC [and the] implicit position that we have something to apologize for and now, we have to move to the middle," he told Broder. "I don't personally feel that I have to move two inches."[1] And Jackson repaid us for Cleveland by not inviting Clinton to the Rainbow Coalition's June meeting. "He's not a contender," wrote the *Post*'s Dan Balz quoting Jackson.[2] Clinton, in an interview with Ron Fournier of *Associated Press,* responded:

Arkansas Gov. Bill Clinton has this to say to critics of the Democratic Leadership Council: Put up or shut up. . . . "Now it's their turn to say what they're for instead of criticizing us," Clinton said of Cuomo and Jackson. . . . "I like Mario, but once again he and Jesse are criticiz-ing me without being specific about what they disagree with. I didn't say we had to apologize for anything, but I did say that it is a fact that we've been getting beat. And, what's their explanation for why the middle-class folks didn't vote for us in '88 when we had a clear shot. . . . People aren't buying what we're selling."[3]

Near the end of June, about two weeks before we began our pre-campaign swing, Dan Balz spent time with Clinton in Little Rock. Playing off Sam Nunn's joke that Clinton was a "rising star in three decades," Balz's story ran in the *Washington Post* under the headline: "Democrats' Perennial Rising Star Wants to Put New Face on Party." "Arkansas Gov. Bill Clinton (D) is a peacemaker by personality, but he is bracing for an argument," Balz wrote. He noted several new positions that Clinton advocated, but said that, with his commitment to issues like civil rights, family leave legislation, gun control, Clinton was "far different from a Republican clone."[4]

A few days later, on July 2, in the first of a *Los Angeles Times* three-part series on the plight of the Democrats, Ron Brownstein painted a sharp picture of the division in the party. Brownstein held Clinton up as the standard-bearer for the New Democrat movement, quoting his statement, "If you've got to be a Republican to say that work is better than welfare and people ought to pay their child support, then we're in worse shape than I thought."[5]

The lines were drawn, and before we left for our trips we printed a pamphlet that included an introduction by Clinton—largely his Cleveland speech—and the New Choice resolutions that we would arm our supporters with. On the cover, Bruce Reed put "opportunity, responsibility, community," our three main themes. Over the next year, we passed and mailed out tens of thousands of those pamphlets. I teased Reed that putting "opportunity, responsibility, community" on the cover was the smartest thing he ever did.

Before Clinton hit the road, I traveled to New Hampshire for a meeting with the organizers of that state's chapter and to do what the *Boston Globe*'s Curtis Wilkie called "missionary work" for Clinton.[6] The ever-troublesome state party chair in New Hampshire, Chris Spirou, who had amended the title of the New Choice resolutions to the New American Choice in Cleveland, had publicly tried to block our New Hampshire chapter from organizing. Spirou had argued that only the state party could use the word "Democratic" in its name, so our group incorporated as the New Hampshire DLC. Clinton wanted no part of a public dispute with the party chairman in the first primary state, so I made the rounds of the New Hampshire political press core to try to diffuse the dispute by making it clear we had no intention of competing with the state party.

In July, Clinton and I met in Chicago with Bill Daley, who would have led our Illinois chapter had he not been diverted to run the Clinton campaign in the state. Then we walked to City Hall to meet with Daley's brother, Chicago Mayor Richard M. Daley.

As we walked into the mayor's office, Bill Murray and Robert De Niro were leaving. After they were out of earshot, Clinton asked Daley why they were there. "They're making a movie [*Mad Dog and Glory*],"the mayor responded, "and they had a scene in it with a Chicago police officer sleeping in his squad car while on duty." Then he paused and said, "We had to *correct* it."

Clinton began by asking Daley what would he want if a Democratic president told him he could have anything he wanted for Chicago. The mayor looked him straight in the eye and responded: "No urban policy. Let me run my city." Daley meant it. When I was Clinton's domestic policy advisor during the 1992 transition, Daley sent me a several-hundred-page document detailing the burdens federal money placed on the city. Our meeting with the mayor was supposed to last only a half hour. But it went nearly an hour and we had to cancel our next meeting.

After lunch we met with Vince Lane and, surrounded by a phalanx of Chicago police officers, we toured two high-rise public housing buildings on the city's West Side. Lane, head of the Chicago Housing Authority, was a radical reformer who believed in personal responsibility. We had run a feature about him in the May issue of the *New Democrat*. When he took over the Housing Authority, virtually every housing project was drug-, crime-, and rat-infested. In high-rise buildings like one we visited, he instituted police sweeps to clear out the thugs and drug dealers who had moved in illegally. Once swept, he cleaned up the buildings, secured them, and created tenant committees that were responsible for managing them. His policy was straightforward: "We punish the criminals and reward the decent folks. It's as simple as that." The result of Lane's Operation Clean Sweep was a huge drop in crime in every building that was secured.

The two high-rises we toured were less than a football field apart, but they could have been on different continents. One had been swept, the other not. The first building seemed like a normal apartment building in a middle- or lower-middle-class neighborhood. The lobby and the hallways were clean with no graffiti on the walls. Most important, the stairwells were clear and secured. The tenants told us that they could carry on a normal life without having to fear for their lives every time they entered their building or walked out of their apartments.

As we walked toward the second building, the police warned that it was very dangerous and we might not want to go in. That did not deter

Clinton. The contrast was stark. In the second building, every inch of the lobby walls was covered with graffiti. Thugs and drug dealers loitered in the lobby and in the stairwells, where much of the drug dealing took place. The tenants could barely get in and out of the building.

Clinton was clearly moved. He added a hand-written note to the thank you letter he sent Vince Lane. It read: "It was great—one of the best days I ever had in public life. Hang in there!"

Four days later, Clinton was back in New York for two days of press and donors meetings, and a tour with Congressman Stephen Solarz of housing rehabilitation projects run by the People's Firehouse, a community organization in the Northside section of Brooklyn in Solarz's district. It was on that trip that Clinton first met Joe Klein, who would become famous as "anonymous" for writing the novel *Primary Colors* based on Clinton's 1992 campaign.

But it was at an earlier meeting with Tommy Tisch in the Regency Hotel's dining room—"the" place in New York for Democratic power breakfasts—that we learned that there was no such thing as a private meeting in a public place. Tisch, whose family owns the Loews Hotel chain that includes the Regency, suggested that the way to win the black vote was to get your picture taken playing basketball with some kids in an inner city neighborhood, as one of the candidates in 1988 had done. Clinton thought the suggestion was absurd and ignored it. Jay Severin, a Republican operative sitting at the next table, overheard and promptly called the writer of "Page Six," the *New York Post*'s gossip column, and attributed the comment to Clinton. After a lot of damage control by Kiki Moore and Clinton's press secretary Mike Gauldin, we convinced the writer that Clinton hadn't said it, but we couldn't prevent the item from appearing.[7]

That afternoon I told Clinton that I would not work in his campaign. I would do anything I could to help him to get elected president, I said, except go to work in the campaign. I thought I could help him more from the DLC.

Just as in Chicago and New York, we had a packed schedule for a three-day swing through California at the end of July. The highlight of the trip was a visit to the Falcon Program, a community policing program in West Hollywood, run by city attorney Jim Hahn's office. John Emerson, our chapter leader and a deputy city attorney at the time, had arranged our tour, which was covered by C-SPAN as part of its "Road to the White House" series. With Congress out of session for most of August, the C-SPAN tape played frequently.

Community policing was the idea of Reuben Greenberg, the African American, Jewish police chief of Charleston, South Carolina. When Greenberg became chief in the early 1980s he decided that putting police in squad cars and having them do little more than respond to 911 calls was not reducing crime. So he pulled a number of officers out of cars and put them back on the beat, covering the streets on foot, riding bicycles, or on horseback, making them accessible to people in the neighborhoods to which they were assigned. Clinton and I had met Greenberg briefly during a quick stop in South Carolina in December 1990, and our Progressive Policy Institute had developed the community policing idea included in the New Choice resolutions.

It was sunny the morning of July 31 when Clinton and I visited the West Hollywood neighborhood that had been riddled with crime, mostly connected to a thriving drug trade and ever-present gangs. But it was turning around, and the advent of community policing in the Falcon Program was credited as the reason why.

First we talked to an apartment manager who had united her residents against drug dealing in her building. Next we walked across a wide street lined with stucco apartment buildings and an occasional palm tree to meet two community police officers, Mike and Dale. The pair could have come straight from Central Casting—thick mustaches, wavy brown hair, aviator sunglasses, and the short-sleeved police uniform that was made famous by the TV show CHiPs. Clinton walked straight over to the cops for a chat.

"What do you think accounts for the turnaround in public attitude toward the police around here?"

"I think its results," Mike said, "A neighborhood like this is no different than our country, because our country is a bunch of little neighborhoods. The good people feel the frustration. They call us, the bottom level of government who comes out here. If we're unable to help, then they get frustrated. Then they get taken over."

The two cops saw positive developments happening in the community, and the involvement of people like the building manager was a step in the right direction, but Mike said they still needed to do more: "There's not enough of us."

When President Clinton signed his crime bill three years later, they would get their reinforcements. The key provision: 100,000 cops for community policing.

That evening, Clinton spoke at a late dinner that included a small group of Hollywood's liberal elite, including actor Warren Beatty and his wife, actress Annette Bening, and Academy Award–winning producer Sidney Pollack. The first question was: "You're not for charter schools are you?" It was clear the questioner was not. Clinton held his ground. "Yes, I am, and you should be, too. Here's why," he responded, and proceeded to make the case for charter schools.

Clinton arrived home in Little Rock about 7:30 in the morning on Friday, August 2, and was back on the road by Sunday night, traveling to New Hampshire to participate in a forum in Concord sponsored by the New Hampshire DLC.

Although Clinton had been reluctant to go to New Hampshire in June to launch the DLC chapter, its leaders had pushed hard to get Clinton to make the trip. Clinton continued to resist, and finally John Breaux and I cornered him one morning in Washington. We told him he had to go, that our New Hampshire DLC was made up of a Who's Who of New Hampshire politics, and he would need their help in the campaign. "If you're unwilling to go out on the limb for them," I said, "you can't expect them to go out on a limb for you." Finally, he relented and agreed to do an issues forum with the chapter. His condition was that three members of congress—Mississippi's Mike Espy, New York's Steve Solarz, and Indiana's Jill Long—also participate in the forum with him. I was so concerned about the New Hampshire trip that I hired an experienced advance man to lead it.

Clinton began that August Monday morning with an interview with Ron Brownstein of the *Los Angeles Times*, followed by a meet-and-greet, and then the forum. The forum ended about 10:45 and New Hampshire Congressman Dick Swett, serving as peacemaker, had arranged for Clinton to walk a short distance to the state party headquarters where he would meet briefly with Chris Spirou. Spirou, for that morning at least, dropped his resistance and the two posed for pictures.

The New Hampshire trip was a great success: 150 people crammed into the forum, twice the number its organizers expected. Clinton delivered the DLC reform message and because of Spirou's antics, he got considerable more press coverage throughout New England and nationally than a normal DLC state chapter event would have merited. A picture of Clinton, Spirou, and Swett all smiling appeared in the *Manchester Union Leader*. After the photographer snapped it, Clinton turned to Swett and joked that if became president, he'd make Swett Mideast peace negotiator—he appointed him ambassador to Denmark instead.

Clinton's last trip as DLC chairman was a two-day swing through Austin, San Antonio, and Dallas, ending at a dinner with Ross Perot.

In Austin we met with Governor Ann Richards and Comptroller John Sharp, to talk about the reinventing government project Sharp had initiated that found the state billions of dollars of potential savings.

When I first tried to schedule the dinner with Perot, he said he was going to be out of town and asked if we'd have dinner with his son Ross Jr. instead. So I scheduled it with Ross Jr., who had attended our 1990 conference in New Orleans, Tom Luce, Ross Perot's counsel, and their wives.

A few minutes after we sat down, Perot Sr. joined us, saying his plans had changed. Perot spent much of the night telling us how much he disliked President George Bush. Not known for moderation in his views, Perot proceeded to rant endlessly about Richard Armitage, whom Bush had recently tried to appoint to a position at the State Department. Perot and Armitage had crossed swords in the past over the return of the remains of soldiers missing in action during the Vietnam War.

As the evening wore on, I became convinced that Perot might consider a presidential run himself. He made it abundantly clear that he would not support President Bush. And, while he seemed to get along well with Clinton, I could not envision a man so straight-laced that he reputedly disciplined or fired staff members for wearing tasseled shoes supporting Clinton.

Clinton had to catch a late night flight back to Little Rock—he would rejoin us the next day in Jackson, Mississippi—and at about 10:30 Ross Jr. offered to drive him to the airport. As I stood outside the Crescent Hotel trying to hail a cab back to my hotel, a man in a 1984 Oldsmobile pulled up, stopped, and rolled down the window. "Do you need a ride back to your hotel?" Ross Perot asked me. I took up his offer and jumped in. It was a sight to behold. Here was Ross Perot, one of the richest men in the world, driving a seven-year-old car with clear plastic seat covers. "This is the car General Motors gave me when I went on the board," Perot said as he strained to peer over the steering wheel. "They wanted to give me a new car every three months, but I told them this one was perfectly good."

Clinton and I reconnected the next afternoon, Saturday, August 10, in Jackson for a meeting with Mike Espy and members of the Mississippi DLC, followed by a speech at the Jefferson-Jackson day dinner to the Mississippi Democratic Party. Around midnight, Clinton said he was about to head out to the airport to catch a plane back to Little Rock and asked me to ride to the airport with him. When we got into the car, he promptly went to sleep.

He had every right to be tired. I know I was. We had just carried out the game plan we agreed to in Little Rock in May with a month of arduous travel. Our goals were to build momentum for a DLC candidate and to get Clinton into states that would be useful for him in presidential race. "Clinton's already boosted his profile and planted his name in people's minds by traveling across the USA on behalf of the centrist Democratic Leadership Council," wrote Judy Keen a few days later in *USA Today*.[8]

The pre-campaign was over and the campaign was about to begin.

THIRTEEN

TO VICTORY

O n Thursday morning, August 15, 1991, just 100 days after our Cleveland Conference, Bill Clinton announced that he was resigning as chairman of the Democratic Leadership Council and forming an exploratory committee to consider a run for president in 1992.

Moments earlier I had been on the phone with him working out the details of his resignation and the formal statement his press office would release announcing the exploratory committee.

"For the past 17 months," that statement read, "as chairman of the DLC, I've had a wonderful opportunity to talk with Americans from every walk of life about the future of the Democratic Party and the future of our great country. It has been an invaluable experience, and I hope we have made a contribution to the debate about America's future. But it is time now for me and my family to carefully consider the wishes and interests of the people of Arkansas and what is best for us to do for 1992."

In essence, the campaign was on—the DLC had its candidate. While Clinton maintained that he had not made a final decision, forming an exploratory committee is the first formal step toward a candidacy, and it was clear that barring some unexpected occurrence he would run.

In the four months since the Cleveland Conference, the DLC had taken important steps to change from a Washington-centered operation into a national political movement by creating more than two dozen autonomous chapters across the country and officially adopting the title *New Democrat* for our magazine. With a presidential candidate to lead it, that movement was now much larger than the DLC.

After Cleveland, the *Washington Post*'s David Broder praised how far the DLC had come in just six years and said that the DLC had gone as far as it could go.[1] He was right. We had carried the movement a long way. After the Dukakis debacle, we administered reality therapy to a party that never seemed to be able to learn from its mistakes. In New Orleans we had laid out the core principles that would guide our movement. And, in Cleveland we had fleshed out those principles into an agenda that we believed could carry a candidate to the White House. We believed only Bill Clinton could take it across the finish line. Now the most important thing for the movement's success was not what happened to the DLC; it was Clinton winning the presidency.

Our role during the campaign would be different. We would not run the campaign; indeed, under the law we could not even endorse the candidate. But, under our new chairman, John Breaux, we could help by using the tools at our disposal to complement the campaign. The DLC and PPI, our policy institute, had provided the New Democrat DNA for the movement, and we still had plenty to do.

Soon after the start of the campaign, Clinton called me and said he wanted to have a DLC person on the campaign and that he wanted it to be Bruce Reed, who became Clinton's issues director and played an instrumental role in helping Clinton shape the message of the campaign.

We devoted the December 1991 issue of the *New Democrat* to a tough critique of every aspect of the Bush presidency. Before he left to join the campaign staff, Bruce wrote a scathing cover piece called "The Collapse of Bushism." Throughout the next year, we used our magazine to promote themes and ideas of the campaign. We focused the March issue on reinventing government, the idea that differentiated Clinton from his primary opponents. In May we published a special issue on the economy. Rob Shapiro, the PPI vice president for economic policy, who played a key role in formulating Clinton's economic policy, wrote the cover article. In July, as Clinton was calling for a New Covenant of opportunity, responsibility, and community, the *New Democrat* focused on a similar theme: "Forging a New Social Contract."

Nearly all the PPI scholars served as outside advisors to the campaign, Shapiro being the most prominent. His work at PPI on the budget, investment policy, and other economic issues became the foundation for Clintonomics. Shapiro was constantly quoted in the press and wrote op-eds explaining and reinforcing Clinton's economic policies.

We also continued the DLC field operation. We launched new chapters in Maryland, New Jersey, and Pennsylvania. John Breaux, Dave McCurdy, and I were on the road constantly to build new chapters or strengthen existing ones.

The start of the campaign also meant a different role for me. While I kept in regular touch with both Clinton and the campaign, participating in daily 8 a.m. conference calls for instance, I would see him only intermittently as things heated up. My role was largely to support the campaign, reinforce the message, and, as an outsider, to constantly goad them to stay true to New Democrat principles. Occasionally that made me the intervener, stepping in only when I thought the campaign was going off course. Clinton would later say in 2000: "If it hadn't been for the DLC with its constant idea machine, and Al From constantly harping on me not to abandon the reformist path, I couldn't have done it."

I firmly believed that the most important message Clinton could send during the campaign was that he was a "different kind of Democrat." And the DLC's political strategy of appealing to middle-class voters, our themes like reciprocal responsibility, and the ideas we pushed like welfare reform, community policing, and national service were absolutely key to sending that message.

It was vital that Democrats change the perceptions that we were soft on crime and national security, and that we took money from people who worked to give it to people who didn't. Until we changed those voters' views, voters would not even listen to us about the economy, the environment, or education, topics on which they might actually like what we had to say.

That's why welfare reform was the single most important issue in the Clinton campaign. It sent the message that Clinton was, indeed, a "different kind of Democrat." James Carville famously said "It's the economy stupid" and he was right. But voters might not even have heard that message if they thought Clinton was like the Democrats they had been voting against.

It was clear to me that if the DLC and I didn't play the role of protecting the New Democrat DNA in the campaign, nobody would. In 1988 we had seen how the good works of the first three years of a presidential cycle can be destroyed quickly in the fourth year—the only year that really counts—when the liberal activists take over the nominating process. And our experience around the Cleveland conference showed that there would be incessant pressure on Clinton to take a more traditional course.

So as the campaign began, I had three paramount goals.

First, I was determined to do all I could to make sure the New Democrat DNA, our strategies, our themes, and our ideas were at the core of the Clinton campaign.

Second, I knew Clinton's instincts were to run a New Democrat campaign, and I wanted to back up those instincts. Very few Democratic operatives believed, as he and I did, in the New Democrat approach. So I knew that he would face pressure, from within his campaign and without, to move away from the DLC and the New Democrat approach to curry favor with the interest groups that played heavily in the primaries.

Third, I wanted to use the resources of the DLC to validate the message that Clinton was a different kind of Democrat. I knew I was not a favorite of party activists or interest group leaders, but I had taken enough hits over the years to earn respect and credibility in the media on that issue.

On October 3, 1991, standing in front of the old State House in Little Rock, Bill Clinton formally announced his candidacy for the presidency of the United States. In the background, blaring over the loudspeakers was Fleetwood Mac's "Don't Stop Thinking About Tomorrow"—a campaign theme song that had been suggested to Clinton by former DLC intern Shawn Landres as he drove us from meeting to meeting during our July DLC trip to Los Angeles.

As he had in Cleveland, Bruce Reed helped Clinton write the speech, and the message was quintessential New Democrat:

> Today I am declaring my candidacy for president of the United States. Together I believe we can provide leadership that will restore the American Dream—that will fight for the forgotten middle class—that will provide more opportunity, insist on more responsibility, and create a greater sense of community.
>
> The change we must make isn't liberal or conservative. It's both and it's different. The small towns and main streets of our America aren't like the corridors and back rooms of Washington. People out here don't care about the idle rhetoric of the "left" and "right" and "liberal" and "conservative," and all the other words that have made our politics a substitute for action. . . . We don't need another president who doesn't know what he wants to do for America. I'm going to tell you in plain language what I intend to do as president. How we can meet the challenges we face—that's the test for all the Democratic candidates in this campaign. Americans know what we're against. Let's show them what we're for.

> We need a new covenant to rebuild America. It's just common
> sense. Government's responsibility is to create more opportunity. The
> people's responsibility is to make the most of it.

The New Democrat DNA in the Clinton announcement did not go
unnoticed. A *Philadelphia Inquirer* editorial described the substance of
his speech: "The Clinton/DLC approach is often labeled as 'moderate,'
but we don't believe that gives the full picture. It is also radical in the
sense that it goes after problems at their root. On one issue after another, Mr. Clinton is advocating major changes in the status quo. For
detractors of the DLC's agenda—folks such as traditional liberals, conservatives, and libertarians—it's bad news to see it being advocated by
someone as articulate and accomplished as Mr. Clinton. But from where
we sit, this candidacy is exciting and promising."[2]

It was clear from the announcement that the foundation of this campaign was its message. Clinton had meant what he said in New Orleans
in 1990: The intellectual resurgence of the Democratic Party must pre-
cede its political resurgence, and if we stood for the right things, the
politics would take care of themselves. Clinton often said to me that if
we told the American people what we were going to do, if we got the
message right, the rest of a presidential campaign—the money and the
organization—would fall into place.

Of course, the campaign still had to be organized. When he finished
his announcement, we went inside the Old Statehouse for a drink. Clinton turned to a small group of us and said, "You better go over to Bruce
Lindsey's office—(Lindsey was his national campaign director)—and put
together a campaign. I just announced for president of the United States,
and we don't have anybody on board." Of course, Bruce Reed was already working on the campaign, and pollster Stan Greenberg and media
man Frank Greer had already signed up. It was not long before James
Carville, Paul Begala, David Wilhelm, George Stephanopoulos, and the
rest of the campaign team were on board.

Because he believed that ultimately presidential campaigns boil
down to a battle of ideas, message, and issues—and Clinton was determined to win the battle of ideas—he began his campaign with three
speeches at Georgetown University in which he fleshed out his New
Covenant with specific proposals. All three speeches—on responsibility and rebuilding the American community, on economic change, and
on American security—further defined the New Democrat nature of his

campaign and how he differed from both the Republicans and the traditional Democratic orthodoxy. That was particularly clear in his first New Covenant speech on October 23, that focused on responsibility and rebuilding the American community.

> Today we need to forge a new covenant that will repair the damaged bond between the people and their government and restore our basic values—the notion that our country has a responsibility to help people get ahead, but that citizens have not only the right but the responsibility to rise as far and fast as their talents and determination can take them, and most important of all, that we're all in this together. . . . Make no mistake—this new covenant means change—change in my party, change in our leadership, change in our country, change in the lives of every American. . . .
>
> We need a new covenant that will challenge all of our citizens to be responsible, that will say first to the corporate leaders at the top of the ladder, we will promote economic growth and the free market but we're not going to help you diminish the middle class and weaken our economy. We will support your efforts to increase your profits—they're good—and jobs through quality products and services, but we're going to hold you responsible for being good corporate citizens, too.
>
> At the other end of the scale, we'll say to people on welfare: we're going to give you training and education and health care for yourself and your children, but if you can work you must go to work, because we can no longer afford to have you stay on welfare forever.
>
> We will say to hard-working middle-class Americans and those who aspire to the middle class: we're going to guarantee you and your children access to a college education, every one of you, but if you take the help, you have to give something back to your country.
>
> In short, the new covenant must challenge all of us, especially those of us in public service, for we have a solemn responsibility to honor the values and promote the interests of the people who elected us, and if we don't do it, we don't belong in government anymore.

All three speeches were well received, and the campaign was clearly on the rise, particularly in New Hampshire. People in Washington and even foreign leaders were starting to notice. On December 4, 1991, I received a call from a friend of mine in the Israeli Embassy who said Bibi Netanyahu was in Washington and wanted to meet Clinton. Netanyahu at the time was an Israeli negotiator for the Shamir government at the 1991 Madrid Peace Conference, which was about to convene bilateral talks in Washington. Clinton also was in Washington then, and he agreed to the meeting. So at about 11 p.m. that night Bill and Hillary Clinton, Bruce Lindsey, and I went up to Netanyahu's suite at the Madison Hotel. As I sat in the suite's living room with Clinton and Netanyahu, I was sure I was witnessing the meeting of two future leaders of their countries. They got along well that night; it was probably the high point of their relationship. Less than two years later, Netanyahu would oppose one of Clinton's finest foreign policy achievements, the 1993 Oslo Accords.

President George H. W. Bush's approval ratings had run as high as 90 percent after the Gulf War, and though they had fallen significantly by January 1992, most potential Democratic candidates that the press called the A team—Cuomo, Jackson, Bentsen, Gephardt, Bradley, Rockefeller, and Gore—opted not to run. Clinton seemed to be on course to win New Hampshire and sweep to the nomination. On Sunday, January 19, the *Boston Globe* published a poll that showed Clinton comfortably out front in the Granite State, with 29 percent of the vote compared to 17 percent for Paul Tsongas, the former Massachusetts senator, and 16 percent for Nebraska Senator Bob Kerrey.

Four days later on Thursday, January 23, everything changed. I was in New York and stopped off at the *New York Times* for a brief meeting with Arthur Sulzberger Jr., who had just taken over as publisher. Four months earlier, just before Clinton's formal announcement, I had gotten to know Sulzberger on a three-day North Carolina Outward Bound trip in the Smokey Mountains. We had talked about Clinton on that trip, and he was surprised that I thought the Arkansas governor would win the Democratic nomination in 1992. I had not seen Sulzberger since he had become publisher, and I thought this would be a good time to congratulate him and do a little proselytizing for Clinton.

I rode the elevator to the eleventh floor, and when it opened I was surprised to see Sulzberger himself waiting. "You need to call Elaine Kamarck at your office," he said. "It's an emergency." And so I sat in the office of the publisher of the *New York Times* as Elaine read me a story that was about to come out in the supermarket tabloid *The Star,* alleging that Clinton had a 12-year affair with an Arkansas woman named Gennifer Flowers.

When I hung up the phone, Sulzberger suggested we go down to the editorial department to meet with Jack Rosenthal, the editor of the editorial page. I had known Rosenthal for years, and when I founded the

DLC, I had made a friendly bet with him that we would eventually find a candidate who would do what Robert Kennedy did: put together a co-alition of blacks and working-class whites. As Sulzberger and Rosenthal were telling me how smart I was for finding Clinton, I was not about to tell them that when *The Star* hit the supermarkets in 24 to 48 hours, I would not look quite so smart. And, I certainly was not going to facili-tate the story into the mainstream press.

Clinton denied the affair and seemed to have survived the scandal. An ABC tracking poll on February 8 showed Clinton still ahead of Tson-gas 28 to 25. Then the second shoe dropped. A letter Clinton had writ-ten to the head of his draft board during the Vietnam War while he was on a Rhodes Scholarship in Oxford, England, was leaked to the *Wall Street Journal*. The letter was an eloquent expression of feelings about Vietnam—feelings that many of us shared—but the implication was that Clinton had used a promise of joining an ROTC program, which he never did, to avoid the draft. The truth was that Clinton drew a high number in the draft lottery and was not drafted. But with the leaked let-ter, his standing in New Hampshire plummeted, and by February 12, six days before the primary, he was 11 points behind Tsongas in the ABC tracking poll and falling.

With incredible grit, determination, stamina, and political skill, Clinton picked himself up off the mat and came close enough to Tsongas in New Hampshire to be dubbed by the press "the Comeback Kid." Two weeks later, on March 3, he won his first primary in Georgia. In rapid succession he won the South Carolina primary and the Wyoming caucus on March 7, and on Super Tuesday, March 10, he won over-whelmingly in Florida, Hawaii, Louisiana, Mississippi, Missouri, and Oklahoma, losing only in Tsongas's home state. This time Super Tuesday had worked for a New Democrat candidate because he won black voters and held a significant number of moderate and conservative white voters who had flocked to the Republican primaries in 1988.

The day after Super Tuesday, in an editorial in the *Times,* Jack Rosenthal conceded that I had won our bet. "Of all the numbers pour-ing forth from Super Tuesday, one stands out," he wrote. "Bill Clinton, white Southerner, won approximately 75 percent of the black vote . . . that one figure gives healthy evidence, probably for the first time since Robert Kennedy's Indiana primary campaign in 1968, that it's politically possible to bring poor blacks and blue-collar whites together."[3]

And then came the kicker: "The [Super Tuesday] triumphs pile up a formidable heap of delegates to the Democratic National Convention. And, they vindicate the vision of a political analyst named Al From, who in 1985 founded the Democratic Leadership Council as a vehicle to drive Democrats back to middle-class voters."[4]

The next week Clinton swept to victories in Michigan and Illinois and the nomination seemed assured.

Remarkably, Clinton's New Democrat message had come through the primaries to this point virtually unscathed. To be sure, on occasion he sounded like a traditional Democrat. In Florida, for example, to appeal to seniors, he took a more conventionally Democratic position against cuts in social security. But the defining aspects of his message were still the reform themes and ideas that had been at its heart since his Cleveland speech.

What made this all the more remarkable was that with Cuomo not running, Clinton really didn't have a formidable traditional liberal to push off. Instead, his main competition was Tsongas, who was more conservative than Clinton on economics. As a result, by suggesting that he would pay for his middle-class tax cut with higher taxes on the rich—perfectly consistent with the tone of his Cleveland speech—he was perceived as moving to the left on economic issues. That was not correct. Growing the private economy was still the cornerstone of his economic program.

That changed in the lead-up to the New York primary campaign in early April. During a quick respite in Little Rock the day after his March 17 victories in Illinois and Michigan, Clinton played golf at a segregated country club. Former California Governor Jerry Brown, the only candidate still in the race, seized on that issue to attack him in the Connecticut primary and the Vermont Caucus the next week. On March 24, Clinton lost both contests to Brown. Although he was still on the path to the nomination, the Connecticut loss in particular left the door slightly ajar, and to clinch the nomination he had to win in New York, a minefield of old-style, interest-group politics.

To traverse that minefield, Clinton muted his reform message. He still called for welfare reform and continued to push for national service. But he downplayed reinventing government, in the words of Ron Brownstein of the *Los Angeles Times,* "to the point where it has virtually disappeared from his rhetoric in New York City—a city that many analysts say they believe epitomizes the need for the types of reforms he has been touting. Instead, Clinton has used his most visible public appearances—particularly a summit with urban officials last Tuesday— to advance a more traditional liberal agenda: increased federal spending on housing, education, health care and other needs."

Explaining the reason for Clinton's strategy, Brownstein wrote that a "senior campaign official said Clinton's New York state hierarchy—led by veteran liberal activist Harold L. Ickes, a strong supporter of Mayor David N. Dinkens—has forcefully urged the Arkansas governor to avoid rankling the mayor, the municipal unions, black leaders, or other established constituencies. The senior official called Clinton's New York operatives 'an impediment to bold new initiatives.' The official added: 'They want us to run a . . . campaign of mollifying interest groups.'"5

Clinton won the New York primary and, with the field cleared, swept the rest of the primaries. But his image as a reformer and a different kind of Democrat took a hit, and that allowed Ross Perot to grab the reform mantle.

Despite the New York detour, the DLC's role in shaping the message and the strategy of the campaign was clear when Clinton came to our annual conference in New Orleans, where two years earlier he had become DLC chairman. In anticipation of the conference, Michael Kramer recognized this in a *Time* magazine column headed "The Brains Behind Clinton." "In a real sense, Clinton will be going home. . . . The intellectual origins of these themes, and many of their specific applications, can be traced to the DLC and its think tank, the Progressive Policy Institute—which is not surprising, since many of the same people responsible for those prescriptions have been intimately involved with drafting Clinton's tactical and substantive playbooks."6

Our conference occurred at the time of the Rodney King riots in South Central Los Angeles, and Clinton focused much of his speech on race and pulling the country together. There was a celebratory mood in the New Orleans Convention Center among the more than 1,000 DLC elected officials and supporters who welcomed Clinton as the presumptive nominee.

By mid-May, even with the nomination locked up, Clinton was running third in the general election polls, trailing Bush and Perot. Campaigning as an outside reformer, Perot had gained ground fast. Though Clinton was pushing the right kind of policy ideas, it was clear that his message—that he embodied a different kind of politics and that he, not Perot, was the agent of change in the race—was not taking hold. Perot's rise threatened to change the calculus of the race. If he really were to win between a quarter and a third or more of the vote, the best strategy for victory might no longer be to court the forgotten middle class as the DLC had long advocated, but rather to run a campaign aimed at turning out core constituencies.

It was time for my first intervention. Clinton called a strategy meeting at the Governor's Mansion in Little Rock for May 15. The purpose of the meeting was to figure a way to reconnect with the forgotten middle class. Because the focus was to be on economic policy, the campaign invited Rob Shapiro to attend. My instinct told me this was a critical juncture in the campaign and that the decisions about to be made were too important to be left to the economists. So I pulled rank and went myself.

The day before the meeting, I fired off a memo to Clinton about the message of the campaign. "The purpose of this memorandum," I wrote, "is to help you frame a political message that will define your campaign and ignite a political revolution that can carry you into the White House. That's the kind of message that can establish you as the agent of fundamental change and can undercut the rationale for the Perot candidacy."

I thought the seeds of such a message were present in the message he'd been delivering, but that it had to be more than a litany of programs. "Rather, it's a clarion call for a new and different kind of politics that reunites and reaches the values and aspirations of the forgotten middle class," I wrote, "a politics of reciprocity and personal responsibility (no more something for nothing) that puts the debate in the country back on a firm moral basis. That's what the idea behind the 'New Covenant' was all about in the first place."

But to lift his message to the level that it could ignite his campaign and diminish the Perot candidacy would require a much cleaner break with the old politics—in the Democratic Party as well as with George Bush—than he'd been willing to make so far.

I told him that making that distinct break was risky because it could hurt him with the Democratic base, but it was worth the risk: "My view is playing the old politics is playing a losing hand—it can get you close, but it can't win. It gives you 40 to 45 percent and shrinking. Making your campaign a crusade for a new and different kind of politics runs the risk of falling short of that base level, but it holds the promise of attracting a new majority coalition."

I told him that I thought the Perot phenomenon would undoubtedly falter; the reason it took off in the first place was voter discontent with politics, the two parties, and government. Clinton needed to fill that void.

I had given considerable thought to why Clinton's message that included so many of the right ideas wasn't generating the kind of passionate support necessary to propel him to the White House. I came up with three reasons.

First, the campaign was sending many, often contradictory, messages. A political message, I suggested, was more than just positions on issues. "It is all the signals your campaign sends out—through the campaign strategy, scheduling, visuals, endorsements, vice presidential selection processes, convention speakers, etc.—that give voters an idea about what your presidency would be like. And while you talk about change and many of your ideas are new, many of the political signals coming from the campaign look like establishment politics as usual."

I thought his message was becoming too programmatic, that the programmatic details had been important in the retail politics of New Hampshire, but obfuscated his themes when he was trying to communicate with voters through wholesale politics. He had done a much better job of communicating those themes with the New Covenant speeches early in the campaign.

Second, I thought the seeds of a crusade to replace the old politics with a new politics of reciprocity was inherent in the New Covenant message, but when he was delivering it, he was rounding the edges of his message just enough to blunt its impact. As a result, people who did not know his record of promoting changes were asking whether he stood for fundamental change or just incremental adjustments.

"From my perspective, that creates an interesting dilemma," I wrote, "you can give a speech that is arguably on message and off message at the same time. To voters and the press, that phenomenon sends signals you're trying to be all things to all people. You need to eliminate conflicting signals in your rhetoric and that the campaign is sending so that your most compelling message can get out with a real edge on it."

Finally, I thought that the Democrats were at an enormous disadvantage in presidential politics because voters' perceptions of the Democrats came from their 1984 and 1988 candidates, because primary voters were demographically and ideologically far different from general election voters, and because there simply weren't enough Democrats any more. "That's why it's essential that the campaign's message be aimed at transcending the Democratic Party, not unifying its factions. A unified Democratic Party loses presidential elections. Dukakis won a higher percentage of Democrats in 1988 than Carter did in 1976; there just weren't enough Democrats."

The message I suggested: an edgy New Covenant that pushed off both parties.

It's time to replace the Republican politics of neglect and the Democratic politics of entitlement with a new politics of reciprocity grounded in the values of personal responsibility and mutual obligation. This new politics will make it clear that hard work and personal responsibility count in our country once again. It will make clear that there's no more something for nothing. It won't offer the false hope that government can solve all our problems, but it will say to every American, if you'll do your part to be part of the solution and not part of the problem, if you'll give something back to your community or country, we'll make sure that the government is on your side, uses your tax dollars wisely, and offers you help when you need it. That is the covenant I will offer the American people.

We met for the strategy meeting in a ground floor meeting room at the Governor's Mansion. Clinton stood in blue jeans in the front of the room, clearly frustrated. He didn't like the idea of running third. He said he didn't want to meet with party hacks before 4 p.m. because he didn't want to be portrayed on the evening news as just another politician.

James Carville started the discussion by saying that we were looking for the "silver bullet that would turn this election around." The discussion quickly moved to what government programs we could offer that would appeal to middle-class voters. Ira Magaziner and Robert Reich led the discussion. As the day proceeded we discussed every possible idea for offering cradle-to-grave programs for middle-class voters. We would have done the most avid European Social Democrat proud. I have to admit I got caught up in the fervor of the discussion and offered suggestions of my own. But after a couple of hours, I realized that the discussion was going in exactly the opposite direction from what I had proposed to him in the memo the day before. If we really followed through on the ideas we were talking about, Clinton would look just like the Democrats that voters had been rejecting in presidential elections for a quarter century.

So I spoke up, making the arguments in my memo. Clinton, I said, was running far ahead of the field when he was viewed as a different kind of Democrat, and if we really wanted to drive down Perot's vote we had to grab the mantle of reform back from him. That meant Clinton had to quit rounding the edges of his speeches and push off both the Republicans and the old Democrats as he had early in the campaign. My interjection had stopped the headlong dash into social democracy, but the meeting ended with no decision.

Rather than going back to Washington right after the meeting, I stayed in Little Rock to have dinner that night with Betsy Wright, Clinton's former chief of staff. After dinner, she suggested we stop by a party that Bill and Hillary were likely to attend. A few minutes after we arrived, the Clintons showed up. Hillary came over to me and said she and Bill had discussed what I had said and had agreed I was right: To drive down the Perot vote, Bill had to be seen as a different kind of Democrat before the convention. She asked me to talk to Mickey Kanter, who was running the campaign, and to develop a strategy to achieve that goal.

Early the next week I talked to Kanter and agreed to consult with David Osborne, Doug Ross, Bill Galston, and Will Marshall to pull together some specific things Clinton could do to be viewed as the change candidate by the time we went to New York for the convention.

On Wednesday, May 20, even before I finished the complete strategy, I sent another memo to Clinton to follow up on the previous meeting and the brief encounter we had had at the party. I emphasized the importance of reestablishing the insurgent nature of the campaign.

> I'm very heartened by the instincts both you and Hillary expressed about the campaign and its message. I think your points—that you need to make the sum of your message greater than its parts, that your message needs to tell people more about you and to include your Arkansas record, and that you need to emphasize the parts of your message that make you a nontraditional Democrat—are right on target.
>
> Like you, I believe the most powerful—and most presidential—message you can deliver is in your announcement and first New Covenant speeches. . . . Importantly, it is the message that you most believe in and are most comfortable with so when you deliver it you generate the passion necessary to energize a campaign.
>
> I am not as heartened by the direction of the discussion at the message meeting. . . . What I heard from the consultants was a desire to come up with a new, big, silver bullet idea (a program) that would somehow transform the nature of the campaign. They are, in essence, trying to find a part that is greater than the sum of your message—and to fix a character problem with a program. That's ass backwards, and it's not going to happen. You're not likely to come up with a silver bullet program, but even if you do, in my opinion, it's not going to be a panacea for the campaign.

I concluded by arguing that it was critical for him to become an insurgent candidate again.

> The key to becoming an insurgent candidate again is to drive home your differences with the old, traditional Democratic Party. The

single biggest strategic failure of your campaign so far is the failure to separate yourself from the failed past of the Democratic Party. This strategic failure of the campaign has created the opening for the Perot candidacy. . . . If you can convince voters you're different than the Democrats they routinely vote against in presidential elections, you can begin to consolidate the anti-Bush vote and close the door on Perot.

You won't become an insurgent candidate—and be in a position to win the election—unless you are willing to make some of your traditional Democratic friends unhappy. That goes against your nature, but to me, that's the critical decision you have to make. If you're not willing to make traditional Democrats who guard the Democratic status quo unhappy enough to scream, you can hardly expect voters who don't pay much attention to politics to see that you really want change. An accommodator is not an insurgent.

It's time to declare the primary season over—and with it the compromises you needed to make to get to 2,145 delegates. From this day forward you need to re-introduce yourself to the voters as a candidate who transcends the Democratic Party, an insurgent who sees building a new majority based on your New Covenant and not unifying the party as your first priority. Take a lesson from Ronald Reagan who ran an insurgent campaign in the Republican Party and carried it on to the fall. Reagan didn't try to compromise with the GOP establishment he beat in 1980; if he had, he probably would not have won. Rather, he just rolled over the party he had just captured and made it support positions he wanted. You need to do the same.

Eight days later, on May 28, I delivered a memorandum signed by Osborne, Ross, Galston, Marshall, and myself suggesting a series of things he could do between the beginning of June and his acceptance speech.

First, we all agreed, he had to go back to the New Covenant message with a particular emphasis on reinventing government. We argued that the revolution in government theme was crucial because it would demonstrate that he was not wedded to the Democrats' traditional discredited way of governing: bureaucratic government.

Second, we urged him to demand a party platform that articulated his message and themes, and included specific planks that challenged traditional Democratic orthodoxy. Equally important, we urged him to resist the temptation to put every interest group favorite in the platform. We thought reporters would be looking at the platform to see if Clinton was really a different kind of Democrat, and it was important that it show that he was.

Third, we suggested that he use the June schedule to reinforce the campaign message, including challenging Democratic audiences to abandon old orthodoxies and change, going around the press and communicating directly with the voters via television talk shows and town meetings, and, as he did in the DLC pre-campaign, visiting programs like the FALCON program in Los Angeles, where New Democrat ideas were being put into action.

Fourth, and most important in many ways, we suggested that he break with the pattern of choosing a vice president to balance the ticket, and, instead use the vice presidential selection to reinforce his message. All but Osbourne, whose personal favorite was Cuomo, suggested that he consider a new face to reinforce the message of change. We particularly advised that he not use the selection process to placate the old party, and that he stay away from the kind of Noah's Ark exercise that Mondale engaged in to select his vice president. We even suggested he consider another southerner on the ticket—though we did not propose Gore— arguing conventional wisdom wouldn't have two southerners on the ticket. And, we suggested he make it clear early on that, while he respected Jesse Jackson, he simply differed with him on too many issues to put him on the ticket. Jackson wasn't going to be on the ticket, but in 1988, Jackson didn't help Dukakis by pushing to be selected, so eliminating him from contention early in 1992 would save the candidate a lot of headaches.

Fifth, just as he should control the platform, we suggested that Clinton control the convention, making sure that the speakers who best carried his message got the prime-time slots.

And, finally, we said that if he took the steps we had suggested to establish with the voters that he was not the kind of Democrat they'd been rejecting, he would have the credibility to use his acceptance speech to tell them what his presidency would be about. That speech, we said, would be the most important political event of his life, and it should tell voters where his presidency would lead them and exactly what the understanding in the New Covenant would be.

My first intervention was successful. During the six weeks leading up to the convention, Clinton did go back to his New Covenant message. He put a heavy emphasis on reinventing government, including in a speech to the American Federation of State, County and Municipal Employees (AFSCME) a call for the elimination of 100,000 federal bureaucrats.

As press reports began to surface about Perot's past erratic behavior, his campaign began to unravel and his support in the polls dropped.

During the Democratic Convention in mid-July, he dropped out of the race, citing a revitalized Democratic Party as one of his reasons.

In contrast to the experience of most recent nominees, the Clinton campaign, under Bruce Reed's direction, controlled the platform. It was dubbed "A New Covenant with the American People" and issued a clarion call for a "revolution in government" and offered a "third way" between do-nothing government and big government. Invoking New Democrat themes, the platform said, "To make this revolution, we seek a New Covenant to repair the damaged bond between the American people and their government that will expand opportunity, insist on greater individual responsibility in return, restore community, and ensure national security in a profoundly new era."

Clinton named me as his personal representative to the platform drafting committee, so when the drafting committee met in Santa Fe, I was the campaign's spokesman. In a press conference following approval of the platform, I outlined five ways that this New Democrat platform was fundamentally different from Democratic Party platforms of the previous quarter century.

First, its centerpiece was economic growth, not redistribution. It declared that the party's first imperative was to revive the American dream of expanding opportunity by fostering broad-based economic growth, led by a robust private sector generating high-skill, high-wage jobs.

Second, the policies it proposed were grounded in mainstream American values—personal responsibility, individual liberty, faith, tolerance, family, and hard work.

Third, it emphasized a new spirit of reciprocity to replace the old politics of "every man for himself" on the one hand and "something for nothing" on the other. It called both for activist government and for those who benefit from government to give something back to their country and community.

Fourth, it rejected calls for a new isolationism from both political extremes and committed Democrats to an internationalist foreign policy that would defend American interests and promote democratic values in the world. And, it declared this in unequivocal language: "The United States must be prepared to use military force decisively when necessary to defend our vital interests."

Finally, it called for a revolution in government to take power away from entrenched bureaucracies and narrow interests in Washington and put it back in the hands of ordinary people by making government more decentralized, flexible, and accountable, and by offering more choices in public services.

In addition to his speech to AFSCME, Clinton went before the United Auto Workers in Detroit and supported NAFTA. Then, in a speech to the Rainbow Coalition, he famously condemned rap singer Sister Souljah—who had appeared at the group's meeting the night before—for hateful remarks she had made after the Los Angeles riots, remarks suggesting black gangs should kill whites. After those speeches, it was clear that Clinton was not just another Democratic nominee pandering to the party's interest groups. I wasn't with Clinton at the Rainbow Coalition so I don't know whether he told Jackson in private meetings before and after the speech that Jackson would not be on the ticket. But when Jackson reacted angrily to Clinton's remarks about Sister Souljah, it was clear that he would not be Clinton's choice.

The selection of Al Gore, a young senator from a neighboring state who shared Clinton's New Democrat philosophy, to be his running mate broke the tradition of a president balancing the ticket with his vice presidential choice. When he called me to tell me he had chosen Gore, he said the message would be "the changing of the guard." The two young families campaigning together did, as Clinton had suggested, send a clear message that this was a different kind of Democratic ticket and a new day was dawning. I loved the idea of two DLC members on the ticket.

As they had with the platform, the Clinton campaign controlled the convention. The keynote speakers included Barbara Jordan, who had so eloquently made the case for personal responsibility before the DLC in Williamsburg, and Governor Zell Miller of Georgia, who headed the DLC chapter in his state.

Clinton accepted the Democratic nomination in the name of the forgotten middle class. In his acceptance speech, he reclaimed the mantle of change and outlined his New Covenant with the American people:

> My fellow Democrats, it's time for us to realize we've got some changing to do too. There is not a program in government for every problem, and if we want to use government to help people, we have got to make it work again.
>
> Because we are committed in this Convention and in this Platform to making these changes, we are, as Democrats, in the words that Ross Perot himself spoke today, "a revitalized Democratic Party."
>
> I am well aware that all those millions of people who rallied to Ross Perot's cause wanted to be in an army of patriots for change. Tonight I say to them, join us, and together we will revitalize America.
>
> We need a new approach to government, a government that offers more empowerment and less entitlement. More choices for young

people in the schools they attend—in the public schools they attend. And more choices for the elderly and for people with disabilities and the long-term care they receive. A government that is leaner, not meaner; a government that expands opportunity, not bureaucracy; a government that understands that jobs must come from growth in a vibrant and vital system of free enterprise.

I call this approach the New Covenant, a solemn agreement between the people and their government based not simply on what each of us can take but what all of us must give to our nation.

We offer our people a new choice based on old values. We offer opportunity. We demand responsibility. We will build an American community again. The choice we offer is not conservative or liberal. In many ways, it is not even Republican or Democratic. It is different. It is new. And it will work. It will work because it is rooted in the vision and the values of the American people.

Convention week was one of the most exciting and gratifying weeks of my life. With two DLC members on the ticket, the DLC was the toast of the town.

Every major newspaper carried stories about how the DLC had changed the Democratic Party, and the coverage continued throughout the week. "This convention marks the triumph of the [Democratic] leadership council," wrote Robin Toner in the *New York Times*.[7] "After seven years the Democratic Leadership Council . . . is finally getting its way," wrote Richard Benedetto of *USA Today*. "So much so that the Democratic ticket to be anointed Thursday is an all-DLC lineup . . . and the centrist platform Democrats will adopt tonight is a kissing cousin to the statement of principles fashioned last year by the DLC when Clinton was its chairman."[8]

But for me personally, one highlight came the next week, when the *Washington Post* wrote a profile in the Style section headed, "Al From, the Life of the Party: The Head of the Democratic Leadership Council Finding Victory in Moderation."[9]

With Perot having dropped out of the race, Clinton emerged from the Democratic Convention with a 24-point lead in a head-to-head contest with George Bush—a remarkable bounce since he had entered the convention with the race in a dead heat.

In his acceptance speech at the Republican Convention in mid-August, Bush accused Clinton of raising taxes in Arkansas 128 times. Unlike the Dukakis campaign, which sat quietly by as Bush attacked him, the

Clinton campaign responded by trying to correct Bush on the number of times he actually raised taxes and then counterattacked Bush for cutting Medicare. While Clinton continued to lead in the race, polls indicated that Clinton's lead had shrunk by half or more.

My concern was that by the nature of the campaign's response, it might inadvertently play into Bush's strategy of trying to define the race along liberal versus conservative lines as the Republicans had done so successfully in the previous three presidential races.

It was time for my second and last intervention. On Wednesday, September 2, I visited the Clintons at their suite in the Sheraton-Park Hotel in northwest Washington.

My main point was that it was not enough just to answer Bush's attacks. Rather, it was important to answer them in a way that reframed the campaign back on Clinton's terms. I suggested that in failing to respond to Bush, Dukakis had made both tactical and strategic mistakes. His tactical mistake was the failure to answer Bush and to come back with his own counteroffensive. The Clinton campaign had not made that same mistake; it had answered the Bush charges.

But Dukakis's strategic mistake, I suggested, was to allow Bush to frame the race as the same old liberal versus conservative race that Republicans had been waging—and winning—since 1968. Dukakis allowed Bush to define him as the kind of Democrat that the voters have been rejecting for a quarter of a century. His tactical mistakes hurt, I said, but his strategic mistakes cost him the election.

To avoid the strategic mistakes, I suggested that Clinton respond to the Bush charges by saying that he didn't know what Bush was talking about; that he was a different kind of Democrat who supported ending welfare as we know it, favored capital punishment, and asked young people who got student aid to serve their country. In other words, by his answer, he should make the point of his campaign—that he was a different kind of Democrat—and not fall into the trap that Bush was trying to set of having Clinton sound like the liberal in the race.

The next week, on September 9, Clinton presented his welfare plan and the campaign began broadcasting a television ad promoting his plan. Richard Berke of the *New York Times* said, "By calling for an end to welfare dependency in the advertisement, Mr. Clinton seeks to dispel any notion pushed by the Republicans to cast him as a traditional tax-and-spend Democrat."[10]

During the fall campaign, I was on the road constantly. Beginning on September 14, I did a series of eight media tours that took me to

15 states. I met with political reporters and editorial boards, appeared on talk radio shows and local television programs, starting early in the morning and ending late at night. The schedule was intense, but the goal was simple: to validate to the press that Bill Clinton was a New Democrat and was different from recent Democratic candidates.

The morning of Election Day, November 3, 1992, was sunny and warm in Little Rock. Ginger, Sarah, and I, and a number of DLC staffers were at the Little Rock Airport waiting for Bill Clinton to arrive after a marathon final campaign swing across the country.

When Clinton got off the plane, he walked over to Ginger and me, leaned over the rope line, and embraced me in one of his legendary bear hugs. "When we started out running around the country, did you ever dream it would turn out like this?" he asked. "Come see me before you go home."

At about 10 o'clock that night, the DLC staff and friends were gathered in my suite at the Excelsior Hotel in Little Rock when Ohio declared for Clinton, giving him the majority of electoral votes needed to become the 42nd president of the United States. I gave my wife and daughter a big hug. What had begun 18 months before in Cleveland had proven a spectacular success.

As Clinton requested, I stayed in Little Rock to meet with him. As I sat in his office on Thursday morning, we talked about the transition, and I showed him the manuscript of the book of New Democrat ideas called *Mandate for Change* that PPI had compiled for the next president. He pulled out a pen and wrote this cover blurb in his own hand:

The Progressive Policy Institute's *Mandate for Change* charts a bold new course for reviving progressive government in America. It offers creative ideas for tackling America's toughest problems and a new governing philosophy based on opportunity, responsibility and community. This book really looks beyond the old Left-Right debates of the past and tries to move us toward a better future.

—*President-elect Bill Clinton*

FOURTEEN

TRANSITION

It was the afternoon of November 11, 1992, eight days after the election. The phone rang in my DLC office. The caller was the president-elect.

"I'd like you to be my domestic policy advisor in the transition," Bill Clinton said to me. "Bruce [Reed] will be your deputy. You'll work on the DLC ideas and put together the national service plan." The transition is the period between the election and the inauguration during which the president-elect must plan and form his government before he takes office. He appoints his cabinet, White House staff, and other top officials, and begins turning his campaign promises into executive actions and legislative proposals for submission to Congress.

Clinton told me I'd be one of four policy directors during the transition: Sandy Berger would be in charge of national security, Robert Reich would handle economic policy; and Judy Feder would manage healthcare policy.

I was delighted to take the job. Two weeks earlier, I had sent Clinton a "personal and confidential" memorandum telling him I did not want to work in the administration as so many in Washington did, but I did ask him for a top job in the transition: "You undoubtedly are flooded with people—many of whom are much closer to you than I am—who want to lead your transition," I wrote. "What I offer is something different. . . . I am willing to do anything you ask to help your Administration get off to a fast start and stay on course."

I had good reasons for not wanting to be part of the administration. I had worked in the White House before, so I knew it meant strain on my family, endless days, low pay, and the White House operator tracking me down anywhere, anytime. I also knew that the way Clinton worked meant I would have more influence on the overall direction of the administration from the outside than I would have on the inside. Even if he had appointed me to a top job, chances were good that I'd have a limited portfolio. With a direct line to him from the outside, I would be free to advise on anything I wanted.

The transition was different. It was only for 10 weeks, and it offered a chance to help Clinton shape his domestic agenda and move the DLC ideas like national service, welfare reform, community policing, and reinventing government another step toward becoming national policy.

Turning campaign promises into legislative proposals or government policies is a tough and complicated job. Even for a candidate as engaged in the details of policy development as Clinton, the promises are usually reduced to a few lines in a speech and a loosely worded fact sheet written on the run by campaign staffers. The scholars at Progressive Policy Institute (PPI) had written papers on many of the DLC ideas, but the distance between a think tank treatise and a legislative proposal ready to withstand the rigors of the congressional sausage grinder is often vast.

The transition office was located in the federal building in downtown Little Rock. Quarters were cramped and the pace hectic. I shared an office not much bigger than my office at the DLC with Bruce Reed and Liz Bowyer, our assistant, who had worked at the DLC before joining the campaign.

On my second day in the office, as I tried to sift through the mountains of paper that job seekers, lobbyists, and policy experts had delivered to the transition office, the phone rang. A woman on the other end said, "Al?"

"Yes," I said. But when she started talking, I soon realized that I was on the phone with Tipper Gore, calling for her husband, vice president-elect Al Gore.

The intensity of a transition is impossible to imagine. In our case, it had been 16 years since the last Democratic transition so the pent-up demand for government jobs among Democrats was absolutely crushing. When I spoke at my temple in Washington soon after my appointment, the sanctuary was packed, and I went home with over 200 resumes. When I went out to get the newspaper in the morning, I was likely to find half a dozen resumes next to my front door.

Michael Duffy described the transition chaos in his profile of me in *Time*:

Al From doesn't look happy to be back in power. Bill Clinton's chief domestic policy planner for the transition appears to be under siege: the austere Little Rock office that From shares with two assistants is strewn with unsolicited faxes, dotted with little yellow Post-it notes and littered with long-forgotten telephone messages, stamped UR-GENT. From endures surprise visits from special-interest pleaders, insinuating party officials, and reconnoitering reporters. After politely thanking another briefcase-toting visitor for the 75-page list of 'action items,' From sighs. 'This,' he says wearily, 'is my life.'"[1]

The fact is I was happy. I had the chance to help put the New Democrat agenda into action—and there was nothing I wanted more than to help my friend Bill Clinton have a successful presidency. Knowing that I was going back to the DLC and not seeking an administration job was a terrific advantage, because I never had to worry whether something I did or said would hurt my chances for a job I was seeking.

On Sunday, November 15, while I was back in Washington, Clinton brought the congressional leadership—Senate Majority Leader George Mitchell of Maine, House Speaker Tom Foley of Washington, and House Majority Leader Dick Gephardt—to the Governor's Mansion in Little Rock for a get-acquainted dinner. The president-elect knew he would need to win congressional support for his proposals on the economy, health care, and other legislative priorities. I'm sure Clinton also wanted to avoid the fate of Jimmy Carter, the last southern governor to win the White House as an outsider, whose administration floundered, in part, because of rocky relations with the congressional leadership.

By the time that dinner was over, Clinton had agreed to back off two proposals for congressional reforms he had made in his campaign—a 25 percent cut in congressional staffs and the line item veto. I found that disturbing—not because those proposals were particularly significant, but because they had been symbolic of Clinton's intention to depart from business as usual and be different from the Democrats who ran Washington. That symbolism was key to his political success. But truth be told, with all the excitement of his victory and the mayhem of the transition happening at the time, I grossly underestimated the significance that dinner would have on the first two years of the administration.

On Monday, November 16, when I returned to Little Rock, Bruce Reed and I went to the Governor's Mansion to meet with the Clintons, Bruce Lindsey, Robert Reich and his deputy, Gene Sperling, and a small group of transition officials. Clinton told us that by mid-December he wanted us to give him a domestic policy strategy, complete with concrete proposals he could advance at the beginning of the administration.

As we broke up, I said to Clinton that he needed to make sure that appointments in the most critical jobs in his administration would be loyal to his program. I said that I knew he was committed to appointing the most diverse administration ever and that indeed should be his goal. But, I said, it was important for him to identify the jobs that were most essential to carrying out his priorities—and for those jobs the main criterion ought to be loyalty to his agenda and not the appointees' own.

When we adjourned into a larger meeting that included the vice president-elect, Clinton asked me to repeat what I had said in the smaller meeting. But my role in the transition was shaping policy, not appointments, so I had very little influence on them. Before the transition ended, I'm sure the president-elect wished he had followed my advice more closely. By that point, he was clearly frustrated by the dominant role in the appointment process played by those he called "the bean counters," who pushed him to make appointments on the basis of diversity or interests first.

Bruce Reed and I assembled a small staff, including several young aides who had worked for him in the campaign, to work on the details of our proposals. We also brought in some senior people: Bill Galston to work on national service and Paul Offner, Senator Moynihan's legislative director, to work on welfare reform.

Much of my time during the transition was spent dealing with members of Congress and the press. With Reich and Feder, I appeared on *Face the Nation* to explain the new administration's domestic policies, and I did a number of visits to Capitol Hill. I also spent considerable time meeting with visitors, including officials from foreign governments interested in learning about the new administration. Among the international leaders was a young member of the British Shadow Cabinet, Tony Blair, who came to see me with another young member of the opposition, Gordon Brown, and Jonathon Powell, later Blair's chief of staff. We met for about three hours in which Blair probed me about the New Democrat themes we had developed and the role they played as we reshaped our party and broke our losing streak in national elections. Nearly six years later, we would have another chance to discuss the New Democrat movement, this time at Chequers for the first meeting on our political approach that became known as the Third Way.

On Friday, December 4, I traveled to Boston for a session at the Kennedy School on national service and visited City Year, Boston's National Service program. Founded in 1988 by Harvard Law School roommates Alan Khazei and Mike Brown, City Year was similar to the DLC plan—students would do a year of service, receive a small weekly stipend while they were serving, and earn a payment at the end their service that they could apply to college tuition or postsecondary training. Clinton had visited City Year during the campaign, and PPI had written about it several times.

My plan was to go to City Year in the morning, visit with Khazei, Brown, and other key officials, then spend a significant amount of time talking to City Year volunteers. But when I arrived at the City Year office, I was met by Boston Mayor Ray Flynn and a gaggle of press he had brought with him. Flynn wanted a job in the administration—and he was not going pass up meeting with a top transition official coming to his city.

It all turned out for the best, for the mayor and for City Year. The mayor was appointed ambassador to the Vatican, though I'm sure I had nothing to do with that. When I told the press that City Year was the prototype for Clinton's national service program (which became AmeriCorps), it got widespread coverage in Boston and nationally. The *Boston Globe* ran a photo of me talking to City Year kids along with a story that quoted what I had told them: "I want to learn from you. You're changing America. We want to know what you've done here to use it as a model across America, setting the stage for the most exciting endeavor of this administration." Ten days later, *USA Today* ran a cover story on City Year that cited my visit and gave City Year, which now has programs in 24 cities including in London and Johannesburg, a big boost.

In thanks, Khazei and Brown sent me a red City Year jacket with "Al From, Democratic Leadership Council" embroidered on the front, which I still wear proudly almost every winter day.

On Monday, December 7, PPI released the book *Mandate for Change*. Transition books from think tanks seldom garner much attention. But *Mandate for Change* was a smash hit. For several weeks, it was on the nonfiction best-seller list in the *Washington Post*. It was translated into several languages, with 40,000 copies printed in Japan and 5,000 in China. Because of the close relationship between DLC-PPI and the president-elect, my position as transition domestic policy advisor, and

Clinton's cover blurb, every major newspaper did a story on the book's release.

Mandate detailed proposals that Clinton had endorsed, including adding 100,000 police officers; time-limited welfare; expanding the earned income tax credit; national service; an assault weapons ban and a waiting period for buying a hand gun; youth apprenticeship; tax credits to help businesses grow; expanding trade; and using market measures to improve the environment.

On Tuesday night, December 8, I took a break from the transition to attend a black-tie DLC gala dinner, "Celebrate the New Democrats," honoring Clinton and Gore and held at Washington's Union Station. When I joined the transition, I took a leave from the DLC, but we had planned the dinner back in June when Clinton was running third. "If Clinton wins, we'll hold the dinner at Union Station," I had joked to John Breaux, "If he loses, we'll have it in my living room."

The dinner was the hottest ticket in town. More than 2,000 people showed up, including many chapter leaders and supporters from around the country whom Clinton and I had met on our travels. The invitations for the dinner were delivered in Washington on Friday, November 6. That morning a picture of Clinton with me next to him walking down the steps in the Arkansas Capitol after our postelection meeting appeared in papers across the country, including the *Washington Post* and the *New York Times*. As we were about to descend the steps, I had said to the president-elect: "If you talk to me as we're going down the steps, it'll be worth a million dollars to the DLC." I was wrong; it was worth $3.2 million. That might not seem like much today, but in 1992 it was one of the biggest takes ever for a Democratic event.

Some important business did take place at the dinner. We had a large head table for the Clintons, Gores, transition and DLC leaders, and major supporters like Michael Steinhardt. Mike Espy, DLC vice chairman at the time, was sitting across from Clinton. On a piece of paper, Espy wrote down ten reasons Clinton should appoint him secretary of agriculture and handed him the note. Later that month, Clinton appointed him to the job.

On Friday, December 19, Bruce Reed and I sent Clinton a two-inch-thick loose-leaf notebook full of domestic policy options, an analysis of the budget impact of our recommendations, and a list of executive orders that he could issue early in his administration. We began the book with a six-page memorandum to Clinton that we called "Pursuing the

Clinton Revolution" in which we suggested that he make five ideas the cornerstones of his administration: national service; reinventing government (including campaign finance and lobbying reform); welfare reform; youth apprenticeship; and community policing.

> Put into action, these initiatives can fundamentally change our country as well as our government. They can define a Clinton Revolution that will give millions of Americans a crack at the American dream, restore personal responsibility, and begin to repair our nation's tattered social fabric. Moreover, though their impact will be great, they can be phased into place at an affordable cost. By putting these ideas at the top of your agenda, you can assure that they—not the priorities of Congress, the press, or the interest groups—will dominate the national debate next year.

In the next section entitled "The Promise of Your Presidency," we explained why we believed his undertaking this strategy was so important.

> During the campaign you took positions on hundreds of specific issues. But the essence of your campaign—the reason you were elected—boiled down to two large promises that spelled fundamental change. The first was to get the economy moving again; the second was to be a different kind of Democrat who rejected business as usual in Washington.
>
> As president, your top priority must be to keep those two large promises. If you do, your presidency will be successful. If you don't, your presidency will be in trouble, even if you honor every specific promise you made.
>
> The purpose of this strategy is to keep that second big promise: to show by your policies and actions that you are a different kind of Democrat who is not beholden to the status quo. Assuming economic conditions improve during the next four years, keeping that second promise is the most important thing you can do to build a durable governing and political coalition. You must not only maintain the support of the 43 percent of the electorate who supported you, but you must win the loyalty of the supporters of Ross Perot—the 19 percent of the electorate most change-oriented and most hostile to the status quo.
>
> Fighting for a domestic reform agenda (reinventing government and welfare reform) and for new ways of doing business (national service, apprenticeship, and community policing) will be critical to cementing the support of Perot voters.

After outlining a proposed timetable for developing and promoting the signature ideas as well as other legislative proposals and executive orders that were included in the loose-leaf notebook, we concluded our memorandum by explaining the strategic considerations that went into our recommendations.

> First, as president, you'll be judged on your performance and what you stand for. Nothing else is as important. Daily press spin, which was so important during the campaign, matters much less when you're president. Substance matters a great deal; style and process matters much less. If you perform well as president, you'll do just fine with the press and especially with the voters; if you don't, no amount of spin will convince the public to support you.
>
> Second, what you stand for matters because it can be an insurance policy when things go wrong. If voters believe you stand for values they care about, they'll give you the benefit of the doubt in bad times. That's why you need to push definitional issues like national service and welfare reform, so from the outset voters will know you stand for mainstream values like work, opportunity, responsibility, and community.
>
> Third, every president says something during his campaign that comes back to haunt him when he seeks reelection. For Carter it was the misery index; for Bush it was "Read my lips." Your promise to take on permanent welfare could be your albatross if you don't make it happen. Permanent welfare will be very difficult to change—substantively and politically. Already some interest groups are lining up against making welfare recipients work. But welfare is a symbol of three decades of failure on the left and the right, and in your campaign two-year welfare is the cornerstone of your argument that you are a different kind of Democrat. You need to make a major effort to implement it, lest you undermine a key promise of your campaign.
>
> In the coming weeks, many will advise you to cut your losses, make easy choices, and settle for the possible and the popular rather than what you really want. Remember what you told us during the campaign: No President has ever changed our history for the better without challenging the American people to live up to higher standards and a higher ideal.
>
> As you once said, we are not out just to change the Democratic Party or even to change the government. The Clinton Revolution must change America.

With our plan delivered to Clinton, my most important responsibility for the transition was completed. My last month on the job, I urged Clinton and Mack McLarty, his first chief of staff, to put together a small policy team in the White House that would report directly to them and be responsible for driving the new president's signature ideas inside the government. I thought that was important because many of his cabinet appointments were unfamiliar with his New Democrat agenda and might be vulnerable to pressure from interest groups who wanted to blunt it.

I strongly recommended Bruce Reed to lead that group, hoping Clinton would name him domestic policy advisor. I was only partly successful. Clinton gave the job to Carol Rasco, who worked with him in Arkansas. But he named Reed and Bill Galston, whom I had also recommended, as her deputies. Over time, Reed assumed more and more influence driving through New Democrat initiatives, and Clinton made him domestic policy advisor in his second term.

I also made some initial forays to Capitol Hill to push our signature ideas—and I quickly got a sense that, as Bruce and I had predicted in our notebook's introduction, important House committee chairs had their own ideas about what the president's priorities should be.

When I visited with the Judiciary Committee's Jack Brooks to push the proposal for 100,000 cops, I learned that the veteran congressman from Beaumont, Texas, who had been in the motorcade when President Kennedy was shot and aboard Air Force One when Vice President Johnson was sworn in as president, was not particularly interested in authorizing more funding for additional police officers.

And, when I met with Bill Ford, the chairman of the Education and Labor Committee with jurisdiction over national service, the crusty old liberal from Ypsilanti told me to the tell the president-elect it would be no problem. "We'll just pass the college aid bill we passed last congress and change the name to national service," Ford said. "That's not exactly what the president-elect has in mind," I responded.

My meetings with Brooks and Ford foreshadowed a reality the new president would soon face. For his first two years, he would be defined by the congressional Democrats he came to Washington to change. Mandy Grunwald, one of Clinton's media consultants in the campaign, told Ron Brownstein and Dan Balz in their book, *Storming the Gates,* that Clinton's November 16 dinner with the leadership turned out to be the administration's "original sin." It was an important lesson: The members of his own party in the Congress can present a president with his biggest political problems.

But this was not the picture that I had in mind as the inauguration approached and my time in the transition came to an end. I would head back to the DLC confident our eight years of struggle had paid big dividends. We hadn't won the battle yet. But the New Democrat ideas that we had fought for against long odds and tough resistance were now the cornerstone ideas of the new president's agenda. With Clinton's leadership, we had moved the ball deep into scoring territory. Now it was up to the new team he had assembled in his administration to help him carry the ball across the goal line.

FIFTEEN

THE CLINTON YEARS

1993–1994

At noon on Wednesday, January 20, 1993, on the West Front of the Capitol, my friend William Jefferson Clinton took the oath of office to become the 42nd president of the United States. Ginger and I were sitting on the podium a few rows behind him. I had high hopes that the new president would bring fundamental change to our country and to the Democratic Party.

I had no formal role in the new administration. My responsibilities as domestic policy advisor for the transition had ended and the new White House staff was now in place. From now on I would be an outside advisor. As in the campaign, I intended to play the role of Keeper of the Faith. I would do everything possible to keep the administration on a New Democrat path. That meant using the DLC to support the administration's New Democrat initiatives and nudge it back to them when necessary, and it meant going straight to the president when I thought things were veering off course.

When I decided not go into the administration, I had resolved to give the new White House staff at least three months to get their feet on the ground. It was a tough promise to keep. But even as the administration hit early bumps in the road, I vowed not to intervene.

The high point of Clinton's early days in office was on February 17, 1993, when he delivered his first State of the Union Address. The speech embodied the New Democrat themes and sent the message that his administration was about to change business as usual in Washington and that he was, indeed, a different kind of Democrat.

"Our nation needs a new direction," Clinton told the assembled members of Congress. "I believe we will find our new direction in the basic values that brought us here: opportunity, individual responsibility, community, work, family, and faith. We need to break the old habits of both political parties in Washington. We must say there can be no more something for nothing, and we are all in this together."

That speech clearly connected with the voters and Clinton's approval rating jumped 11 points to 64 percent in the CBS-*New York Times* poll.

Then things quickly went downhill.

Clinton's promise to lift the 50-year old ban of gay personnel serving in the military was an early lightning rod. Because it was the first controversial issue facing the new administration, it took on more of a definitional character than it might have if Clinton had raised it a year or two later, after he had cemented his reputation as a different kind of Democrat. "The big problem—the image that lingers—is his association with the very sort of peripheral 'values' issue that torpedoed Democrats for a quarter century before 1992, and that Clinton skillfully managed to avoid during the campaign," wrote *Newsweek* columnist Joe Klein. In the campaign, Clinton, with his positions on welfare and crime and his emphasis on personal responsibility, seemed to understand better than Bush the moral and ethical concerns of working Americans. "He never hedged his support for gay rights," Klein wrote, "but that was acceptable—indeed, honorable—in the larger context [of the campaign]: this guy seemed to share America's moral priorities, a 'different' kind of Democrat."[1]

Then some early appointments ran into trouble. Clinton had vowed, rightly, to make his administration the most diverse in history, and right out of the gate he was under intense pressure to appoint interest and constituency group favorites to key positions. The troublesome appointments included his first two nominees for attorney general who were caught in the scandal dubbed Nannygate because they employed undocumented immigrants as household help or failed to pay social security taxes for them. But no nomination more exemplified Clinton's problem than his appointment of Lani Guinier, a professor at the University of Pennsylvania Law School, to be assistant attorney general for civil rights. Guinier's nomination ran into big trouble because some of her legal writings raised questions about the legitimacy of majority rule and asserted that racism excluded minorities from ever becoming part of the governing coalitions. This raised the ire of Republicans and even some moderate Democrats because it seemed to run counter to the New Democrat principle of equal opportunity, not equal outcomes. After a bitter fight, Clinton eventually withdrew Guinier's nomination.

The president's first budget also drew challenges from both sides of the aisle. There was much good in it, including the expansion of the earned income tax credit, a DLC idea that moved millions of people out of poverty and was the largest, most significant antipoverty program in history. There were also significant budget cuts. But he dropped the middle class tax cut; proposed tax increases, including an energy tax to encourage conservation and clean fuels; and included fewer cuts than many of his moderate Democratic allies would have liked.

In retrospect, that budget plan, which passed in August with Al Gore providing the deciding vote, would put the country on the path to a balanced budget and become the foundation for the economic successes of the Clinton years. But that outcome was not apparent during its rocky run through the Congress. Congress rejected a stimulus package in the plan and replaced the broad-based energy tax with a small tax on gasoline. Spending tax dollars with discipline, like reforming welfare, was in the minds of voters a defining difference between New and old Democrats. So when he was criticized by a number of moderate Democrats in Congress, including a number of DLC members, for too many tax increases and too few cuts, it left the impression in the eyes of many voters that this was just another tax-and-spend Democratic administration.

The high-profile fights over gays in the military, early appointments, and the budget led to a difficult beginning for the administration. A lot of voters saw Clinton as coming down on the wrong side of two critical fault lines that divided old and New Democrats: tax and spend versus cuts, and cultural liberalism versus mainstream values. My fear was that until the American people saw him crossing those fault lines—as they did during the campaign—Clinton's approval ratings would fall and not rebound.

Still, I maintained my self-imposed silence. I did not want to interfere with an administration just learning the ropes, and I had confidence that Clinton would soon get his sea legs and right the ship.

But on April 16, 1993, after a trip to Buckhannon, West Virginia, the home of West Virginia Wesleyan College, I finally decided it was time for me to intervene. I had traveled to Buckhannon because my older daughter, Ginny, was then a senior at Wesleyan, and I had promised the president of the college, Tom Courtice, that I would give a talk to the political science classes before Ginny graduated the next month.

Buckhannon is a small, sleepy college town, nestled in coal mining country of Upshur County. When the college arranged a press conference before my talk, I really wasn't expecting tough questions. Boy, was I surprised. When the press conference began, the single reporter/

cameraman started to hammer me over and over again with questions about "this new tax that Clinton was proposing."

The "new tax" that he was asking about was actually not a Clinton proposal but a comment made by Donna Shalala, the secretary of Health and Human Services. Shalala told the USA Today editorial board during tax week that a value-added tax (VAT) was under consideration as a way to fund health-care reform. This created a major stir in D.C. because only two months earlier the president had said that he would not consider a VAT. I had no idea that the issue had traveled all the way to small-town America. And yet, there I found myself, in the middle of West Virginia, thirty miles from the nearest small airport, a world away from Washington, D.C., defending the administration from itself.

The next morning, I awoke at 4:30 a.m., not my best hour, to catch one of the few flights out of the tiny Clarksburg airport at 6:10 a.m. I made it onto a little 19-seater prop plane and as the plane took off, I thought about the trouble that the president was in and how the administration seemed to be sliding off track. At that point, his approval ratings had only just begun to slip a little, but my experience in Buckhannon convinced me that they would soon begin a more precipitous slide. In fact, his approval rating in the Gallup Poll dropped 10 points at the end of April.

Suddenly, the plane hit an air pocket and we dropped several hundred feet. The drop was so steep and so sharp that my reading glasses shot out of my shirt pocket and slammed into the ceiling of the plane. A woman in the front row began screaming, "We're all gonna die! We're all gonna die!" over and over, the rest of the way to Washington. It didn't feel like a good omen to me.

By the time I reached my office at 8:00 a.m., I had decided that holding my silence any longer was not helping the administration or the country. So I sat down at my computer and began hammering out a memorandum to the president. I titled it simply "The Next Hundred Days."

There is a pervasive and growing perception that something about the Administration is not quite right. The grumbling is increasing. Among many moderate and conservative Democrats there is a growing feeling that you're just not dancing with the ones who brought you to the dance. . . .

I think that people—including a lot of your political allies—are having a hard time figuring out who you are and what you really stand for. Only once in your first three months—in your State of the Union address—did you really articulate clearly your New Democrat ideology. As the impact of that speech wore off and the messages from the White House became decidedly more mixed, voters (who after all are just getting to know you) have legitimately begun to wonder what you're really all about.

Think of it from the perspective of a typical member of the "forgotten middle class" you courted so assiduously during the campaign. What messages is he hearing? He's seen you drop that middle class tax cut and fight for a stimulus package that—when you get past all the political rhetoric about the good or bad it will do—is not likely to benefit him at all. His kids aren't likely to go to Head Start; he's not likely to see CDBG money; his kids are most likely vaccinated; and he's skeptical about the value of temporary public employment programs. . . . after telling him that you wouldn't raise his taxes, you've slapped him with an energy tax and, in the last few days, he's hearing you're thinking of another new (and hidden) tax—all the while members of your own party are telling you that you didn't cut spending enough. Finally, he's concerned about the values message you've delivered so far, and the public institution he most respects (the military) is suspicious of you. All the while he'd still like you to succeed, but he has to question how you're different than the Democrats he's been voting against for a quarter century.

Your strongest and most natural coalition should be built from the center out and include some Republicans, not from the left in. The bottom line is this: if the change you seek is indistinguishable from what the congressional Democratic leadership wants, it won't look like real change to the American people.

In the rest of the memo, I offered a number of suggestions, including that Clinton use public venues such as his commencement speeches that spring to reinforce New Democrat themes: "While much of your effort will be on selling your health-care plan, devote half of your time to driving your 'different kind of Democrat' agenda into the American peoples' psyche. . . . You need to be viewed as pushing hard for two-year welfare, national service, tough anticrime measures . . . reinventing government, youth apprenticeship, school reform and charter schools, etc., so that people will really understand who you are and what you believe in."

I sent the memo to Nancy Hernreich, the head of the Oval Office who had been Clinton's scheduler in Arkansas. Nancy passed it on to the president. Clinton called me that day and suggested that we have a meeting the next week to talk about the issues I raised.

The following Friday afternoon, April 23, I was summoned to the White House for a meeting in the Roosevelt Room, just across the hall from the Oval Office. The key players in the administration sat around a long conference table: Hillary Clinton, Vice President Al Gore, chief of staff Mack McLarty and his deputy Mark Gearan, Clinton's chief confidante Bruce Lindsey who was personnel director, political director Rahm Emanuel, communications director George Stephanopoulos, press secretary Dee Dee Myers, National Economic Council director Robert Rubin, domestic policy advisor Carol Rasco, and her deputies, Bruce Reed and Bill Galston. Pollster Stan Greenberg and political consultant James Carville sat in chairs along the wall. I was at the end of the table nearest the Oval Office

Clinton sat in the middle of the table, holding a piece of paper. On it was a list of the New Democrat ideas that he and I had put together during his years at the DLC. Clinton wanted to find out where we were on each.

He started going through items—enterprise zones, community development banks, welfare reform. Then he came to community policing and the crime bill.

The crime bill was a collection of proposals aimed at making Americans more secure, including reforms to everything from prisons to police recruitment. But its cornerstone idea called for 100,000 new cops to implement community policing in cities and communities across the nation.

Glancing down at his list, Clinton turned to Stephanopoulos and asked, "George, where are we on the crime bill?"

He responded, "Mr. President, I've talked to Chairman Brooks and he said if you call him next week, he'll move the crime bill." Brooks might move *a* crime bill, but I was skeptical that he would advance *our* crime bill. I knew from my meeting with him during the transition that, for whatever reason, he was not likely to support the 100,000 new police officers.

"George, how many cops will be in this bill that the chairman is going to report out?" I asked Stephanopoulos.

He answered that the chairman was planning to hold the 100,000 cops until later, but he would report out many of the other provisions of the bill.

"Mr. President, don't take that deal," I responded immediately, "because all you care about in this crime bill is the 100,000 cops. From a political perspective, you want somebody to look out his window in 1995 and see a police officer on the street and say 'I feel safer because my president put him there.'"

I don't know whether Clinton called Jack Brooks the next week or not, but the 100,000 cops did remain as a centerpiece of the president's crime bill. That strategy—and the crime bill when it passed after a difficult legislative road over a year later—changed the entire system of policing in America and resulted in a decade-long reduction in crime.

The Roosevelt Room meeting didn't define Clinton as a New Democrat again, but it did help focus the attention of key people in the White House on New Democrat ideas.

A week later, the president called me. It was a few days before a DLC retreat in New Orleans, and he told me that he wanted to announce his national service plan, which would become AmeriCorps, at the event. National service was a quintessential New Democrat idea. It too had become a cornerstone of the Clinton agenda, and it was just the kind of initiative that I thought would show the American people that he meant what he had said on the campaign trail. The announcement at the conference in New Orleans was also a chance for Clinton to start the process of reconnecting with his DLC friends on an issue that they championed.

Throughout May, there were overt calls in the press for Clinton to get his administration back on track, to tighten up its focus and stick to the message that got him elected, by bringing in a New Democrat to be deputy chief of staff. Among the names being tossed around in the press were Roy Neel, vice president Gore's long-time chief of staff, John Podesta, then White House staff secretary, and, surprisingly enough, me, though the president knew I still had no intention of entering the administration. By mid-May, press reports surfaced that president had decided to bring on Neel.

Neel wasn't the only staffing change. On Saturday, May 29, 1993, Clinton announced that he was shaking up his White House staff, including bringing on David Gergen, a moderate Republican who had served presidents of both parties, as a senior counselor to help keep the administration on a centrist path. The president also replaced Stephanopoulos, who had developed a testy relationship with the press at the daily White House briefings, with Dee Dee Myers.

The night before the announcements, Neel called me at home to tell me what the president was planning and to get my views on the impending changes. I told Neel that I agreed with the president's moves, and after a short conversation, we agreed to continue our discussion in person. The next week, we scheduled a meeting at the White House for the afternoon of Wednesday, June 9.

On the morning of June 9, we had a meeting of the Progressive Policy Institute Board of Trustees and nearly every trustee showed up, for possibly the first and last time. The group was chaired by Michael Steinhardt and included Jon Corzine, then a top executive at Goldman Sachs. When I told them that I had to go to the White House for a meeting that afternoon, Steinhardt pushed me out the door, telling me, "you have to be on time for the White House."

When I arrived at the White House, I met with Neel in his first floor office, just a few doors down from the Oval Office. After about an hour, Neel mentioned that the president wanted to speak with me as well but was running late—par for the course for Clinton, who operated on what we called "Clinton time." In the West Wing with some time to kill, I wandered into Bruce Lindsey's office.

Lindsey was dutifully entertaining me when Neel popped in and said the president was ready and he'd walk me over to the East Wing. Suit jacket flung over my shoulder, I marched with Neel past the press room and the Rose Garden to the East Wing elevator.

When the elevator door opened on the second floor, I peered into the State Dining Room and my jaw dropped. The first person I saw was not the president, but my 83-year-old father, who lived across the country in Arizona. Then I saw my wife, Ginger, standing next to President Clinton and Hillary Clinton. It had all been an elaborate ruse, perpetrated by my wife, my staff, and the President of the United States. What I had walked into was not a meeting but my own 50th birthday party, a surprise party hosted by the president and first lady in the State Dining Room.

As I looked around the room at my parents, Ginger's mother, my two daughters, and the dozens of friends and colleagues whom the first couple had invited to the White House, I was absolutely speechless. Bill Clinton doubled over in laughter—he said he had "never seen me speechless before."

The fact is that my silence was a stunned one. My birthday is actually May 31, and Clinton had already sent me a gift. It was a gift that I had always wanted and still hangs in my office: a large framed picture of Clinton taking the oath, with Ginger and me seated with other dignitaries on the podium behind him. His inscription read: "To Al From—with high hopes of 50 more years of fighting for good causes and good people—you have helped make America a better place. Happy Birthday—Bill Clinton."

Throughout the summer, Clinton's approval ratings hovered in the low- to mid-40 percent range, and I continuously reminded him and top White House staff of my concern that voters weren't seeing the president's promised New Democrat credentials. Work was being done on all of his New Democrat policies inside the administration, but fights over the budget and gays in the military put him on the wrong side of the "tax and spend" and mainstream values fault lines.

In June the DLC commissioned from Stan Greenberg a poll of Perot voters to see how the president could get back on track with those critical swing voters. In our introduction to that study, "The Road to Realignment: Democrats and the Perot Voters," Will Marshall and I wrote: "President Clinton faces an urgent political imperative: crafting a substantive and political strategy for expanding his base beyond the 43 percent plurality that elected him. Such a strategy is a prerequisite for governing effectively in the short term and seizing a rare opportunity to realign U.S. politics around a new Democratic governing majority. To expand his base, the President must go hunting where the ducks are. That means targeting the nearly 20 million voters who backed Ross Perot in last year's election."

The DLC's study provided a road map to realignment. In 1992 the Perot voters had lost faith with the Republicans, but six months into Clinton's first term, they hadn't found a home in the Democratic Party. In fact, the study revealed that Perot voters had grown increasingly skeptical since the election about the president's ability to fundamentally change the nation's course.

Greenberg's data showed that the starting point for expanding his base was to reestablish his credentials with voters as "a different kind of Democrat" but that in the first half-year of his presidency, the reverse had happened. Fewer voters saw the president as a new-style Democrat in late June than in February, and as a result his support among the electorate as a whole had plummeted.

In February 1993 when the president's approval rating stood at 60 percent, 61 percent of the electorate told the ABC News/*Washington Post* poll that Clinton was a "new-style Democrat who will be careful with the public's money," while only 35 percent said he was "an old-style, tax and spend Democrat."

By late June our poll showed Clinton's approval rating had dropped to 43 with 50 percent disapproval, and just half the voters saw the president as a new-style Democrat while 45 percent thought he was an old-style Democrat. More significantly, voters who viewed Clinton as a New Democrat approved of his performance in office by more than three-to-one and those who viewed him as an old Democrat disapproved of his performance by more than five-to-one. Moreover, the drop in the percentage of voters viewing Clinton as a new-style Democrat was dramatic among voters that the president would most need most if he were to expand his base: people earning $30,000 to $50,000, independents and whites.

Not surprisingly, Greenberg's research also provided strong evidence that Clinton could make substantial inroads into the Perot bloc if he governed as a "different kind of Democrat." The study revealed a five-part strategy that Clinton could pursue to hold on to his voters and win over Perot supporters.

First, he needed to grow the economy and create jobs. Reviving the economy was the top concern of both Perot and Clinton voters. But Perot voters had little faith in the conventional economic prescriptions of either party. They were pragmatists who would judge this president—as they had his predecessor—on the basis of the economy's performance.

Second, he needed to take aggressive steps to reform and reinvent government. Perot voters had little faith in government's ability to do anything right. So before Clinton could expect to win their support for major new public initiatives, he had to convince them he was "fixing" a government that they believed was broken. Clinton needed to pioneer a new form of non-bureaucratic activism that was more effective, efficient, and responsive. He also had to make good on his promises to curb the power of special interests and to "end welfare as we know it."

Third, he had to demonstrate that he would spend the taxpayers' money with discipline. A *Los Angeles Times* survey showed that 51 percent of Perot voters believed government wasted half of every dollar it spent. Therefore, it was essential to achieve deficit reduction primarily through spending cuts rather than tax increases. For Perot voters, the federal deficit was a powerful symbol of national decline and political irresponsibility. To be perceived as a strong leader, Clinton had to face down the special interests that defended wasteful spending programs and clamored for expansive government. In short, tackling the deficit was less an economic imperative for Perot voters than a test of character and political accountability.

Fourth, he needed take a more assertive approach toward Congress. The DLC study showed that, even when they agreed with Clinton's positions, Perot voters doubted his ability to overcome the forces of inertia in Washington. From their point of view, the worst thing that could happen to Clinton was that he permit himself to be captured by the Washington establishment. To underscore his "outsider" credentials, the president needed to push Congress harder to enact a program of radical change. This would require more than simply siding with Democrats in the old partisan debate in which Perot voters rejected both sides. Clinton could break gridlock and win their support only by forging new and sometimes bipartisan coalitions around an agenda that moved beyond the polarized left-right debate.

Fifth, he needed to invoke the middle-class values of work, family, and individual responsibility that the president had articulated so clearly during the campaign. Many Perot voters believed that these mainstream values were no longer honored or rewarded in America. If their sense of economic insecurity inclined them toward the Democrats, their sense of middle-class grievance impelled them toward the Republicans. The GOP advantage on values constituted a serious obstacle to a Clinton strategy for building a new presidential majority. "To neutralize that advantage," we said, "President Clinton needs to identify once again with the interests and values of middle America." To do that, we recommended that the president "press vigorously ahead with initiatives . . . that dramatize his commitment to a new ethic of responsibility. And, while tolerant of all points of view, the President must resist demands from activists and pressure groups that he embrace values or cultural policies that are at odds with the moral convictions of most Americans."

This road map was similar to the New Democrat agenda the president had campaigned on and to the Clinton revolution, which Bruce Reed and I had recommended during the transition. For Clinton and the Democrats, the Greenberg study showed that the key to realignment was converting unaligned voters. This could only be accomplished on the basis of new governing approaches that actually solved problems and gave people their money's worth from government.

On August 28, 1993, David Gergen called me with a problem. The president was planning to unveil his health-care plan in September, and at a strategy session in the White House, it was decided that the president would devote almost all his attention to selling that plan all fall and spend only a week pushing for passage of legislation implementing NAFTA. "If we only push NAFTA for a week, we'll lose it," Gergen said. "You need to talk to the president and convince him to give it higher priority." I told Gergen that I'd send a memo to the president the following Monday.

Trade, like fiscal discipline and welfare, separated New Democrats from old. Democrats had historically been the free trade or low tariff party. The Smoot-Hawley tariff that deepened the Great Depression was sponsored by Republicans; Franklin Roosevelt had reinstituted a policy of expanding trade, and every Democratic president since had supported new trade rounds. In the years following World War II, when the American economy was the only economy left standing, organized labor supported free trade. But when the German and Japanese economies rebounded and proved to be tough economic competitors, labor turned protectionist, and more and more Democrats followed suit. The DLC was the outlier, supporting expanded rather than restricted trade in our New Orleans Declaration and fast-track consideration for NAFTA in our New American Choice resolutions.

Expanded trade was one of three essential parts of the Clinton-New Democrat economic growth strategy. The first was fiscal discipline to assure a firm foundation for private investment and growth. The second was investment in people and technology to stimulate innovation and assure that every American had the tools to get ahead. The third was expanded trade and opening markets abroad so that more American goods and services were sold in the international economy. Competition from imports—as long as it was fair—also helped keep prices and inflation down, which benefited low-income people, those on fixed incomes, and American manufacturers concerned with the cost of supplies.

Clinton's support for NAFTA was not popular with Democrats, but he believed deeply that expanded trade was critical to growing the economy. At a meeting at the Washington Court Hotel back in September 1991, just a week before he announced he would run for president, a number of his supporters urged him to back off on NAFTA and trade. Clinton listened and listened for a day and a half. Then, just before the meeting ended, he said: "If you want me to become an isolationist or a protectionist, get another candidate because I won't do it."

The real battle over NAFTA was in the House. There was little doubt that the Senate would ratify the treaty. But even if ratified, the treaty could not go forward without the passage of implementing legislation. That gave the House a chance to scuttle the treaty, and a majority of House Democrats, led by Majority Leader Dick Gephardt (Missouri) and Majority Whip Dave Bonior (Michigan), were intent on doing just that.

I knew the memo I promised Gergen was important when early Monday morning Mack McLarty called and asked where it was. I delivered the memo called "A 'Make or Break' Fall" later that day. It was one of the toughest I ever sent the president. The bottom line was that he was in danger of losing some New Democrat support and that getting NAFTA ratified and implemented would be the best thing he could do to strengthen his presidency in the fall.

> Most voters care at least as much about strong presidential leadership as about ideology. Unfortunately, after seven months, the percentage of Americans who see you as a strong and decisive leader has dropped precipitously (from 59 in April to 41 percent in the most recent *Washington Post*-ABC News Poll). You clearly need to reverse that trend.
>
> As the tough questions come to the forefront this fall, they'll be watching to see whether you set the national agenda or whether you accommodate the agenda of the congressional leadership and the powerful interest groups. In a sense, this fall will be about who's running this town. The American people thought they elected you to do that, but so far you haven't convinced them that you're in charge.

I told him that time was running out, that Labor Day would likely mark the end of his grace period. After that it would become harder for many New Democrats in the Congress, in the press, and in the DLC to continue to give him the benefit of the doubt. What troubled me most is that most of the objective indicators—unemployment, inflation, interest rates, etc.—had improved since the first of the year, but his approval ratings had gone down and remained low.

I thought he entered the fall in a very precarious political position. Winning the budget fight allowed him to stay afloat, but he came out of the budget fight perceived much more as a taxer and spender than he was going in. With diversity, gays in the military, HIV-positive immigrants, federal funding for abortion, ties with Hollywood and the eastern liberal establishment, I believed he'd put himself too far left on the cultural divide. And, I was clearly not alone. In an August *Washington Post*-ABC News poll, 41 percent said his views were too liberal for them. At the end of the convention in July 1992, that number had only been 19 percent. For Dukakis in 1988, it was 32.

> The issues on the table this fall—reinventing government, NAFTA, health care, and, perhaps, another round of spending cuts and

welfare reform—offer you an incredible opportunity to redefine and strengthen your presidency. But that opportunity is not without risks, and those issues, particularly health care, contain land mines that you need to avoid because they could severely—even mortally—wound your presidency.

The best scenario for you this fall is to offer a bold reinventing government package; to go all out and score a big victory on NAFTA; to offer a health-care plan that begins a debate that can lead to a bipartisan health-care package; to pass another round of spending cuts that convinces people you're spending their tax dollars with discipline; and, to propose the initial steps of a time-limited welfare plan that puts you on the way toward honoring your campaign promise to end welfare as we know it. And if along the way, you can pass national service and a crime bill with 100,000 cops and you can beat back the effort by House liberals to gut your education reforms, all the better.

The worst scenario for you is for your reinventing government package to be underwhelming; for NAFTA to go down with you perceived as only fighting for it halfheartedly; for your health-care package to conjure up images of costly, overregulated, entitlement-oriented liberalism and immediately set off a bitter partisan fight like on the budget; for you to appear to be paying off individual members for their budget votes with additional spending instead of pushing for more cuts; and, for welfare reform to be delayed or weakened by the opponents of two years and off . . .

Of all the opportunities you have this fall, NAFTA presents the greatest. Passing NAFTA can make your presidency. NAFTA presents both an economic and political opportunity. Getting the economy off the ground is still the most critical challenge you face, and NAFTA is the most important policy—and maybe the only one—you can pursue this fall to do that. A victory of NAFTA will both create real jobs and demonstrate that you have the vision to lead our country into the world economy at a defining historic moment. It would make it clear that you speak for the national interest, while NAFTA's adversaries, including Perot, are playing special interest politics as usual.

Politically, a victory on NAFTA would assert your leadership over your own party by making it clear that you, not the Democratic leadership in Congress or the interest groups, set the Democratic Party's agenda on matters of real national importance. And, it would establish the kind of bipartisan coalition on a major issue that you'll need down the road on health care and welfare reform.

I can't tell you how much better it would make your life and how much it would strengthen your presidency for you to beat Bonior and organized labor on NAFTA. That would reestablish presidential leadership in the Democratic Party, something that hasn't happened since 1966.

Then I proceeded to tell him that I believed health care contained the most land mines of any of the issues that could come up in the fall, and that it would be difficult to build a majority on health care, as he had on the budget, with Democratic votes only because many Democrats had already taken positions much different than the plan he was likely to propose, including members of the DLC.

The stakes in the health-care battle are enormous. As I see it, there are two dangerous outcomes, either of which would severely damage (and, perhaps, mortally wound) your presidency. The first is for you to come out with and become indelibly identified with the old liberal stereotypes of big entitlement and regulation driven government. That would put you on the wrong side of the tax and spend fault line forever. The second is for you to come out with a plan that is roundly defeated in Congress. It seems to me that the best—and perhaps only—insurance policy against both would be to have a substantial number of Republicans signed on to your plan when it is introduced. For that reason, I urge you to sign up some Republicans for your plan before you draw any lines too firmly in the sand.

After outlining the specific steps he could take in the fall to push NAFTA and a New Democrat agenda—and explaining the advantages and risks of my strategy—I ended the memo with a candid assessment of where he stood with his colleagues at the DLC.

The bottom line is this. A number of us involved in the DLC have devoted a good portion of our lives to promoting the kind of change in our party and in the country that allowed you to be elected president. You were a partner in the effort. We believe we played a pretty significant role in your election. And we want more than anything else for your presidency to succeed. But we believe it will not succeed if the same forces in Congress and the interest groups that have run the Democratic Party into the ground for the past 25 years continue to dominate the party. We're prepared to fight preferably with you—but without you, if necessary—to make sure that doesn't happen. Preserving the integrity of the movement in which you played so vital a part demands no less.

About two hours after my memo was delivered to the White House, the president called me—and he was not happy. He did not agree with my assessment, and he let me know that in emphatic terms. I listened as he went on for more than half an hour by my watch. Then, having gotten his anger off his chest, he said, "What do we have to do?"

I told him that I thought NAFTA was an important defining issue for him and that it would not be ratified without a vigorous White House campaign for it. He asked me to come down and meet with Bob Rubin, head of the National Economic Council, to talk about putting together such a strategy.

The president did launch a major campaign to ratify NAFTA. Rahm Emanuel was put in charge in the White House, and he brought in Bill Daley to lead the campaign. The focus was on implementing legislation in the House. That meant working with the Republicans since a majority of Democrats were opposed to NAFTA.

The DLC did its part. Our policy institute's trade expert, Paula Stern, who would later chair the International Trade Commission, wrote a strong case for NAFTA that we circulated on Capitol Hill. We hired organizers to work with our chapters to lobby members in their home districts. For the first and only time in my life, I registered as a lobbyist so I could lobby members on the Hill. I spoke in favor of NAFTA to the World Affairs Council in Los Angeles, and I traveled to several states to do public and media events supporting passage, including New Mexico, Arizona, California, Washington, and Ohio. When it appeared we might have trouble with Republicans, I connected the White House with Billy Pitts, who had worked the House floor for Minority Leader Bob Michel when I was head of the Democratic Caucus. Pitts played an important role in locking down needed Republican votes.

The night of November 18, 1993, after a 13-hour debate in which an astonishing 245 members spoke, the House passed NAFTA by a vote of 234 to 200. As expected, with Gephardt and Bonior leading the opposition, the Democrats voted 156 to 102 against the treaty. Republicans supported it 132 to 43. Bernie Sanders, the liberal independent from Vermont who organized with the Democrats, voted against it. "Tonight's vote is a defining moment," Clinton said at the White House. "At a time when many of our people are hurting . . . we chose to compete and not retreat." A few days later, the Senate approved NAFTA, 61–38, and Clinton signed the implementing legislation on December 8.

Also in November, at the Memphis church where Dr. Martin Luther King Jr. delivered his last sermon, the president delivered an important speech on race and responsibility, invoking King's name and legacy to condemn family disintegration and violence in black neighborhoods.

His NAFTA victory demonstrated that Clinton was the political leader of the government. His Memphis speech showed that he was the moral leader of the nation. In both cases, the president stood above partisan politics and transcended the old left-right debate. As a result, he bounced back in the polls.

As 1994 began, I was feeling much better about the direction of the administration. Clinton's initial speech on health-care reform was well received. By late January, right after his State of the Union Address in which he promised to push a welfare reform bill, his approval ratings in the Gallup poll reached nearly 60 percent. While he didn't move welfare reform—the most definitional of New Democrat ideas—in his first year, his budget plan included both the expanded earned income tax credit and empowerment zones. He had appointed Vice President Al Gore to lead the reinventing government effort, and Gore's first report in September 1993 called for the elimination of 252,000 federal bureaucrats. Congress peeled off the Brady bill from the crime bill and on November 30 Clinton signed it into law. And, most important of all, Congress passed the national service bill and Clinton signed it on September 21, creating AmeriCorps.

"The president entered 1994 with a lot going for him," I wrote in my February column for the *New Democrat*. "The economy continues to look strong. More importantly, on crime and welfare Clinton has thrown his Republican opposition off balance by occupying political ground they've held for most of the last 25 years. In addition, he's forced Republican strategists to try to make the case that our health-care system isn't broken, a tough sell to the public. If Clinton stays the New Democrat course, Republicans will have little choice but to join him as they did on NAFTA."[2]

While I was delighted to see him back on the New Democrat path, I had seen how easily those New Democrat initiatives (sans welfare reform) could be overshadowed by other issues as had happened on fiscal discipline and gays in the military. And I was concerned that could happen again as health care and the crime bill made their way through Congress.

I was particularly worried that the president's greatest challenge would be avoiding land mines planted by factions in his own party, particularly in the House, where elements within the Democratic coalition in Congress were maneuvering to derail a tough crime bill and honest welfare reform, and to make compromise on health care more difficult.

My concerns were legitimate. Youth apprenticeship and legislation authorizing charter schools passed in 1994, but their political impact was completely overshadowed by what happened on health care, crime, and welfare reform. Both the Republicans and the liberal Democrats helped drive his approval numbers back down by the middle of the year, and they would not recover until after the midterm election.

The health-care proposal, drafted by Hillary Clinton and her health-care advisor, Ira Magaziner, was attacked by the health-care industry and Republicans as big government that would come between you and your doctor. Many Democrats, including a number of DLC-ers, opposed it as well, preferring a less intrusive bill proposed by Representative Jim Cooper of Tennessee and Senator John Breaux.

Even before the draft was finished, I had met with Hillary Clinton and Magaziner in the summer of 1993 in her West Wing office and urged them to pursue a center-out rather than left-in political strategy. I thought if they started in the political center with allies like Cooper and Breaux and perhaps a centrist Republican or two, they might be able to build a coalition in the middle that could actually pass a bill. The alternative strategy was to start on the left with supporters of a single-payer system and then try to add more votes by moving toward the center. There was no doubt that the biggest single block of supporters in the House was the single-payer block. The problem, as I saw it, was that there were not nearly enough of them to pass a bill, and the single-payer block would never expand.

The warning signs of trouble for the health-care plan were apparent by mid-November when Mack McLarty called me. Clinton was scheduled to speak at the DLC annual conference in Washington in early December and Mack didn't want Clinton and the DLC to be on opposite sides on health care. He asked me to meet with Magaziner and report back to him about whether I thought there was any possibility of working a rapprochement. If not, he said, he'd ask Roger Altman, the deputy treasury secretary and a DLC supporter, to negotiate on behalf of the administration with Cooper and Breaux.

I reported back to McLarty that Magaziner, who was from Rhode Island, believed that John Chafee, his state's Republican senator, would eventually support the administration proposal and bring other Republicans with him. I thought that was highly unrealistic, that with each passing day the prospect of any Republican support was slimmer and slimmer. So Altman came up to the DLC and met with Cooper and Breaux. They agreed to a set of broad principles and to what the president and Breaux would say in their DLC speeches to avoid the appearance of conflict. The key was that Cooper and Breaux accepted universal coverage, the president's nonnegotiable demand, and the president agreed to flexibility in how to get there. The DLC conference went off smoothly, and I was hopeful that we might actually be able to reach a compromise, but it just wasn't in the cards.

Finally, with no Republican support and no chance of passage, Mitchell pulled the bill in the Senate and announced it would not be considered until the next Congress.

A tough crime bill with 100,000 cops seemed on its way to quick passage. Different versions passed the House and the Senate in late 1993, but then the two houses did not move to reconcile the differences. As time passed, a combination of liberal amendments that made the bill look soft on crime and opposition to an assault weapons ban gave the Republicans the opportunity to torpedo the bill. To save it, Clinton was forced to negotiate a compromise with the Republicans. Although the bill's most important provision—the 100,000 new cops—had a profoundly positive impact on the nation's crime rates over the next decade, in political terms for Clinton and the Democrats in 1994, the damage was already done.

The welfare bill, which the leadership and most House liberals opposed, never saw the light of day.

As 1994 wore on, Clinton was less and less perceived as the different kind of Democrat he had promised to be.

On several occasions throughout the year, I met with Clinton and sent him memos urging him to get back on the New Democrat path. In one I argued that Clinton's approval rating should have been about 15 or 20 points higher based on objective conditions in the country and his actual performance. But he was so tied in the public mind to the congressional Democrats that short of a big public blowup—which was not in his nature—there was nothing that could change that perception.

One of my memos to Clinton was the subject of a column in late August in the *Wall Street Journal*. "Like a struggling hitter working out of a slump, President Clinton gets plenty of unsolicited advice these days," Jerry Seib wrote. "But none is more important than a six page memo he got a couple weeks ago from Al From." After citing my appeal to the president to push New Democrat approaches, to stand up more to the old-line Democrats in Congress who don't share his agenda, and to redefine the fight on his terms, Seib continued: "In fact, the Clinton Administration has done some of that. The problem is that its own Democratic allies in Congress resist. A prime example is Vice President Al Gore's reinventing government initiative. It calls for reducing the civilian federal work force by 252,000 over five years. But in Congress, lawmakers are quietly undermining that effort by slipping into bills language that shields various agencies from the president's knife. . . . In other cases, Congress has drained money away from New Democrat initiatives to fund Old Democrat programs."[3]

To me, the saddest part about what happened to Bill Clinton was that he really was a New Democrat—he really believed in New Democrat principles and ideas. Often during his presidency, he would call me and say, "One of these days our critics are going to understand I really believe in these ideas." But in his first two years, he was plagued by the inability to separate from the old-style Democrats who ran the Congress. This problem was foreshadowed in the dinner at the Governor's Mansion in Little Rock with congressional leaders the first weekend of the transition. It was exacerbated because many of the White House staff interfacing with the Hill in the first two years had come from Congress and tended to want to work on the inside through regular channels. It was like taking the bat out of his hand. Clinton had won the nomination and the White House by challenging those old ways.

In November 1994, the voters took out their frustrations with business as usual in Washington on the Democrats. Republicans won 54 seats in the House and nine in the Senate, grabbing control of both Houses. Now Clinton had to deal with the Republican leadership: Newt Gingrich and Bob Dole. And he needed to get himself up off the floor and get ready for his own reelection in 1996. He knew he had to reestablish himself as a New Democrat before he faced the voters. The turnaround was about to come.

SIXTEEN

THE REBOUND

1995–1996

"Tonight we must forge a new social compact to meet the challenges of this time," President Bill Clinton told the American people and the assembled members of Congress in his 1995 State of the Union Address.

> As we enter a new era we need a new set of understandings, not just with our government, but even more important, with one another as Americans. . . .
>
> I call it a New Covenant. But it is grounded in a very, very old idea, that all Americans have not just a right but a solemn responsibility to rise as far as their God-given talents and determination can take them, and to give something back to their communities and their country in return. Opportunity and responsibility: they go hand-in-hand. . . . And our national community can't hold together without both.
>
> Our New Covenant is a new set of understandings for how we can equip our people to meet the challenges of a new economy, how we can change the way our government works to fit a different time, and, above all, how we can repair the damaged bonds in our society and come together behind one common purpose. We must have dramatic change in our economy, our government, and ourselves.

With those words, Clinton returned to the New Covenant, the New Democrat theme that he had ridden into the White House. Clinton, who earned the title "the Comeback Kid" in the New Hampshire primary three years earlier, was beginning another political comeback.

The day before the speech, Clinton sent me a draft for review, and I responded with a short memo saying I thought the speech themes should all come under the rubric of the New Covenant. After reading my memo, he called me the morning of the speech and said: "Rewrite it and send it to me."

I called Bruce Reed and together we worked on framing sections that could make the themes of the speech clear. About 4:30 p.m. on the day of the speech, I sent our suggestions to the president. Clinton's chief speechwriter Don Baer, a New Democrat through and through, skillfully wove them into the fabric of the speech he had written, as it was being put on the teleprompter.

The actual words may have been inserted at the last minute, but the return to the New Covenant theme and the New Democrat message had been carefully thought out over a 10-week period between the election and the speech. I had a hand in that process but so did many others inside and outside the administration. In the end, Clinton went where he wanted to go—back to the New Democrat philosophy and agenda.

For Clinton and the Democrats there was no way to sugarcoat the results of the 1994 election. He called it a good country licking—and it was. The Republicans won control of both Houses of Congress, the House for the first time in four decades. Their gains were enormous: 54 House seats, 9 senators, and 10 governors. Moreover, they defeated some of the biggest name Democrats like Governors Mario Cuomo of New York and Ann Richards of Texas. In the Senate, Harris Wofford of Pennsylvania and Jim Sasser of Tennessee both lost, majority leader George Mitchell retired and the Republicans won his seat. In the House, the Republicans ousted Judiciary Committee chairman Jack Brooks, a 42-year incumbent, Ways and Means Committee chairman Dan Rostenkowski, a 36-year member, and Speaker Tom Foley, marking the first time a speaker had lost reelection since 1862.

I was the Democratic commentator that night for the hour special on Public Broadcasting television, and I remember searching to find a single one of my friends who had won. Thank goodness for Colorado Governor Roy Romer, a DLC vice chairman, whose reelection gave me something positive to talk about.

There were undoubtedly many reasons for a landslide that great. In the South, the inevitable happened. Democratic incumbents, who had survived in House districts that had been voting Republican for more than three decades in presidential elections, survived no more. But the biggest reason for the overwhelming defeat was that voters were disgusted with business as usual in Washington, and they took it out on the Democrats in charge.

Even before the returns were in on Election Day, I had sent a blunt memorandum to the president suggesting a postelection strategy.

"The course I suggest will require real strong presidential leadership," I wrote. "That's something that most voters haven't consistently seen from you, but when they have—as in the NAFTA fight, they've responded very favorably. Strength is the most important quality voters want to see in a president.

"I've long said that the most important thing you could do was to reassert strong presidential leadership in the Democratic Party. That is still the case. But now time is short. Think of yourself as a cat in its ninth life. You have one more opportunity to seize control of our party and of the national agenda. Please take it. Your presidency and the future of progressive politics in America are at stake."

Ironically, I wrote, the election could save his presidency and that he needed to see it as an opportunity to get his presidency off to a much-needed fresh start. After two years in office and despite a record for which he deserved more credit, too many voters still didn't know who he was and what he stood for. For too many voters, his presidency was defined by gays in the military, big government health care, and his personal character as defined by both his private behavior and public indecision.

"That may not be fair," I wrote, "but it's a reality, and it's critical that you change it. I believe you can."

I argued that while the Republican gains were likely to be large, they did not have to be lasting. The American people, I suggested, were of two minds about government.

Like in the 1960s, Americans see lots of problems in their communities and they want to solve them. But, like in the 1980s, they have very little faith in the government's ability to do anything right. When those two strands come into conflict—as they did in the health-care debate—the antigovernment side always wins. That's what happened in this election—and the Republicans took the antigovernment side. Their essential message was "we won't make it worse and the Democrats will because they're for high taxes and big government." That's a potent argument, but it doesn't solve the problems voters want solved. So in the long term, it will leave voters even more frustrated than they are now.

The only way to relieve the voters' frustration is to solve the problems they want solved. And that requires not antigovernment rhetoric, but a new synthesis that marries public activism with nonbureaucratic means and progressive ideas with mainstream values. The candidate or party that develops and promotes that new synthesis will be positioned to win in 1996. *Therein lies your opportunity.* That new synthesis is embodied in the New Democrat agenda you ran on in 1992, and nobody knows it better than you do.

I told him that despite the conventional wisdom, he was well positioned to seize the political initiative and govern as a New Democrat. Even though voters were fed up with partisan polarization, the new Congress was likely to be far more polarized than the last, with the Democratic caucuses being more liberal and the Republican caucuses more conservative.

The increased polarization in Congress is an opportunity for you to seize the vital center of the political spectrum. The Republicans have left it wide open for you. Plant yourself firmly there. Don't let the Democrats pull you to the left, and if the Republicans move right to deny you legislative victories, welcome that—presidential elections are won in the center not on the left or the right. Remember that positioning matters more than legislative victories. Besides if you're in the vital center where the voters are, sooner or later members of Congress from both sides of the aisle will join you there.

Finally, I argued that the New Democrat agenda is right both politically and substantively. If this election told us anything, it was that the old liberalism had run its course. No one ran as an unabashed old-fashioned liberal—and with very few exceptions candidates who tried to put together the old New Deal coalition failed. But the answer to the death of liberalism was not simply to turn right: Candidates who tried to become instant conservatives also didn't do well in the election.

The bottom line is that old liberal and conservative approaches don't fare well politically because most voters see them as increasingly irrelevant to the problems they face in their everyday lives. That's why voters are seeking a new synthesis. And, as long as that new synthesis is progressive—like the New Democrat agenda—it holds out the most promise for turning your 43 percent plurality in 1992 into a majority in 1996. The New Democrat message allows you to appeal to both the base and the middle class at the same time—in Bill Galston's words, it unites those in the middle class struggling to stay there with those aspiring to get there.

I concluded the memo by recommending that his agenda for the next two years fit into a framework of three big themes that respond directly and clearly to the real problems and frustrations the voters were feeling in their everyday lives: restoring the American dream, repairing the social fabric, and getting government under control. And I recommended specific policy proposals to reinforce those themes.

At the DLC, I commissioned Stan Greenberg to do a postelection study that included a national poll and a series of focus groups both to understand why the election turned out the way it did, and to figure out the Democratic route to recovery. Independent voters, who we oversampled, were very clear: They were voting against the president's big government health-care plan and his pursuit of a liberal agenda on gays in the military. To recoup, the Greenberg study recommended a New Democrat course.

It is doubtful that any of the findings of the DLC poll surprised Clinton, but he was not happy about it. Clinton's anger flashed during a private Oval Office meeting with a half dozen DLC leaders on Tuesday, December 6. We were in the middle of our annual conference and he was scheduled to speak that night at our tenth anniversary gala. Dave McCurdy, who replaced Breaux as the DLC chairman, had lost a bid for a Senate seat in Oklahoma. He blamed Clinton for his loss and, a month after the election, he was still bitter. Clinton let McCurdy know that he did not appreciate that. As we were walking out of the Oval Office, I said to Clinton: "Remember, we're your friends."

"Then act like it," he shot back.

That night, both the president and first lady came to the DLC gala. Clinton was charming, and while his 35-minute speech was slightly defensive, he reconnected with his DLC and New Democrat roots while softly chastising us for not fully appreciating all the progress he had made on DLC ideas. He also did something that he would continue to do in the face of political adversity—he went back to the New Orleans Declaration. "Some time in the next two or three days if you want to know how to state our principles with clarity," he told the DLC crowd, "go back and read the New Orleans Declaration. That's just as good as it gets."

Then he read the principles—every one of them—saying that if we believed in them, we had a great future. To an audience that was skeptical about his commitment to that New Democratic agenda, he said: "Now this is what I want to say to you: You have to decide what your mission is in this new world, because the truth is we are already making a difference in the new Democratic Party. In the last two years, despite the atmosphere of contentiousness and all the difficulties, more of the DLC agenda was enacted into law and will make a difference in the lives of the American people than almost any political movement in any similar time period in the history of the United States. And, you ought to be proud of that."

He was right, of course. DLC ideas—national service, community policing, and the expanded earned income tax credit—had become law. He had pushed reinventing government against opposition inside his administration and Congress, and he had rolled over the congressional Democrats on NAFTA. But in the public eye all of those achievements had been overwhelmed by gays in the military, big government health care, and his seeming willingness to yield to congressional Democrats on spending cuts, some parts of the crime bill, and, most important, on welfare reform. As a result, voters—and many in the DLC—tended to give him too little credit. I understood the president's frustration: Never had so much seemed like so little. The reality was that would not change until he grabbed control of the budget debate and passed welfare reform. He listed all of the DLC ideas he had passed and then looked to the future: "The answer is not to reverse what we have done, but to build on it. The answer is to reach out to the middle class and say, 'We know why you're angry. We know why you're frustrated. We got the message of the elections. We're not going back on our principles but we're coming right at you because we are hired to help you build a better future for yourselves. That is our only purpose.' If we do these things, their predictions of our demise will be entirely premature."

He concluded his speech by challenging his DLC audience to help him.

What's your responsibility? It's to join me in the arena—not in the peanut gallery, in the arena, and fight, and roll up your sleeves, and be willing to make a mistake now and then, and be willing to put your shoulder to the wheel, be willing to engage, be willing to struggle, be willing to debate and enjoy this.

He observed that Americans were "going through a great period of change," and that the resulting conflict of ideas could be good for the party and the people:

> The responsibility we have is not to win elections. It is to fight for the people about whom elections are fought. If we fight for them and their children, then the elections will take care of themselves. And if they don't, we'll still be doing what is right. That's my commitment, and it ought to be yours.

Throughout December, I continued to consult with the president, nudging him to return to the New Democrat message and to reconnect with the forgotten middle class. On December 15, he delivered a ten-minute address from the Oval Office in which he proposed a "middle class bill of rights" that included easing the tax burden on middle class families raising kids or sending kids to college, to be paid for with cuts in government spending resulting from his reinventing government initiative.

I sent him a short memo the next day telling him that he "did good last night. . . . Your speech sent the right message—your proposals are solid, New Democrat ideas, grounded in the right values and the right approaches to governing. I particularly liked the tone: tough, aggressive, yet optimistic—a tone that sounded, in a word, presidential. . . . This speech was very important for you to give. . . . It laid a solid foundation for the next two years. It is the beginning of a long march back. It reforged the bond between you and the forgotten middle class."

On January 8, 1995, David Osborne wrote a 7,000-word piece in the *Washington Post Magazine* telling Clinton that he needed to be a New Democrat again to save his presidency. Osborne began his article by quoting one that Clinton and former Colorado Governor Richard Lamm had written 10 years earlier in the *Christian Science Monitor,* in which they had suggested how Democrats could rebound from the Mondale debacle:

> Our problems are rooted in our priorities and lack of discipline. Our No. 1 priority . . . should be to get America's economy growing again. . . . Second, the Democratic Party must learn what New York Mayor Fiorello La Guardia called the most important lesson of politics: how to say no to your friends. . . . Third, the Democratic Party

should take the lead in reforming the very systems it had the foresight to initiate. Clearly many of these systems cannot be sustained as they now exist. . . . The election is over. The people sent us a message. Now they are waiting for us to send one back. . . .[1]

Now Osborne, in the form of a public letter to Clinton, was urging the president to take his own advice, and he did not hold back:

Much of the public has tuned you out. The way to regain people's ear—and gradually their trust—is with action. And that action has to hurt. You have to fire some of your closest friends. You have to eliminate some of your favorite programs. You have to give up on one of your fondest dreams, universal health insurance. If you do not, no one will believe you are serious.

Your new agenda comes right out of the Democratic Leadership Council, a group you chaired until you ran for president. But you chose not to pursue it in 1993, and few believe you will deliver on it now. The critical question is: Can you discipline yourself and your administration over the long haul? Unless you have the courage to go all the way—unless you embrace a new agenda, new advisers, new values and a new communication strategy, and stick to them—you'll never win the disillusioned voters back.[2]

David Osborne got Clinton's attention. Clinton had known Osborne for more than a decade and respected him. Indeed, as governor, Clinton had been featured in Osborne's first book *Laboratories of Democracy*, that focused on innovations in state government.

The next afternoon, I spent more than two hours in the Oval Office with Clinton and Leon Panetta. We talked about Osborne's piece, about Clinton's standing in the polls, about how to respond to the new Republican Congress, and about New Democrat issues. But most of all we talked about how he could make a comeback before the 1996 election. When we were finished, Panetta asked me to summarize what I told them in a memo to the president.

In that memo, I outlined a Clinton survival plan designed to deal with the two big problems of character and ideology.

First, you need defining fights against the Republicans. But those fights must be New Democrat vs. Republicans, not Old Democrat vs. Republicans. We can win fights on New Democrat positions; Republicans win fights against Old Democrats.

Second, you have to transcend the Mondale-ian instincts of your political advisors. The presidency is about macro politics; your advisors focus on micro politics. Successful presidents send big messages like cutting back government; unsuccessful president's worry about small messages to narrow constituencies, like the political impact of specific program cuts on particular constituencies. To send big messages and govern as a New Democrat, you need New Democrats in your inner circle.

Third, your strength is in the Senate, not the House, because the GOP doesn't have 60 votes in the Senate and because the top House spokesmen—Bonior, Frank, Gephardt—are a (political) disaster; they tend to define Democrats in ways that help the Republicans.

My advice was blunt. Among my suggestions were:

- A major speech setting the context for the policies he had announced on December 15. Without that context, those policies appeared to be pandering. The best policies in the world wouldn't sell if they didn't fit into a larger and understandable context.
- Get more edge and cuts into his program—especially spending cuts. The spending cuts offered were mushy. To counter the balanced budget amendment, he needed to challenge the Republicans with a hard-nosed list of specific cuts that would make them resist.
- Emphasize the job training part of the Middle Class Bill of Rights, call it the Middle Class GI Bill so it's easily recognized, and use it, not tax cuts, to try to differentiate himself from the Republicans on economic policy.
- Follow Osborne's advice and put New Democrats in key political, substantive, and communications jobs in the White House. The most important White House change he needed to make was to put in a New Democrat as communications director.

I had proposed a pretty tough recovery regime, but I believed he was in deep, deep trouble, and he could not finesse his way back.

The State of the Union was a true New Democrat speech. Not only did the president return to the New Covenant concept, he also hammered away at New Democrat ideas like fiscal discipline, empowering workers, reinventing government, political reform, a GI bill for the American worker, and a campaign to reduce teenage pregnancy. He included spirited defenses against Republican attacks on national service, the Brady Bill, and the assault weapons ban. On welfare reform, he drew the line as I suggested, repeating lines from the campaign, saying he "wanted to end welfare as we know it" and that "welfare should be a second chance not a way of life."

"I want to work with you, with all of you to liberate people and lift them up from dependence to independence, from welfare to work, from mere childbearing to responsible parenting," he challenged the Republicans. "Our goal should not be to punish them because they happen to be poor."

The speech went 81 minutes and was panned by a number of pundits. But I believed the 1995 State of the Union address importantly restated what Clinton really believed and might be a starting point for his turnaround. A couple of days after the speech, I sent him a short note of encouragement: "Don't let the op-ed writers and the pundits get you down. Your State of the Union address was terrific and, despite its length, ordinary people watched the whole speech and liked it. Most importantly, the speech outlined a framework that, if followed up properly, will allow you to transcend the day-to-day debate. The New Covenant—a new set of understandings between the people and the government—is the kind of big idea that defines presidencies more than programs do."

But the speech was only a start. Shortly after the speech, Bruce Reed and Don Baer sent a memo to Erskine Bowles, another New Democrat who had recently become deputy chief of staff, suggesting ways Clinton could reinforce its message. Clinton then held a number of events, including a summit at Blair House, and directed executive actions that kept welfare reform in the public spotlight. In April, at the end of the first one hundred days of the Republican-controlled Congress, Clinton urged the Republicans to work with him on issues like welfare reform and reducing the size of government, saying, "I do not want a pile of vetoes." But he made clear that if they sent him legislation from their Contract with America with which he disagreed, he would veto it. The New Democrats on his staff, like Reed and Baer, saw the "pile of vetoes" speech as an important juncture in his relationship with the Republicans.

Then, in a televised address on June 13, Clinton, over the objection of many in his administration and congressional Democratic leaders, announced he would balance the budget in 10 years. He would balance it on his terms: protecting education; reducing health-care costs, not services, to lower the cost of Medicare; providing tax cuts for the middle class, but not the wealthy; and cutting welfare but helping people move from welfare to work. Republican congressional leaders had proposed a balanced budget in seven years, but Clinton argued that his plan would be better for economic growth. His support for a balanced budget didn't end his squabble with Congress, but it did help him change the dynamic of the budget debate. Now that Clinton was on record for a balanced budget, he could shift the debate from whether to balance the budget to the priorities for getting there.

Despite these steps forward, for most of 1995 the congressional Republicans dominated the debate and Clinton seemed on the defensive. Once he was even forced to argue to the press that he was still relevant. Other than for a brief period after the Oklahoma city bombing in late April, his approval ratings never got out of the 40s.

DLC supporters, particularly our major donors, were becoming increasingly impatient. Three of them, Michael Steinhardt, Barry Diller, and Mitch Hart, financed a project in our foundation to write a "New Progressive Declaration," based on the New Democrat themes that they thought Clinton was not pushing hard enough. Their thought was that if Clinton didn't get back on the New Democrat path—and soon—the declaration could be the basis of a third party candidacy. In July, Michael Kramer wrote a column in *Time* that quoted Steinhardt and Diller about their discontent with Clinton. I tried to temper the piece, saying we'd work to get Clinton to pursue our formula, but it concluded with a quote from Steinhardt interpreting my statement: "Al feels a loyalty to Clinton because he feels responsible for electing him, but what we're planning is bigger than some psychological thing. We'll just have to see if Clinton buys our new stuff. If not, and somebody else takes it on, then we'll probably fracture."[3]

The president was none too happy about the piece, and he called me at home to let me know that in no uncertain terms.

I wasn't ready to abandon Clinton and jump to a third party, but I was extremely concerned about his seeming inability to convince voters he was a New Democrat. I expressed those concerns in my July/August *New Democrat* column:

As he approaches reelection, the President faces a choice. He can continue to play to the status quo within our party as he has done in the first third of 1995, and hope to squeak back into office with the aid of

Republican mistakes and the right third party candidate. Or, he can try to do what FDR did—articulate a clear, forward-looking, and easily understood road map that will assuage the fears that prevent Americans from embracing the challenges ahead. He doesn't have to run as a third party to do that. But . . . he will have to take on his party's base.

I continued the drumbeat in the September/October issue, though I said the president's decision to support a balanced budget was a good sign:

President Clinton must choose whether to run on idea-based politics of Hart [or] the interest-group politics of Mondale. He chose the former in 1992, offering himself to the people as a "different kind of Democrat." The President's recent decision to support a balanced budget is a tipoff that he understands this. That's why liberals complained so loudly when he announced it. . . .

   Dick Morris, the President's latest political advisor, calls this strategy "triangulation." That means running to a third point—against both Republican and Democratic orthodoxy. . . . Triangulation doesn't mean the President will disregard core Democratic constituencies every time—witness his July speech on affirmative action. But the object of Morris's strategy is to leave no doubt in the voters' minds come November 1996 that President Clinton is no liberal Democrat who reflexively adheres to party pieties. For President Clinton triangulation is a political necessity. Barring unforeseen circumstances, he can't win without the support of voters outside his base.

Then in November 1995, Gingrich overplayed his hand and Clinton quickly and shrewdly seized control of the debate. Clinton and Gingrich had battled over the budget throughout the year. The Republican House had spent months pushing measures in their Contract with America that couldn't pass the Senate and holding hearings to attack Clinton, and it missed the deadline for enacting spending bills and legislation to raise the debt ceiling that were necessary to keep the government running. That was not unusual; Congress often failed to pass all spending bills before October 1, the beginning of the fiscal year. To keep the government going, the Republicans passed a continuing resolution that funded the government through November 13.

As this deadline approached, the Republican Congress sent Clinton a bill that would raise the debt ceiling and fund the government, but only if the president agreed to increase Medicare premiums, raise taxes on the working poor, slash funding for education and the environment, and repeal environmental and public health regulations. If the president didn't go along with their radical budget, they threatened to shut the government down.

Standing by his June promise to use the veto pen when necessary, Clinton vetoed the bill. True to their word, the Republicans forced a government shutdown, once in November, and then again from December 16 until January 6.

On November 13, the day that he vetoed the debt ceiling bill, Clinton spoke at the DLC's annual conference:

> The Republican Congress has said to me with brutal simplicity, "you will sign our cuts in Medicare, education, the environment, or we will shut the government down. You will agree to support our budget and all of its major elements. You will agree to support what we have called regulatory reform, repealing 30 years of bipartisan commitment to a clean environment and a safe food supply or we will push the government into default."
>
> Well, America doesn't respond very well to those kinds of pressure tactics. It's no way to find common ground. So this morning, just before I came here, I vetoed their bill on the debt ceiling. I did not relish doing this. My job as President is to take care of the American people. . . .
>
> I think it is very important that you understand that this great debate in Washington is not, *is not,* about balancing the budget. It is about balancing our values as a people. The American people want and deserve a balanced budget. Five months ago, I proposed a balanced budget that eliminates the deficit, cuts hundreds of wasteful and outdated programs, but preserves Medicare and Medicaid, invests in education, technology, and research, protects the environment, and defends and strengthens working families. And it maintains the ability of the United States to lead the world toward peace and freedom and democracy and prosperity. My budget reflects those values and fulfills our interests. The Republican congressional budget simply does not. . . .
>
> As long as they insist on plunging ahead with a budget that violates our values in a process that is characterized more by pressure than constitutional practice, I will fight it. I am fighting it today. I will fight it tomorrow. I will fight it next week and next month. I will fight it until we get a budget that is fair to all Americans.

Clinton had shifted the debate. It was no longer about the Republicans trying to force Clinton to accept a balanced budget. The showdown had allowed Clinton to convince the American people that he was indeed for a balanced budget, a significant part of convincing them he was the "different kind of Democrat" he had promised to be. The debate was now about values and priorities—and Clinton would win that hands down.

My friend Jack Kemp, who would be the Republican vice presidential nominee a year later, told me once that Gingrich's problem was hubris. Kemp was right. The week before the November showdown, Gingrich had flown on Air Force One to Yitzhak Rabin's funeral. He had apparently wanted Clinton to negotiate with him during the flight. But Clinton, who was extraordinarily close to Rabin, spent most of the flight in the front of the plane grieving with former presidents Carter and Bush. When the plane landed at Andrews Air Force Base, Gingrich was asked to exit through the rear door, which was the normal procedure for passengers on Air Force One. Only the president exits through the front door. But Gingrich threw a tantrum and the *New York Daily News* ran a giant front-page headline over a caricature of the Speaker that read, "CRY BABY." At his best, Gingrich was a brilliant strategist who engineered the Republican victory in 1994, but in the budget showdown, he let hubris cloud his judgment.

In all major polls, voters blamed Gingrich for the shutdown by a margin approaching two to one. Clinton's approval ratings had begun to improve in the Gallup poll in early November, rising above 50 percent for the first time, other than after Oklahoma City, in 18 months.

Clinton's numbers sagged again during the second shutdown. But the 1996 State of the Union gave them a boost. The speech, like the State of the Union a year earlier, was an important touchstone for the president in reestablishing his New Democrat credentials. Dick Morris played a major role in shaping this speech, and I reviewed the final draft with him. As Clinton's last State of the Union Address before his reelection campaign, the speech had to build a good foundation for the campaign.

Declaring that we live in "an age of possibilities," Clinton detailed the progress the country had made during his first three years in the White House: the healthiest economy in three decades; the lowest combined rates of unemployment and inflation in 27 years; nearly 8 million new jobs, over a million of them in basic industries; America selling more cars than Japan for the first time since the 1970s; a record number of new businesses started; strong world leadership bringing hope for new peace; and progress in restoring fundamental values. He continued, "The crime rate, the welfare and food stamp rolls, the poverty rate, and the teen pregnancy rate are all down. And as they go down, prospects for America's future go up."

The speech contained a bushelful of values-laden New Democrat ideas. It reiterated his calls for a balanced budget and action on welfare reform. He talked about national service and his support for charter schools, and called for higher standards, character education, and expanded help for kids to go to college. And, reminding them of his veto, he told the Republicans not to cut the earned income tax credit.

But the most noteworthy part of the speech was his declaration that the "era of big government is over."

> I believe our new, smaller government must work in an old-fashioned American way, together with all of our citizens through state and local governments, in the workplace, in religious, charitable and civic associations. Our goal must be to enable all our people to make the most of their own lives—with stronger families, more educational opportunity, economic security, safer streets, a cleaner environment in a safer world.

By declaring an end to big government on the heels of his agreement to balance the budget, Clinton clearly demonstrated his distance from the big government, tax and spend liberals.

The voters responded positively, his approval rating bouncing up to 52 percent after the State of the Union. And it would stay up, never falling below 50 percent for the rest of his two terms in office.

All but one of the initiatives Bruce Reed and I had proposed as cornerstones of the Clinton revolution were now in place. The one that remained was the most defining of the New Democrat issues and the most important promise of Clinton's 1992 campaign: ending welfare as we know it.

The welfare system had become the symbol of broken government. During the Depression, Franklin Roosevelt created Aid to Dependent Children to alleviate the burden of poverty for families with children and to allow widowed mothers to maintain their households. But by the 1980s, it subsidized a seemingly never-ending cycle of dependency and poverty. Welfare laws in most states discontinued payments if there was a "man in the house," thereby discouraging welfare recipients from marrying the father of their child. All too often, the children of welfare mothers repeated the same pattern of teen pregnancy and welfare, creating a new generation of dependency every 15 years.

Not surprisingly, most Americans resented welfare, viewing it as taking their hard earned money and giving it to people who didn't work and didn't have any prospect of working. Even welfare recipients didn't like the system. Too often they were trapped in poverty with no hope of escaping. The antiwelfare attitude was prevalent across society. Mike Espy had urged me for years to poll welfare in minority communities, arguing that we would be surprised how antiwelfare they were. In our first eight years, the DLC was always strapped for funds, and we never had the money to do the polling, but in 1992 I asked Dan Yankelovich to conduct focus groups on welfare in working-class black and white neighborhoods. Espy was right: The prevalent attitude among working-class blacks in Philadelphia was: If you want to have six kids go to it, but not on my dime. I work too hard.

While many Democratic governors like Clinton supported replacing welfare with a work system, congressional Democrats, tended to defend the existing system. Republicans from Reagan to Gingrich had used it to define Democrats as wasteful, big-government, big spenders.

"Welfare," Clinton had said over and over in the campaign, "was a second chance, not a way of life." He was committed to offering recipients training, health care, and day care, but telling them at the end of two years that if they were able to work, they had to get a job or work in community service. In his first two years, he offered a plan, but the Democratic leadership in Congress wouldn't consider it. The new Republican-controlled Congress twice sent Clinton punitive welfare bills and twice he vetoed them. Then in August 1996, they sent him a third bill that he thought was not perfect but met most of his objections to their earlier ones. The question was whether he would sign it.

Inside the administration, key players in the White House and at the Department of Health and Human Services (HHS), including former Robert Kennedy aide and HHS assistant secretary Peter Edelman, urged Clinton to veto. Bruce Reed and Rahm Emanuel advocated signing. Nancy Hernreich, Clinton's Oval Office chief, said the president wanted my advice. I scheduled a call with the president and quickly faxed Clinton a note urging him to sign the welfare reform bill and committing myself to do all I could to rally support for that decision. I suggested he consider several points:

1. You have presided over a historic ideological transformation of the Democratic Party. Over the weekend, I read the party's platforms from 1980 through 1996. We are truly a *New Democratic* party. You deserve enormous credit for that.

2. The challenge before us is now operational. We must demonstrate the ability to put the big ideas of this new ideology—like ending welfare as we know it—into action. The pressure you are getting to not sign this bill proves the difficulty.

3. For you personally, signing a welfare bill—and Bruce Reed assures me this is one you can comfortably sign—will not only cement your credentials as a New Democrat, but it will also end any talk of your campaigning one way and governing another.

4. Finally, signing the welfare bill will redeem your most important promise of 1992. At the same time it will take Dole's most powerful potential issue away from him. Veto a third welfare bill—and no matter the explanation—Dole has an issue.

In a cab crossing the Triborough Bridge in New York City, I flipped open my cell phone and called the president of the United States. The cab driver, a recent Asian immigrant, couldn't believe it. He particularly couldn't believe it because when we were talking, the call dropped three times, and I had to call back. He turned to Holly Page, who was traveling with me, and said, "Is he really talking to the president?" Holly assured him I was. And when Clinton and I finished our discussion, I was confident that he would sign the bill.

At a Rose Garden ceremony of August 22, Clinton signed the bill ending welfare as we knew it. It was a long slog, taking almost his entire first term. In the end, he signed a bill nearly half the Democrats in both the House and Senate had voted against. Democratic leader Dick Gephardt voted against it, a strong indication that had Democrats still controlled the House, passing welfare reform would have been even harder. As Clinton always said, change is never easy. When he signed the bill, the final cornerstone of our Clinton revolution was in place. There would never again be a doubt that he was a different kind of Democrat.

After he signed welfare reform and was renominated the following week at the Democratic Party's 1996 Convention in Chicago, Clinton's approval rating in the Gallup poll shot up to 60 percent—the highest it had been since he entered the White House.

For the convention issue of the *New Democrat,* I wrote a cover story about the ideological shift in the Democratic Party. I compared the 1996 platform to the 1980 platform, the previous time an incumbent president had run for reelection. The transformation was striking: "In 1996, the party stands for New Democrat values, beliefs, and policies that an overwhelming majority of Americans can support. In 1980, it did not. It's that simple."

In November, running as a New Democrat, Clinton won a smashing reelection victory over Bob Dole and Ross Perot, taking 31 states and the District of Columbia for a total of 379 electoral votes.

He came to celebrate his victory on December 11 at the DLC's annual conference. The night before the conference, Clinton called and asked me to go jogging with him at Fort McNair the next morning. I was supposed to give one of the opening speeches at the conference, but what could be better than telling your supporters and donors that you'd have to delay your speech because you were going running with the president?

Later that morning, Clinton's speech began: "You know, I went jogging with Al From this morning. And the original theme of my speech was the era of big government is over. The new speech will be: the era of Big Al is over. He's lost 75 pounds in 15 months. If that's not enough to make you optimistic about America, I don't know what is." The *Washington Post* picked up Clinton's remark and ran before and after pictures of me in its gossip column, "The Reliable Source." Papers across the country picked up the item, and I probably got more attention for my weight loss than anything I've ever done in politics.

Then Clinton turned serious:

> A year ago when I spoke here, our nation was facing a time of great decision. That day the congressional majority was pressing its budget plan upon the nation, and I told you why I didn't like it, but I hoped we could pass a balanced budget. That night at midnight the government was shut down. It was a moment of fundamental decision about the direction of our nation, the role of our government, the strength of our values. That day I said the great question before us was: can the center hold?
>
> Well, today the clamor of political conflict has subsided. A new landscape is taking place. The answer is clear: the center can hold, the center has held and the American people are demanding that it continue to do so.

As Clinton looked forward to his second term, his New Democrat policies were in place. Overcoming resistance from many in his own party on the balanced budget and NAFTA, he was pursuing a New Democrat economic policy of fiscal discipline, investment in people and technology, and expanded trade aimed at growing the private economy—and the economy was growing and creating jobs.

With the enactment of welfare reform, all five cornerstones of the Clinton revolution were a reality. AmeriCorps was already bigger than the Peace Corps at its height. A vigorous effort to reinvent government was underway, reinforced by his declaration that the era of big government was over. He had passed a tough crime bill, more cities were turning to community policing, and the deployment of the 100,000 new cops was well underway. Youth apprenticeship and charter schools were now the law of the land. Welfare reform had replaced the broken system that encouraged dependency with a new system to promote work.

We knew from the election—he was the first Democrat to be elected twice since Franklin Roosevelt—that New Democrat policies were good politics. The next four years would tell us if they were good for America.

SEVENTEEN

THE CLINTON RECORD

C linton gave America eight years of peace and prosperity.

When he left office in January 2001, America was on a roll. The economy was the best it had been in the lifetimes of most Americans, with the longest period of sustained economic growth in American history. Employment was at an all-time high and unemployment at a three-decade low. Inflation was low and under control. Incomes and wages were going up. Child poverty was down, and the welfare rolls were cut nearly in half. The violent crime rate was the lowest in a quarter century. The federal government was the smallest since the Kennedy administration. And his environmental record was the best since Theodore Roosevelt. Not surprisingly, Clinton left the White House with a 66 percent approval rating in the Gallup poll, the highest rating for a president leaving office since Gallup began rating presidents during the Truman administration.

One by one, with his New Democrat/Third Way approaches, Clinton took the issues that had been central to the Republican's political success away from them. He was threatening to redefine national politics going into the new century. Gingrich and the Republicans in the House could not fathom that, and with all their issue arrows removed from their quivers, they chose the only line of attack available to them—they attacked his admittedly inappropriate personal behavior.

For the most part, Clinton's second term was devoid of the kind of intraparty disputes that hampered the president during his first term. To be sure, the old Democrats in the interest groups and in Congress, led by Dick Gephardt, the first DLC chairman who signed the New Orleans Declaration, didn't just roll over. They challenged the president from time to time, particularly on trade, but the Clinton policies were work-ing so well, growing the economy and creating jobs, that they were un-able to gain any sustained traction.

There was some liberal grumbling in 1997 when Clinton moved ahead on a balanced budget agreement. David Obey, the ranking Demo-crat on the House Appropriations Committee, was particularly critical. As we rode to an event together, Hillary Clinton turned to me and asked, "Don't they understand what we're trying to do?" I answered that that they did and they didn't like it.

But when the vote on the balanced budget bill came in late July, it passed 346 to 85, with 52 Democrats voting against it—almost all liber-als, including Minority Leader Gephardt, Obey, and Charlie Rangel, the ranking Democrat on the Ways and Means Committee.

In late 1997 House Democrats, again led by Gephardt, were able to stop Clinton from renewing fast-track authority, which allowed for expedited approval on trade agreements. The fast-track vote was a strong indication that the growing protectionism in the once pro–free trade Democratic Party had not abated. Indeed, it would continue after Clinton left office. Trade would be one policy area where Democrats would not follow the New Democrat lead. That reality underscored that Clinton was a different kind of Democrat every time a trade mat-ter came up. Still, with the exception of the fast-track loss, on the main trade fights during his administration the pro-trade president was able to prevail.

Nonetheless, I was concerned about the fast-track defeat—and about Gephardt's role in consistently opposing the president on his key New Democrat initiatives. At the time I still thought we had work to do to win the battle for the soul of Democratic Party. Gephardt, who came to Congress as a moderate, had cast his political lot with organized la-bor and the old Democrats. I was also concerned that he might pose a potential challenge to Al Gore for the presidential nomination in 2000.

In early June 1997, even before the budget and fast-track fights, I had joined the battle with Gephardt in a *Wall Street Journal* op-ed headed "New vs. Old Democrats" in the *Wall Street Journal*.

I wrote that Gephardt was fighting Clinton's transformation of the party by "attacking the heart of the president's spectacularly successful economic policy" and trying to undermine Clinton's efforts to transcend interest group politics.

"So Democrats will face a choice," I concluded. "Will we complete the transformation of our party in accordance with the New Democrat course President Clinton has laid out? Or will we reverse course and fall victim again to the old approaches that left us in the political wilderness for much of the past quarter century?"

Right after the fast-track loss in November, I wrote a memorandum to the president putting the fast-track defeat in perspective as "a temporary setback, not a crushing defeat," and at the same time underscoring the importance of continuing the battle for the soul of the party:

> It [the fast track fight] is not insignificant because it shows how little most House Democrats think they need you. They don't appreciate what you've done—that you're the most successful Democratic politician in half a century. They never have liked you because you came to Washington to change them. They don't trust you, in part because your ideas are different than theirs and because they don't believe you really care about them. And, as they see your presidency winding down, they don't fear you because you've never really made them pay for crossing you. Those are realities we need to deal with.
>
> It is a very clear warning that for you to succeed, New Democrats have to win the battle for the soul of the Democratic Party. That battle goes on—our adversaries, led by organized labor and Dick Gephardt— are powerful and will not give up, and to a very great degree your legacy and the political prospects of the vice president hang in the balance.

I suggested that the prevailing situation was untenable, that Clinton couldn't have the organized interest groups that make up the infrastructure of his own party work against him and spend money against issues that he pushed to redefine our party, and that he could not allow his minority leader in the House to continue to act with abandon as the rallying point for his opposition. I told him that would not change until New Democrats were the clear and unequivocal winners in the battle for the soul of the Democratic Party.

The scandal over Clinton's personal behavior and the politically inspired impeachment proceedings would limit Clinton's abilities to push new initiatives and new reforms. With the Republicans nearly unanimous in their effort to oust him from office, Clinton needed the support of all Democrats for his survival, including those like Gephardt who had opposed the president on his most defining New Democrat initiatives. He could no longer afford to push off against Gephardt. Without the support of the leader of his party in the House, his presidency would be in severe jeopardy.

As Clinton prepared for the 1998 State of the Union address, he seemed poised to propose another round of New Democrat initiatives. In the November/December 1997 issue of the *New Democrat,* we had looked ahead to the last three years of his presidency.

> Five years into his presidency, Bill Clinton has already built a legacy of achievement, a record that could earn him a place in the upper tiers of American chief executives. But as his recent setback on fast-track legislation demonstrates, and impressive as his record is, his accomplishments are reversible, and it is early yet to cast his legacy in stone. Looking forward, we believe the route to securing his place in history as a truly transformative figure leads to four major challenges: equipping Americans to succeed in the new economy; building a world-class education system; breaking the cycle of inner-city poverty; and modernizing the entitlements.

Early in January 1998, Clinton invited a small group, including Erskine Bowles, Bruce Reed, his chief speechwriter Michael Waldman, HUD Secretary Andrew Cuomo, and a handful of others to a meeting in the residence on the third floor of the White House to discuss his upcoming State of the Union. We discussed the ideas in the DLC magazine and a proposal Cuomo had made for a new urban antipoverty plan aimed at closing the opportunity gap.

About a week before the speech, the *Washington Post* ran a story accusing Clinton of having an Oval Office dalliance with a White House intern, which led to the House investigation and impeachment.

Clinton of course didn't mention the story and gave a solid State of the Union speech. He talked about a Third Way, articulated his accomplishments, used some of the themes that the DLC and Cuomo had suggested, and fit the speech into a construct of opportunity, responsibility, and community. With everything else going on, it was not the time for new big initiatives; he offered none.

In 1999 Clinton did propose one more important new initiative, a New Markets plan aimed at bringing growth, jobs, and opportunity to areas of the country that had not benefited from the prosperity of the 1990s. He launched the initiative with three trips to underserved areas in Appalachia; Newark, New Jersey; the Mississippi Delta; rural Arkansas; East St. Louis, Illinois; the Pine Ridge Indian Reservation in South Dakota; and suburban Chicago. I accompanied him on the first two New

Markets trips. On December 14, 2000, just a little more than a month before he left office, the New Markets initiative was enacted into law.

Clinton had another significant, though contentious, victory in his last year in office. The fight over normal trade relations for China had come up nearly every year, and Clinton had been able to prevail. But in 2000 he proposed legislation to make normal trade relations with China permanent (PNTR) so that it would no longer require annual renewal. A significant majority of House Democrats opposed it and did their best to beat the president. One night at the White House, Erskine Bowles, Clinton's chief of staff, walked over and asked me to run a meeting with the president and about 40 DLC-type Democrats on PNTR. He said he had met with a group of House Democrats who had verbally beaten him up so badly that he wanted to stay out of the path of incoming fire that night.

Almost all of organized labor opposed PNTR, including the Teamsters union, whose position showed how complicated the trade issue was for labor in an increasingly international economy. The United Parcel Service (UPS) was lobbying hard for PNTR because the agreement would allow them to win new flight routes to China, an enormous market. Mike Eskew, the chairman of UPS, said that the agreement would result in 40,000 new UPS jobs—one for every 17 packages—all of them Teamsters. So, the Teamsters were lobbying the Transportation Department to approve the UPS flight routes to China at the same time they were lobbying against PNTR.

I visited a number of House members on the president's behalf. With most of them, I didn't have to argue the merits of his position. They knew he was right. But they feared repercussions from labor if they voted against them. For an ordinary Democratic congressman, unions might provide a quarter to a third of his campaign funds, and they were afraid that they could not replace the money. One $500 check from a business organization would not replace $250,000 in contributions from labor.

In the end, Clinton prevailed on PNTR. Most House Democrats voted against it, but the president was able to convince 73, about a third of the Democratic Caucus, to support him.

As his two terms drew to a close, it was clear that Bill Clinton had changed America and modernized the Democratic Party. He offered new and innovative ways to further the Democratic Party's cherished values and highest ideals. He reconnected it with its first principles and grandest traditions.

Opportunity for all, special privilege for none has been our party's first principle since the days of Andrew Jackson. Under Clinton's leadership, we became the party of opportunity again by restoring fiscal discipline to government and delivering sustained, noninflationary economic growth.

He reunited our party's policies with the values most Americans share—work, family, responsibility, individual liberty, faith, tolerance, and inclusion—by passing welfare reform and the Medical and Family Leave Act, expanding the earned income tax credit, and reducing crime.

He reconnected our party with John Kennedy's civic ethic of mutual responsibility by creating AmeriCorps and by asking citizens to give something back to their country.

He restored our party's historic global outlook by promoting democratic and humanitarian values throughout the world and by expanding trade to foster prosperity and upward mobility at home.

And, he reconnected our party with Franklin Roosevelt's true legacy of innovation by modernizing government, diminishing bureaucracy, and giving people the tools they need to solve their own problems in their own communities.

Just as Franklin Roosevelt and the New Dealers—with new ideas to fit their times—modernized the Democratic Party for the industrial era, Bill Clinton and the New Democrats modernized their party for today. By embracing this innovation, the New Democrats, like the New Dealers, led an economic resurgence. By tempering the excesses of capitalism, Roosevelt saved capitalism. By modernizing progressive governance, Clinton saved progressive governance.

In short, President Clinton has created a modern, progressive political philosophy for the information age.

EIGHTEEN

GOING INTERNATIONAL

1997–2000

At 10 a.m. London time, on Saturday, November 1, 1997, I walked into a large living room at Chequers, the country home of the British prime minister. A few minutes later, Tony Blair walked in, pulling a piece of paper from his pocket.

"Opportunity, responsibility, community," Blair said. "These are the notes from our first meeting during the Clinton transition."

I had come to Chequers in 1997 as part of a small delegation led by Hillary Clinton to begin a dialogue on Third Way politics—the reform politics that manifested itself as New Democrat in the United States and New Labour in Great Britain. Those discussions would continue intermittently for the next three years, and eventually involve more than a dozen leaders of center-left governments from around the world, all of whom committed, in varying degrees, to our Third Way reforms.

I first met Tony Blair in January 1993 in the Clinton transition office in Washington, D.C. Recently appointed the shadow home secretary, Blair was accompanied by Gordon Brown, the new shadow Chancellor of the Exchequer, and Jonathon Powell, who was working in the British Embassy in Washington and would later become Blair's chief of staff. For nearly three hours, we discussed our efforts to change the Democratic Party. The British Labour Party had been out of power since 1979. Blair was particularly interested in the themes, messages, and ideas Clinton had used to break the Democratic Party's losing streak. He wanted to know how we handled tough social issues like crime and how we were able to emphasize private sector growth in our economic message.

Blair listened carefully and took notes. Blair and Brown had come to Parliament at the same time and worked together to reform the Labour Party. Both wanted to be Labour's leader, but they agreed only one of them would run for the job. Brown, who was slightly older than Blair, believed he had the inside track. But when Labour's leader John Smith died unexpectedly in May 1994, Blair outfoxed Brown to become the reform candidate. Running as the moderate candidate who would lead the party away from its leftist roots and using many of the New Democrat themes, Blair was elected Labour Party leader on July 21, 1994, winning 57 percent of the vote in a three-way race against two left-ish candidates.

Once in office, he moved quickly to change the party and separate himself from the party's losing status quo. At Labour's conference in October 1994, he shocked the delegates by proposing to rewrite the party's charter to remove Clause Four, the commitment to state ownership of industry. The next month in the *New Statesman*, a magazine closely associated with the Labour Party, Blair wrote a piece titled "No Favours" which created distance between his New Labour Party and the trade unions. Unions "have a legitimate and important part to play in the economy and the workplace," he wrote. "They do not want, nor will they get favours from a Labour government."[1] In late January 1995, Blair launched a grassroots campaign to win support of the party's rank and file for overturning Clause Four, and in March 1995 the party executive committee approved a new charter granting Blair's proposal.

Two years later, on May 1, 1997, Blair's New Labour Party routed the conservatives, ending 18 straight years of Tory rule.

A few weeks after Blair's election, Clinton told me at a reception at Blair House that Tony Blair was interested in forming a DLC-like organization in Great Britain. One night near the end of September, Hillary Clinton called me at home. My daughter Sarah had gone off to Vassar a couple of weeks earlier, and Chelsea Clinton was about to leave for Stanford, so we spent a few minutes chatting about being empty-nesters. Then she said she was giving a speech in Northern Ireland at the end of October and that Tony Blair wanted to host a small seminar at Chequers to discuss the future of New Democrat-New Labour politics. She asked me to join her for that discussion. On October 20, I received formal invitation from Blair.

Joining Hillary Rodham Clinton on the nine-member American group were Treasury deputy secretary Larry Summers, OMB director Frank Raines, HUD secretary Andrew Cuomo, Hillary's chief of staff Melanne Verveer, Sid Blumenthal of the White House staff, Joe Nye of the Kennedy School, former White House communications director Don Baer, and me. The British group was led by Blair and included Gordon Brown, Labour MPs Peter Mandelson, Patricia Hewitt, and Stephen Byers, David Miliband, Blair's chief policy advisor, and Tony Giddens, head of the London School of Economics, who has written extensively on the Third Way.

Blair had called the meeting to discuss how to avert what he called "the danger of winning power but not the battle of ideas." Unless we defined the political territory with our ideas, he said, people would grow disillusioned with our parties, just as they had with the governments they had replaced.

After twelve hours of discussion with our British counterparts, I came away more convinced than ever that if we continued to move forward and consolidate our victories, the New Democrat and New Labour movements would not prove transitory. Together, we could define a new progressivism that would shape center-left politics all over the globe well into the twenty-first century.

Most striking were the similarities between the two movements. Both were born out of political defeat: consecutive losses in national elections resulting from the two parties veering far to the left and losing touch with ordinary voters. Both had the same political goal: to build a majority coalition of those in the middle class and struggling to stay there with those aspiring to get there. Both had emerged from the political wilderness by offering new progressive ideas grounded in their parties' first principles while clearly rejecting the excesses of their parties' recent pasts.

In the opening session, Blair said that the new progressive politics stood for progress and justice. He defined its core ethic as enlightened self-interest—what New Democrats called mutual responsibility—the simple notion that as citizens of a community we have obligations to others, not just ourselves.

Economically, Blair said, we stood for a Third Way—the concept of enabling government. We believed that government contributes to creating wealth through public investments in education and infrastructure—in short, by giving citizens and communities the tools they need to get ahead. We believed in fair taxes, not tax and spend.

Socially, he said, we stood for inclusion and opportunity for all. We believed in a new concept of welfare that moved people into the work force, not welfare that kept them dependent on the one hand, or no welfare at all on the other. We believed in strengthening civic, community, and family bonds. And, we believed we should be both tolerant of differences and tough on crime.

Politically, he said, we stood for the concept of citizenship. We believed that government could not do everything and we needed to develop the voluntary sector to do what government could not do.

And, internationally, he said, we stood for engagement, not isolationism.

In sum, Tony Blair's new progressive politics rested on three cornerstones of our New Democrat movement: equal opportunity, mutual responsibility, and empowering government.

But if we had a clear philosophy and it had proven successful politically in recent elections for both President Clinton and Prime Minister Blair, how did the New Democrat and New Labour movements continue to grow and prosper after these two leaders passed from the scene? After all, that prospect that was only slightly more than three years away in the United States.

To do that, Blair said, our twin challenges were to brand our politics and colonize the political territory around us. Branding meant giving the politics a clear definition so that voters would instantly recognize the values and ideas associated with it and be able to differentiate them from those of political adversaries. Colonizing the political territory around us meant expanding and strengthening our base, holding on to our traditional allies on the left and winning over new supporters in the political center.

For New Democrats, those were still very formidable challenges and were very much interrelated. The party discipline of the parliamentary system ensured that all of Labour must act as New Labour, like it or not. But our system was different. All Democrats were not New Democrats—the experience with fast track had shown that. New Democrats had not yet cemented brand identity or captured the political territory around us, even in our own party. On welfare reform, the balanced budget, and trade—three of the most defining New Democrat issues— powerful Democratic Party interest groups and their key congressional allies had opposed President Clinton. And, in the United States, that was the biggest obstacle we faced in carrying New Democratic politics into the next century.

To me, the most important key to meeting the two challenges the prime minister posed was to define the left. Whether we or the remnants of the old left captured the progressive brand in politics could determine the long-term success of our movements. If ordinary voters thought of

New Democrat-New Labour values and ideas when they thought of left-of-center politics, the movements would triumph over a bankrupt right and continue to win increasing numbers of voters in the political center. But if those critical voters believed they were really buying the tired ideas and excesses of the old left when they voted Democrat or Labour, they would once again turn to the Republicans and Tories just as they had for most of the 1970s and 1980s.

In the end, it came down to where Tony Blair began. If we wanted the new progressive movement in world politics to prevail, we needed to win not just political power, but the battle of ideas as well.

Because our countries were so different and our meetings so intermittent, the aim of our talks with Blair and later with other Third Way leaders was to brand our politics globally. The talks gave legitimacy to a kind of politics that pundits within one country or another might pass off as political expediency. But if leaders across the globe governed by same philosophy, it was much harder to dismiss.

That first session at Chequers and the other meetings that followed always included sessions in which we talked about New Democrat ideas. And even with our national differences, those exchanges were often useful. After the Chequers meeting, for example, Gordon Brown asked me to send him Rob Shapiro's work at the Progressive Policy Institute (PPI) on the earned income tax credit. It wasn't long before the Blair government enacted the working families' tax credit, the British version of our tax credit.

Shortly after I arrived home, I received a handwritten note from Tony Blair dated November 2, the day after our meeting. "It was great to see you at Chequers and renew our friendship. I understood once again why you have made such an extraordinary contribution to the rebirth of the Democrats. Thank you and best wishes."

We continued our Third Way discussions with Blair and his team at the White House on a Friday afternoon in early February 1998, when the prime minister was in Washington for an official visit.

The Blair visit was quite a time for Ginger and me. On Thursday night, we were among the 240 guests at a State Dinner honoring Blair in the East Room of the White House. The dinner was the largest during the Clinton presidency, and the hottest ticket in Washington, with a guest list that included Barbara Streisand, her fiancé James Brolin, John Kennedy Jr., Carolyn Bessette, Tom Hanks, Harrison Ford, Steven Spielberg, Ralph Lauren, Tina Brown, Anna Wintour, Carol Channing, Warren Buffet, and Peter Jennings. Ginger's favorite part was meeting

Tom Hanks. She talked to him during the cocktail reception and we sat behind him during the entertainment.

The next morning, we were invited by Vice President Al Gore to a breakfast he and Tipper were hosting for the Blairs in the Benjamin Franklin State Dining Room at the State Department, one of the most elegant rooms in Washington for receiving foreign visitors. Originally I demurred, citing the State Dinner the night before and my scheduled meeting with Blair that afternoon. But Morley Winograd, the parliamentarian at the DLC's Cleveland meeting who was now running the reinventing government effort for Gore, called and told me I had no choice—it was a command performance. When we arrived, we found out why. We were seated at the head table with the Blairs and the Gores.

At the breakfast, Blair spoke about his Third Way initiatives: "fiscal and financial prudence," education reform, reforming the welfare state to cut dependence, constructive internationalism, and reinventing government. "It is indeed a third way," he said, "not old left or new right, but a new center and center-left governing philosophy for the future."

We reconvened at the White House after lunch, and for four hours we discussed the new economy, social policy, and community, and how to build a new majority around the Third Way. We also talked about writing a Third Way statement of principles, which we eventually did two years later.

In late January 1999, Will Marshall and PPI hosted a Third Way policy retreat at the Airlie Center in the Virginia countryside, not far from Washington. There, I approached Miliband about the possibility of Blair participating in a DLC-sponsored event after the April NATO summit in Washington. A week later, Miliband emailed me with Blair's response. "The PM has replied enthusiastically to the idea of a Third Way event on the afternoon of Sunday 25th April. The first step is obviously to try and get the President committed to the event (and/or Vice President?). However the PM also thinks it necessary to involve fellow European leaders—starting with Schroeder and Jospin (and Kok?). Overall, this is excellent news, but now we need to put something really good together." Miliband also responded positively to having a number of state and local officials who were putting Third Way ideas into action make presentations at the event.

I sent a memo to the president asking him to participate. I told him that this high-profile event had two purposes: It would be an important part of "branding" our ownership of the Third Way, the politics we created, and, by having European leaders from center-left parties discuss "common themes, values, and ideas that define the Third Way throughout the democratic world," the Third Way would be "seen as a substantive governing philosophy and not just an electoral tactic." In addition, I wrote, "it would focus on a cornerstone of the Third Way, New Democrat philosophy—a new kind of activist government that equips or empowers citizens with the tools they need to solve their own problems in their own communities."

All seemed to be going well. Then Sid Blumenthal reported that the National Security Council had said Clinton shouldn't participate. I had sent Clinton the note on February 8, but I doubt he focused on it then because the vote on the impeachment charges was scheduled in the Senate for the following week. So the request got sent to the NSC, which was not eager to have the president participate in a public political event with international leaders; they were undoubtedly aware that hostilities were likely to break out in Kosovo before the end of the month.

When I told Miliband that the president would probably not participate, he reported back that Blair was "keen to go ahead anyway," and would try to involve other European leaders. I promised him that I would continue to try to get the president, the first lady, or the vice president—but I suspected the same obstacles would preclude their attendance.

We continued to plan the meeting assuming the president would not attend. Hillary wanted to participate, though she was running into resistance from the NSC too. She invited Wim Kok of the Netherlands to come, and he was eager to do so. Blair invited Germany's Gerhard Schroeder and France's Lionel Jospin, and Schroeder accepted. Massimo D'Alema, the Italian prime minister, had heard about the event and asked to come, a request we were happy to grant. I also arranged for four of our New Democrat stars at the state and local level to make presentations— Maryland's lieutenant governor Kathleen Kennedy Townsend on crime, Colorado's governor Roy Romer on education, Mike Thurmond, Georgia's labor commissioner, on moving people from welfare to work, and Denver's mayor Wellington Webb on encouraging investment and entrepreneurship in big cities.

As the event neared, the NSC relented on Hillary Clinton, so we put her on the program and promoted her attendance and Blair's in our publicity. Meanwhile, I worked on John Podesta, White House chief of staff, about having the president come. I was convinced that when he focused on it, he would not want to miss an event on his politics with

Blair, Schroeder, Kok, and D'Alema. I'm sure Hillary Clinton pushed hard as well.

In the end, about two days before the DLC event we learned the president would participate, but we could not announce his attendance publicly.

Of all the public Third Way events, this one was the most focused on building the brand. I had a big background banner made that read:

THE THIRD WAY: Progressive Governance for the 21ˢᵗ Century

New Democrat
New Labour
New Middle

The NATO summit had ended about 4 p.m. and it took some time for Clinton, Blair, and the others to get to the National Press Club. To make the focus absolutely clear, I began the program with a short welcome in which I defined the Third Way.

Whether they're called New Democrat, New Labour, or the New Middle, the values, ideas, and approaches to governing of the Third Way are modernizing center-left politics around the globe. They are grounded in a public philosophy that embodies fundamental progressive principles, furthered by innovative ideas and modern means.

The Third Way philosophy can be summarized this way. Its first principle and enduring purpose is equal opportunity for all, special privilege for none. Its public ethic is mutual responsibility. Its core value is community. Its outlook is global. And, its modern means are fostering private sector economic growth—today's prerequisite for opportunity for all—and promoting an empowering government that equips citizens with the tools they need to get ahead.

Then I turned the meeting over to Clinton to lead the discussion. "Basically, our lodestars have always been, in the United States, the concept of opportunity, responsibility, and community," Clinton said. "We've worked on this for years. We've tried to think of simpler and more complex ways to say what we stand for, but we've never done any better than that." He then spoke about why people were choosing Third Way leaders.

I believe it is because the social arrangements which were developed within countries and the international arrangements among them are no longer adequate to meet the challenges of the day. Most of the parties of the right made a living by saying how bad [our parties] were—we were always for more government, and they were for less of it, and if you thought [government] by definition bad, then less is always better than more. So they had quite a run in the 1980s. And then it became readily apparent that that didn't solve any problems and that there were serious questions that demanded serious answers.

Each of the leaders confirmed, in his own way, the Third Way's defining principles. "The Old Left tried to resist change. And our parties became associated with high taxes, special interests, big government," Blair said. "The New Right thought the solution to everything was just to get rid of government. I think it was indifferent to what was actually breaking apart the bonds of society. Our parties of the center-left are on a voyage of rediscovery. I believe what we're really about is the politics of community, opportunity, responsibility."

The Third Way, said Wim Kok, "is symbolic for renewal. I am proud to be a citizen of a country where we have a very high social standard. But if you're not careful this can be dangerous. People need to be protected in terms of social standards, of social care. But people must also feel the urgency of responsibility. Opportunity is one thing; responsibility is the other thing."

"For 10 years or more we've asked is there an alternative to the near-liberalism on the one hand and orthodox state socialism on the other hand?" said Schroeder, speaking through an interpreter. "People have sought a third way because both of these tracks have been discovered to be misorientations. We need to make sure that as many people as possible can share in the opportunities and responsibilities within the society. If that is understood, then I think you have found a third way."

The four European leaders who appeared at the DLC forum were representative of the Third Way trend that was sweeping the continent. For most of the 1980s, conservative governments dominated European capitals. But that was rapidly changing.

In the next issue of the *New Democrat,* Martin Walker, European editor and former U.S. bureau chief of Britain's *The Guardian* newspaper, wrote: "Never have European leaders looked so ready for change. Eleven of the E.U.'s 15 member states are now led by socialist or social democratic governments. Socialists are in the governing coalitions in two more. A clear majority of these leaders can be placed squarely in the Third Way camp. They are determined to achieve the mix of balanced budgets, steady growth, welfare reform, and job creation that have marked the Clinton decade in America."[2]

Third way leaders met in Florence in November 1999 and again in Berlin in June 2000. In Berlin, leaders of center-left governments from 14 nations including Britain's Blair, Germany's Schroeder, Chile's Lagos, and South Africa's Mbeki signed a progressive manifesto defining their common progressive approach to governance. The themes were opportunity, responsibility, and community. President Clinton's New Democrat philosophy, first articulated in New Orleans and Cleveland, was modernizing progressive politics all over the globe. That was his true legacy and the legacy of the New Democrat movement.

NINETEEN

A LOOK AHEAD

Bill Clinton and the New Democrats saved the Democratic Party from the political wilderness.

The American people had simply lost faith in the party's ability to govern the country. Bill Clinton and the New Democrats restored that confidence.

Before 1992, Democrats had lost the popular vote in five of the six previous elections. Since 1992, they have won the popular vote in five of six elections.

That is not to say that President Barack Obama, a transformative political figure, would not have been elected in 2008 had it not been for Bill Clinton and the New Democrats. But his road would have been much steeper. He would have had to convince the voters—as Clinton had to—that Democrats could be trusted with national power.

But what about the future? Do New Democrat principles still apply?

Yes. Times have changed. America has seen dramatic changes demographically, socially, and technologically in the last two decades. The challenges are different today than they were in the 1990s, and so the policies must be different to meet them.

But the core principles of the New Democrat movement—its animating principle of opportunity for all, its ethic of mutual responsibility, its core value of community, its global outlook, its emphasis on economic growth and empowering government, and its embodiment of values like work, family, faith, individual liberty, and inclusion—are as viable and useful for meeting today's challenges as they were for meeting the challenges of the 1990s.

I believe that in those principles and in the history of the New Democrat movement, there are lessons for both political parties today. And I believe that if either party—and I certainly hope it would be the Democrats—puts together an agenda for the future that furthers those principles, it would both break today's polarized political gridlock and build an enduring political and governing majority.

For my party, it means thinking big, promoting a new politics of higher purpose. It's time to go beyond class warfare and identity politics. Class warfare offers politically appealing rhetoric, but it divides our country and provides no real solutions to our nation's problems. Identity politics tends to protect the status quo and offer equal outcomes while tamping down the promise of equal opportunity (our pre-Clinton problem) by using government redistribution policies to hold our coalition together.

I'm all for redistribution—that's why a progressive tax system is the only fair way to pay for government. But without private sector growth, a redistribution strategy is self-defeating. That's why Democrats cannot afford to lose our appreciation for business and the private sector. It is a growing, prospering private sector that lets us do all the good things we want to do with government—we have to create and grow wealth to have wealth to redistribute.

So what would a New Democrat agenda to tackle today's and tomorrow challenges look like? Here are some ideas.

First, we need to make clear our higher national purpose: to grow the economy, create jobs, and bring America together again.

Second, we need to get back to the fundamentals to create a sound environment for growth. We need to get our fiscal house in order. Whether it's a plan like the one offered by former Clinton chief of staff Erskine Bowles and former Republican Senator Alan Simpson or some other plan, we need to adopt and enforce a blueprint that will cut the deficit and build confidence in the private marketplace. Such a plan will undoubtedly require spending reductions, modernizing entitlements, and increasing revenue by reforming the tax code, and it will require investments in people, infrastructure, and energy that will help grow the economy.

Third, we need to overhaul the tax code to lower rates and eliminate costly loopholes. In closing loopholes, we should follow a simple policy of cut and invest: We will invest in activities that help the whole economy grow, but we will eliminate subsidies that go to individual industries, particularly subsidies to prop up dying industries.

Fourth, we should eliminate the payroll tax, the tax on work, and replace it with a carbon tax on polluters. The payroll tax is among the most regressive taxes on the books. To recruit professionals and high-income workers who are in high demand and short supply, an employer will gladly pay both the employer and employee parts of the payroll tax. But for less skilled, low-income workers who work in jobs for which workers are readily available, an employer can, in essence, make them pay both sides of the tax in the form of lower wages. If they don't like it, the employer can simply hire somebody else for the job.

I know the argument that we can't cut the payroll tax because it pays for Social Security. I believe it's a phony argument. For decades, we've been borrowing from the Social Security trust fund to pay for general operating expenses of government, basically using the trust fund as a piggy bank to fund the deficit.

No single action we could take would create more jobs than cutting the tax on work and lowering payroll costs significantly for employers. And replacing the payroll tax with a green tax would be an effective, market-oriented way to improve the environment by putting a real cost on polluting. If a carbon tax or another green tax does not raise enough revenue to keep Social Security in the black, then we could supplement it with general revenues raised from a reformed and more progressive income tax.

Fifth, we need to end the demagoguery on all sides and modernize entitlements. Fixing entitlements like Social Security and Medicare is necessary to save them. Avoiding needed reforms under the guise of protecting beneficiaries is a fool's mission. If we do nothing, these programs will run out of money and no one will receive benefits. Fixing Social Security may be the easier of the two. Raising the retirement age gradually for future recipients—say, those now under 50 or 45 years old—would probably do the job.

On Medicare, I believe a plan offered by Senator Ron Wyden of Oregon, a Democrat, and Congressman Paul Ryan of Wisconsin, a Republican, is headed in the right direction. That plan would allow future Medicare recipients—those now under 55 years old—to go into the current Medicare program or to choose to receive a premium support to purchase a Medicare-approved private health-care plan. The idea behind the plan, which has all sorts of safeguards for recipients, is to use competition to drive down Medicare costs. Because Ryan was the Republican vice presidential nominee in 2012, that plan became somewhat of a political football. But, I believe it's a good idea and merits careful consideration.

Sixth, we need a new round of reinventing government, this one focused on cleaning up and simplifying the federal regulatory maze.

Seventh, we need a fundamental restructuring of our public school system, especially in the big cities. In the information age, what you learn is what you earn, and too many kids in inner city schools aren't learning anything. I believe we need to follow the New Orleans model in every major city and make every school a charter school or charter-like school. Rather than have schools run by overstaffed, costly, and sclerotic school administrations, every school should be put on a five-year charter or performance contract. At the end of five years, if the school meets its goals, its charter should be renewed and expanded. If it doesn't, it should be closed or put under new management.

In the digital age, I also believe we need to dramatically expand the use of online learning. I'm well aware of the concern about home schooling—and I'm wary about that myself—but those concerns are outweighed by the opportunities to get up-to-date online curricula, textbooks, and individual learning programs to kids who would otherwise be trapped in failing schools with out-of-date, worn textbooks or no textbooks at all.

Eighth, we need to expand AmeriCorps into a universal system of national service. I believe *every* American should do a year or two of service either in the military services or in AmeriCorps. As citizens, we all have an obligation to give something back to our community or country. And we all would benefit by having a common experience with our fellow Americans from all walks of life. I'd like to see colleges make service a condition of admission. And, my personal preference would be a system that ties federal student aid and student loans for college or postsecondary training to service. I know that is controversial; it ran into hostile opposition when it was proposed 25 years ago. But my thinking is simply this: If you want your country to provide you the opportunity to go to college, you need to accept the responsibility of giving something back to your community.

Finally, we need to make a national commitment, once and for all, that no one in America who works full time year-round to support a family should be poor. The earned income tax credit—or some other system of tax subsidies to people in full time employment—needs to be expanded to meet that goal. If people work full time, they should not be poor.

Those nine proposals won't solve every challenge America will face, but it would represent a good start and a significant break from the status quo toward a society that offers opportunity to all, demands responsibility from all, and brings our people together in a community of all.

Now what can today's Republicans learn from the experience of the New Democrats? I'm not in the business of helping Republicans, but I'd give them three pieces of advice based on our experience.

First, they need to heed the words of Bill Clinton at the DLC's 1990 annual meeting in New Orleans that the intellectual resurgence of their party needs to come before its political resurgence. They need to start standing for ideas that ordinary Americans who go to work every day and play by the rules can feel comfortable supporting. If they do that, as Clinton told us, the candidates will take care of themselves.

The Republicans will nominate a candidate in 2016. But the chances of any Republican winning—barring a national catastrophe—will be severely diminished if they don't change their party. So, I'd suggest that they declare a moratorium on candidate talk during 2014—and encourage all the potential candidates to work together to forge a new, forward-looking, inclusive agenda that appeals to voters they've been losing or turning away and that a candidate can take into the general election. Then in 2015, the candidates can fight over whom can best carry their new agenda to the American people.

Second, that new agenda has to be more inclusive. Mitt Romney's message of self-deportation for undocumented immigrants did not offer a welcome mat to Hispanics, the fastest growing constituency in the changing electorate. In our case, with a much different electorate, we couldn't win without increasing our appeal to what Clinton called the "forgotten middle class" who had been leaving our party in droves. In today's electorate, I believe it will be hard for the Republicans to win without a vastly more appealing message to Hispanics. The Republicans have a harder road to hoe than we did. Because we were already a diverse party, bringing back middle-class voters did not fundamentally change our coalition. After all, they had been part of it before they left. But the Republicans are a homogenous, nearly all-white party. Bringing in Hispanics will require a big change in their coalition.

Third, they need to become more tolerant on cultural issues. The Republicans will likely always be the more conservative party on cultural issues, and that doesn't have to change. But they can't allow intolerant, extremists on the cultural right to dominate their party. If they do, the voters they need won't even listen to them about the issues they might agree on.

Republicans ought to look carefully at how Clinton talked about the abortion issue in 1992. He said abortions should be legal, safe, and rare. By saying abortions should be legal and safe, he was reassuring his pro-choice supporters. Because Clinton was clearly pro-choice, he was never going to win votes from the most extreme pro-life voters. But most voters are not on the extremes of the abortion issue—whether pro-choice or pro-life. In 1992, a substantial part of the electorate was what I characterize as soft pro-life. They were against abortion most of the time but not in every instance. By saying abortion should be rare, Clinton was telling those voters that while he disagreed with them, he understood why someone may have concerns about abortion. As a result, many of those soft pro-life voters were open to examining Clinton's positions on other issues, and when they did, many of them voted for him.

In the years before 1992, columnist Michael Barone used to call the Democrats the "stupid" party. If the Republicans don't change—and fast—they'll earn that appellation.

Can the Republicans pull off the kind of turnaround the New Democrats did between 1988 and 1992? It's possible, but I think it will be much harder for them to do it than it was for us. The reason is that their party is much more ideologically homogenous than ours was. In the early 1990s, despite the conventional wisdom, there were twice as many moderates and conservatives in the Democratic Party as there were liberals. The liberals made the most noise, the press paid the most attention to them, and they dominated the nominating process. But two-thirds of rank and file Democrats were not self-identified liberals. That meant if we could talk to them—and if they heard us—we had a good chance to win their votes in the primaries and the general election with a mainstream message that moved the party toward the center.

The Republican problem is more difficult. The overwhelming majority of Republicans are self-identified conservatives, meaning there is not a huge primary constituency to appeal to for moderates with an eye on the general election. That, in essence, is what happened to Mitt Romney. When Bill Clinton was labeled a moderate, it helped him, even in the primaries. When Mitt Romney was called a Massachusetts moderate in the primaries, it hurt him and forced him to take positions that he would regret in the general election. So to do what we did, the Republicans are going to have to redefine conservatism in a way that both holds the conservatives and broadens the party's appeal to moderates so that a candidate can move smoothly to the center in the general election. Not impossible, but difficult.

In June 2009, I retired as CEO of the DLC, but stayed on as chairman of the board. In early 2011, when Bruce Reed, my successor as CEO, left to become chief of staff for Vice President Biden, I shut down the DLC—and it's now part of the Clinton Foundation. That was the New Democrat thing to do. We had accomplished our mission and there was no reason to keep it going.

We created the DLC in 1985 to forge a new national agenda for the 1980s and 1990s that would make Democrats competitive again in national elections. We did that. With Bill Clinton, we helped end the party's losing streak in presidential elections. Our ideas helped save progressive politics in the United States and around the globe. And I believe they changed America for the better.

NOTES

CHAPTER 1: THE WILDERNESS

1. Brownstein's comments were made at the Clinton Library in Little Rock on a panel entitled: "Reimaging the Progressive Tradition—The Clinton-Gore Campaign and the Emergence of a Democratic Agenda for the 21st Century," September 28, 2012.

CHAPTER 4: THE HOUSE DEMOCRATIC CAUCUS

1. Edward Cowan, "Democrats Offer New Policy to Sustain Growth," *New York Times,* Sept. 19, 1982.
2. Editorial, "The Democrats and MITI-Minus," *New York Times,* Sept. 22, 1982.
3. Howell Raines, "Debate Among Democrats Draws Sharpest Exchanges of Campaign," *New York Times,* Jan. 16, 1984.
4. Ibid.

CHAPTER 5: EARLY DLC

1. Rowland Evans and Robert Novak, "Democrats: A New Split," *Washington Post,* Feb. 1985.
2. Ibid.
3. Phil Gailey, "Dissidents Defy Top Democrats; Council Formed," *New York Times,* March 1, 1985.
4. Ibid.
5. Ibid.
6. Jack W. Germond and Jules Witcover, "Kirk Shows Up the Soreheads," *Baltimore Sun,* Sept. 23, 1985.
7. Kevin Merida and Sam Attlesey, "Democratic team blitzes Texas in campaign to polish image," *Dallas Morning News,* July 2, 1985.
8. Jeff Brown and Arnold Hamilton, "Democrats Won't Be Written Off," *Dallas Times Herald,* July 2, 1985.
9. Paul Taylor, "Democrats' New Centrists Preen for '88," *Washington Post,* Nov. 10, 1985.
10. Ibid.
11. Ibid.
12. Ibid.

CHAPTER 6: BREAKING NEW GROUND IN THE IDEAS WAR

1. David Broder, "A Welcome Attack of Sanity Has Hit Washington," *Washington Post,* Oct. 7, 1985.
2. Richard E. Cohen, "Democratic Leadership Council Sees Party Void and Is Ready to Fill It," *National Journal,* Feb. 1, 1986.
3. Phil Gailey, "Democrats Assail Reagan Credibility on Military," *New York Times,* March 14, 1986.
4. Richard Stengel, "Rising Stars from the Sunbelt," *Time Magazine,* March 31, 1986.
5. Editorial, "Hard Truths About Race," *New York Times,* April 26, 1986.
6. Lena Williams, "Democrats Urged to Reassess Impact of Public Welfare Programs," *New York Times,* June 24, 1986.
7. Larry Eichel, "Top Democrats Leave Welfare Forum Without Firm Plan," *Philadelphia Inquirer,* June 24, 1986.
8. Michael Kinsley, "Democrats Should Be, Well, to the Left," *Washington Post,* May 22, 1986.
9. Arthur Schlesinger, Jr., "For Democrats, Me-Too Reaganism Will Spell Disaster," *New York Times,* July 6, 1986.
10. Ibid.
11. Ibid.
12. Al From, "Worthy Heirs of the Democratic Legacy," *New York Times,* July 20, 1986.
13. Carl Irving, "Robb Hoping Democrats Pursue New Policy Paths," *San Francisco Examiner,* July 23, 1986.
14. Peter T. Kilborn, "Democrats' Ideas on the Economy Shift: Many in Top Posts Differ With Party's Longtime Policies," *New York Times,* Aug. 12, 1986.
15. Ibid.
16. Paul Taylor, "Military Buildup Faulted By Democratic Centrists; 'Bad Bargain,' Says Leadership Conference," *Washington Post,* Sept. 17, 1986.
17. E.J. Dionne, Jr., "Democrats Fashion Centrist Image in New Statement of Party Policy," *New York Times,* Sept. 21, 1986.
18. Robin Toner, "Reporter's Notebook; Democrats Savoring Plans," *New York Times,* Dec. 15, 1986.
19. Richard Fly, "How the Democrats' Young Turks Are Seizing Power," *Business Week,* Dec. 15, 1986.
20. Jon Margolis, "'Progressive' Democrats Becoming Norm," *Chicago Tribune,* Dec. 14, 1986.
21. Robert A. Rankin, "Democrats Focus on New Directions," *Philadelphia Inquirer,* Dec. 20, 1986.

CHAPTER 7: THE ILLUSION OF POWER

1. Rhodes Cook, "Will 'Super Tuesday' Mean Southern Trouble?" *Congressional Quarterly,* May 9, 1987.
2. Carl Irving, "Democrats Pondering the South," *San Francisco Examiner,* June 22, 1987.
3. Editorial, "Democrats Talk Foreign Policy . . ." *Washington Post,* Sept. 27, 1987.

4. Paul West, "Gore Challenges his Rivals in Fla. Democratic Debate," *Baltimore Sun*, Oct. 6, 1987.
5. Donald Kimelman, "Democrats Signaling Another War on Poverty," *Tulsa Daily World*, March 10, 1988.
6. Dennis Farney, "Middle Ground: The Democrats Recast the Party to Win Back Suburban Voters They Lost to Reagan," *Wall Street Journal*, July 19, 1988.
7. Editorial, "Mr. Bush Adopts Youth Service," *New York Times*, Oct. 13, 1988.
8. David S. Broder, "There's Another Candidate Who's No Jack Kennedy," *Washington Post*, Oct. 7, 1988.

CHAPTER 8: THE ROAD BACK, PHASE 1

1. E. J. Dionne, "Party Told to Win Middle-Class Vote," *New York Times*, March 12, 1989.
2. Richard Benedetto, "Dems scold Jackson for 'divisiveness,'" *USA Today*, March 13, 1989.
3. Richard Benedetto, "Moderate Democrats Tell Jackson to Expect a Fight," *Gannett News Service*, March 12, 1989.

CHAPTER 10: THE ROAD BACK, PHASE 2

1. Mark Shields, "Tying Entitlements to Duties," *Washington Post*, Feb. 4, 1989.
2. Robert J. Shapiro, "The Minimum Wage Deal," *Washington Post*, July 3, 1989.
3. Paul West, "The Democratic Party Brain Dead?" *Baltimore Sun*, Aug. 13, 1989.
4. David Broder, "The Democrats Need a Policy Voice," *Washington Post*, Sept. 24, 1989.
5. Paul Taylor and Maralee Schwartz, "Jackson's Unity Address Baffles, Irks Some Moderate Democrats," *Washington Post*, March 25, 1989.

CHAPTER 11: THE ROAD TO CLEVELAND

1. Seymour Martin Lipset, "Equality and the American Creed," Progressive Policy Institute backgrounder, June 1, 1991.
2. Margaret Carlson, "The Neoliberal Blues," *Time* magazine, April 2, 1990.
3. David S. Broder, "Sen. Nunn: Democrats' Shadow Commander," *Washington Post*, Dec. 16, 1990.
4. David S. Broder, "Moderate Democrats Trying to Grow Grass Roots; Leadership Conference, Launching New Chapters, Hopes to 'Build a Network' for 1992," *Washington Post*, Dec. 12, 1990.
5. Adam Nagourney, "Group Hopes to Steer Democrats Right," *USA Today*, April 23, 1991.
6. Ibid.
7. Howard Fineman, "Duel of the Democrats," *Newsweek*, April 8, 1991.
8. A. L. Maypolitics, "Brown optimistic that Democrats can win on kitchen-table issues," *Atlanta Journal Constitution*, April 25, 1991.

9. Basil Talbott, "DLC Convention: No Invites for Jackson, McGovern," *Chicago Sun-Times,* April 15, 1991.
10. Editorial, "Slighting Jesse Jackson," *Baltimore Sun,* April 22, 1991.
11. Bill Clinton, *My Life,* (New York: Alfred A. Knopf, 2004) 366.
12. Christopher Matthews, "Democratic Conservatives Find a Voice," *San Francisco Examiner,* May 9, 1991.

CHAPTER 12: THE PRE-CAMPAIGN

1. David S. Broder, "Cuomo Says Party Needs Program, Not 'New Faces'; New York Governor Plans Speeches Around Nation to Help Shape Democrats' Agenda," *Washington Post,* June 7, 1991.
2. Dan Balz, "Jackson Struggles to Define '92 Role: Racially Divisive Issues Trouble Two-Time Presidential Contender," *Washington Post,* June 8, 1991.
3. Ron Fournier, "Governor Says DLC Critics Need to Say What They're For," *Associated Press,* June 12, 1991.
4. Dan Balz, "Democrats' Perennial Rising Star Wants to Put New Face on Party," *Washington Post,* June 25, 1991.
5. Ronald Brownstein, "Democrats Search for Identity," *Los Angeles Times,* July 2, 1991.
6. Curtis Wilkie, "Democratic Faction Seeks N.H. Welcome," *Boston Globe,* June 28, 1991.
7. Page Six, "Hat's in the ring, head's in a sling," *New York Post,* July 19, 1991.
8. Judy Keen, "Arkansas gov tests waters prior to plunge," *USA Today,* Aug. 14, 1991.

CHAPTER 13: TO VICTORY

1. David S. Broder, "The DLC at Six" *Washington Post,* May 12, 1991.
2. Editorial, "The Moderate Radical," *Philadelphia Inquirer,* Oct. 6, 1991.
3. Editorial, "Bill Clinton, in Black and White," *New York Times,* March 11, 1992.
4. Ibid.
5. Ronald Brownstein, "In N.Y., Clinton Silent on Government Reform," *Los Angeles Times,* April 6, 1992.
6. Michael Kramer, "The Brains Behind Clinton," *Time,* May 4, 1992.
7. Robin Toner, "Democrats in New York–Party Leadership; 1992 Ticket Puts Council of Moderates to Stiff Test," *New York Times,* July 15, 1992.
8. Richard Benedetto, "Ticket clings to centrist roots // Liberals feeling left out," *USA Today,* July 14, 1992.
9. Lloyd Grove, "Al From, the Life of the Party: The Head of the Democratic Leadership Council Finding Victory in Moderation," *Washington Post,* July 24, 1992.
10. Richard L. Berke, "The 1992 Campaign: The Ad Campaign; Clinton: Getting People Off Welfare," *New York Times,* Sept. 10, 1992.

CHAPTER 14: TRANSITION

1. Michael Duffy, "A Public Policy Entrepreneur: Domestic-issues coordinator Al From yanked the Democrats back to the center," *Time,* Dec. 14, 1992.

CHAPTER 15: THE CLINTON YEARS

1. Joe Klein, "Clinton's Values Problem," *Newsweek,* April 26, 1993.
2. Al From, "On a Roll," *New Democrat,* Feb. 1994.
3. Gerald F. Seib, "New Democrat: An Old Concept Worth Revisiting," *Wall Street Journal,* Aug. 24, 1994.

CHAPTER 16: THE REBOUND

1. David Osborne, "Can this President Be Saved? A Six-point Plan to Beat the One-Term Odds," *Washington Post Magazine,* Jan. 8, 1995.
2. Ibid.
3. Michael Kramer, "Clinton's Troops Turn Away," *Time* magazine, July 10, 1995.

CHAPTER 18: GOING INTERNATIONAL

1. Tony Blair, "No Favours," *New Statesman and Society,* Nov. 18, 1994.
2. Martin Walker, "Europe's Third Way Labs," *New Democrat,* May/June 1999.

INDEX